Better Homes and Gardens®

Best of Knit It

Favorites from the Editors of KNIT IT® Magazine

For general information about our other products and services, please contact our Customer Care
Department within the United States at (800) 762-2974, outside the United States at (317) 572-3993
or fax (317) 572-4002.

Wiley also publishes its books in a variety of electronic formats and by print-on-demand. Some content
that appears in standard print versions of this book may not be available in other formats. For more
information about Wiley products, visit us at www.wiley.com.

ISBN 978-0-470-88708-0

Printed in the United States of America

10 9 8 7 6 5 4 3 2 1

Better Homes and Gardens®

Best of Knit It

Favorites from the Editors of KNIT IT® Magazine

WILEY

John Wiley & Sons, Inc.

contents

women's garments

bags & purses

accessories

kids

babies

home decor

plus...

women's garments

Find your perfect sweater among this collection of stylish shrugs, cardigans, pullovers, and jackets.

Dressed up or dressed down, this fisherman shrug is the perfect topper for a shell, a tank, or a tee.

FISHERMAN shrug

Designed by **The Knitting Tree**
Photographed by **Olivia Graham**

■■■■□ Intermediate

Sizes

S/M (L/XL)

Instructions are written for the smaller size with changes for the larger size given in parentheses. When only one number is given, it applies to both sizes.

Note: For ease in working, circle all numbers pertaining to the size you're knitting.

Finished Measurements

Length (Back) = 24 (26)"
Width = 61 (65)" from cuff to cuff

Materials

Yarns

Super bulky wool or wool blend, 540 (648) yds. [490 (588) m] in ivory

Needles & Extras

- Size 13 (9 mm) needles OR SIZE NEEDED TO OBTAIN GAUGE
- Size 15 (10 cm) 32" or 36" circular needle OR SIZE NEEDED TO OBTAIN GAUGE
- Blunt-end yarn needle

Notes

Gauge

9 sts and 12 rows = 4" (10 cm) in St st pat (knit all RS rows, purl all WS rows). TAKE TIME TO CHECK YOUR GAUGE.

Knit

BACK

Using needles, cast on 38 (42) sts.
Row 1: Knit.
Row 2: Purl.
 Cont in St st and inc 1 st at each edge every 6th row 3 times. Work until piece measures 8 (10)"—44 (48) sts.

Shape armholes

Row 1: K1, ssk, k to last 3 sts, k2tog, k1.
Row 2: Purl.
 Rep Rows 1 and 2 thirteen (14) more times. Place rem 16 (18) sts on holder.

SLEEVE (MAKE 2)

Using larger needle, cast on 28 (30) sts.
Row 1: *K2, p2; rep from * across row; end k0 (2).
Row 2: P0 (2); *k2, p2, rep from * across row.
 Cont in rib pat until piece measures 8 (10)". Change to smaller needles.
Next row: Knit, inc 1 st at each end of row.
Next row: Purl.
 Cont in St st and inc 1 st at each edge every 6th row two times—34 (36) sts. Work even until piece measures 17 (19)".

Shape armhole

Row 1: K1, ssk, k to last 3 sts, k2tog, k1—32 (34) sts.

Row 2: Purl.
Row 3: Knit.
Row 4: Purl.
 Rep Rows 1–4 five times, then rep Rows 1 and 2 three times. Place rem 16 (18) sts on holder.

FRONT (MAKE 2)

Using smaller needles, cast on 22 (24) sts (line BC).
Row 1: Knit.
Row 2: Purl.
Row 3: K1, ssk, k to last 3 sts, k2tog, k1.
 Rep Rows 2 and 3 until 1 st rem.
 Bind off.

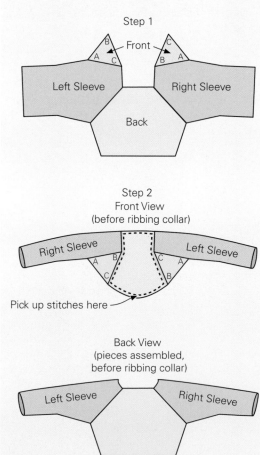

FINISHING

Sew raglan edge of each Sleeve to corresponding raglan edge of Back as shown in Finishing diagram Step 1, *right*. Referring again to Step 1, sew one Front along line AB to the other raglan edge of the Right Sleeve; sew the other Front along line AC to the other raglan edge of the Left Sleeve.

Referring to the Finishing diagram Step 2, *right*, sew line BC of the Front (the one attached to the Right Sleeve) to the edge of the lower Back; sew line BC of the Front attached to the Left Sleeve to the other edge of the lower Back easing shaping as necessary.

Sew sleeve seams. With size 15 circular needle, pick up and knit 100 (108) sts around entire circumference (BC of each Front, held sts from tops of Sleeves, and top and bottom edges of Back) as shown in Step 2. **Note:** You should pick up and k approx 1 st every other row or st. Work in k2, p2 rib for 4½". Bind off very loosely.

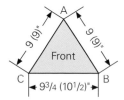

Front
9 (9)"   9 (9)"
C   9³/4 (10¹/2)"   B

Sleeve

7 (8)"
9 (10)"
9 (9)"
8 (10)"
15 (16)"
26 (29)"
12¹/2 (13¹/2)"

Back

7 (8)"
9¹/4 (10)"
8 (10)"
19¹/2 (21¹/4)"
17¹/4 (20)"
17 (18¹/2)"

Finishing

Step 1

B C ← Front → C B
A   A

Left Sleeve   Right Sleeve

Back

Step 2
Front View
(before ribbing collar)

Right Sleeve   Left Sleeve
A B   C A
C   B

Pick up stitches here

Back View
(pieces assembled,
before ribbing collar)

Left Sleeve   Right Sleeve

An interesting slip-stitch pattern results in a double-thick fabric that lasts through lots of wear. Worn with a slouchy belt, this three-quarter-length wrap coat flatters every figure.

wrap coat

Designed by **Mari Lynn Patrick**
Photographed by **Tony Lattari**

Sizes

S (M, L, 1X, 2X, 3X)

Instructions are written for the smallest size with changes for larger sizes given in parentheses. When only one number is given, it applies to all sizes.
Notes: For ease in working, circle all numbers pertaining to the size you're knitting. The back has a center slit at the lower edge, and the sleeve cuffs are slit at the outside edges.

Finished Measurements

Bust = 34 (38, 42, 46, 50, 54)"
Length (Back) = 32½ (33, 33½, 34, 34½, 35)"

Materials

Yarns

Bulky weight wool blend, 1,650 (1,800, 2,025, 2,175, 2,400. 2,475) yds. [1,509 (1,646, 1,852, 1,989, 2,195, 2,264) m] in brown (MC)

Bulky weight wool, approx 75 yds. (68 m) in variegated brown (CC)

Needles & Extras

- Size 11 (8 mm) needles OR SIZE NEEDED TO OBTAIN GAUGE
- Size 10 (6 mm) needles
- Size H/7 (4.5 mm) crochet hook
- Stitch holders
- Stitch markers
- Two ⅞"-diameter buttons
- Blunt-end yarn needle

Notes

Gauge

16 sts and 23 rows = 4" (10 cm) in pat st using larger needles. TAKE TIME TO CHECK YOUR GAUGE.

Special Abbreviations

inc 2 sts = On RS rows, k4, yo, k1 into front and back on next st. On the next row, work pattern as established.

Knit

PATTERN STITCHES

(Odd number of sts; 2-row rep)
Row 1 (RS): Knit.
Row 2: *K1, sl 1 with yarn in back (wyib); rep from *, end k1.
    Rep Rows 1 and 2 for pat st.

BACK

Left edge

Using larger needles and MC, cast on 39 (43, 47, 51, 55, 59) sts. Work in pat st for 48 rows or 8½", end with a WS row. Place sts on holder.

Right edge

Using larger needles and MC, cast on 47 (51, 55, 59, 63, 67) sts. Work in pat st for 48 rows or 8½", end with a WS row.
Next row—Joining (RS): K34 (38, 42, 46, 50, 54) sts of right edge, place left edge behind the rem sts of the right edge and (k1 st from the right side tog with the 1 st of the left edge) 5 times, k to end—81 (89, 97, 105, 113, 121) sts. Work 1 row even.

Shape sides

Dec 1 st at each side on next row, then every 12th row twice more, every 4th row 5 times, then every other row twice—61 (69, 77, 85, 93, 101) sts. Work even until piece measures 19" from beg. Inc 1 st at each side on next row, then every 4th row 3 times—69 (77, 85, 93, 101, 109) sts. Work even until piece measures 23" from beg.

Shape armholes

Bind off 4 sts at beg of next 2 rows, 3 sts at beg of next 0 (0, 0, 2, 2, 2) rows, then dec 1 st at each side every other row 2 (4, 6, 4, 7, 11) times—57 (61, 65, 71, 73, 73) sts. Work even until armholes measure 8 (8½, 9, 9½, 10, 10½)".

Shape shoulders

Bind off 4 sts at beg of next 8 (8, 4, 4, 4, 4) rows; bind off 5 sts at beg of next 0 (0, 4, 4, 4, 4) rows. Bind off rem 25 (29, 29, 35, 37, 37) sts for Back neck.

RIGHT FRONT

Using larger needles and MC, cast on 57 (61, 65, 69, 73, 77) sts. Work even in pat st for 8½", ending with a RS row. Work side shaping as for Back at end of RS rows only—51 (55, 59, 63, 67, 71) sts. Work even until piece measures 23" from beg.

Shape neck and armhole

Shape armhole as for Back and AT THE SAME TIME, when armhole measures 1½ (2, 2½, 3, 3½, 4)", inc 2 sts (see Special Abbreviations) at beg of next 2 RS rows and every 10th row twice more. Work even on 53 (55, 57, 60, 61, 61) sts until armhole measures 5 (5½, 6, 6½, 7, 7½)".

Shape lapel

Next row (RS): Work 25 sts, place marker (pm), join a 2nd ball of yarn and bind off next 3 sts, work to end. Cont to shape the lapel side as foll: Bind off 5 st at beg on next 5 WS rows and AT THE SAME TIME shape neck side as foll: Bind off 2 (2, 2, 3, 3, 3) sts at beg of next 3 (3, 3, 4, 4) RS rows, then dec 1 st every other row 3 (0, 0, 0, 0, 0) times, then every row 0 (5, 5, 5, 3, 3) times. When armhole measures same as Back to shoulder, shape shoulder as for Back at beg of WS rows.

LEFT FRONT

Work as for Right Front, reversing all shaping.

LEFT SLEEVE

Note: Designation of left edge or right edge of Sleeve is with Sleeve laid flat and RS facing.

Left edge

Using larger needles and MC, cast on 27 (27, 27, 29, 29, 29) sts. Work in pat st for 1½", ending with a WS row.
Next row (RS): K2, yo, k2tog (for buttonhole), k to end. Work even until piece measures 3", ending with a WS row. Place sts on holder.

Right edge

Using larger needles and MC, cast on 23 (23, 23, 25, 25, 25) sts. Work in pat st for 3", ending with a WS row.
Next row—Joining (RS): K18 (18, 18, 20, 20, 20) sts of right edge, place left edge over rem sts of right edge and (k1 st from right edge tog with the one st of left edge) 5 times; k to end—45 (45, 45, 49, 49, 49) sts. Cont in pat as established, inc 1 st each side every 14th (12th, 8th, 8th, 8th, 10th) row 4 (5, 8, 8, 8, 10) times—53 (55, 61, 65, 65, 69) sts. Work even until piece measures 18" from beg.

Shape cap

Bind off 4 sts at beg of next 2 rows, 3 sts at beg of next 2 rows, dec 1 st at each side every other row 9 (10, 13, 15, 15, 17) times, bind off 3 sts at beg of next 2 rows. Bind off rem 15 sts.

RIGHT SLEEVE

Left edge

Using larger needles and MC, cast on 23 (23, 23, 25, 25, 25) sts. Work in pat st for 3", ending with a WS row. Place sts on holder.

Right edge

Using larger needles and MC, cast on 27 (27, 27, 29, 29, 29) sts. Work in pat st for 1½", ending with a WS row.
Next row (RS): K to last 4 sts, k2tog, yo (for buttonhole), k2. Work even until piece measures 3" from beg, ending with a WS row.
Next row—Joining (RS): K22 (22, 22, 24, 24, 24) sts of right edge, place the left edge behind the rem sts of the right edge and join as for Left Sleeve. Cont as for Left Sleeve.

FINISHING

Block pieces to measurements. Sew shoulder seams. Using smaller needles and MC, beg at markers on lapels, pick up and k77 (77, 83, 93, 99, 99) sts evenly across neck edge. Work in k1, p1 rib for 3 rows. Change to larger needles. Beg with Row 1 and work in pat st for 3". Bind off kwise on a WS row

Set in Sleeves. Sew side and sleeve seams.

Using crochet hook and MC, sl st firmly on WS along line of picked-up sts along Back neck to create a firm seam so the collar does not stretch.

Using crochet hook and 2 strands of CC held tog, work a Surface Chain Stitch from RS just inside the edge around the cuff, center fronts, lapels, and collar edges as foll: Hold a CC sl knot beneath surface of knitting; insert crochet hook into work from top to underside and pull the sl knot through to top of work, *insert hook into knitting, pull up a CC loop, and draw through loop on hook; rep from *. (See photo on *page 11*.) Sew buttons on cuffs opposite buttonholes.

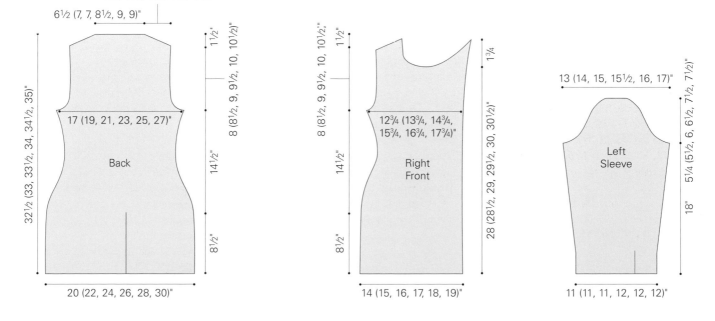

4 (4, 4½, 4½, 4½, 4½)"
6½ (7, 7, 8½, 9, 9)"
1½"
8 (8½, 9, 9½, 10, 10½)"
17 (19, 21, 23, 25, 27)"
32½ (33, 33½, 34, 34½, 35)"
14½"
8½"
Back
20 (22, 24, 26, 28, 30)"

8 (8½, 9, 9½, 10, 10½)"
1½"
1¾
12¾ (13¾, 14¾, 15¾, 16¾, 17¾)"
28 (28½, 29, 29½, 30, 30½)"
14½"
8½"
Right Front
14 (15, 16, 17, 18, 19)"

13 (14, 15, 15½, 16, 17)"
5¼ (5½, 6, 6½, 7½, 7½)"
18"
Left Sleeve
11 (11, 11, 12, 12, 12)"

mosaic JACKET

Designed by **Elena Malo**
Photographed by **Akin Girav**

■ ■ ■ ■ ■ **Experienced**

Sizes
One size: S/M

Finished Measurement
Bust = 39"
Length (Back) = 24½"

Materials
Yarns
Bulky weight acrylic blend, 500 yds.
(452 m) in dark red (A)

Bulky weight acrylic blend, approximatley 460 yds. (420 m)
in orange (B)

Needles & Extras
• Size 10 (6 mm) needles OR SIZE NEEDED
  TO OBTAIN GAUGE
• Size 9 (5.5 mm) needles
• Size 9 (5.5 mm) 29" circular needle
• Stitch holders
• Blunt-end yarn needle
• Six buttons about ¾" diameter

Notes
Gauge
10 sts and 18 rows = 3" (7.5 cm) in pat st using larger
needles. TAKE TIME TO CHECK YOUR GAUGE.

Knit
PATTERN STITCHES
Mosaic Pattern Stitch

(12 + 3 sts)
Note: On all RS rows, slip all stitches
with yarn in back; on all WS rows, slip all
stitches with yarn in front.
Beg to work from Mosaic Chart, *page 18.*
Row 1 (RS): Using A, knit.
Row 2: Using A, purl.

Row 3: Using B, k1, *sl 1, k11; rep from
* to last 2 sts; sl 1, k1.
Row 4 and all WS rows: P all sts that
were knitted on previous row with same
color, and sl all the same sts that were
slipped on previous row.
Row 5: Using A, k2, *sl 1, k9, sl 1, k1;
rep from * to last st; k1.
Row 7: Using B, (k1, sl 1) twice, *k7,
(sl 1, k1) twice, sl 1; rep from * to last 11
sts; end row with k7, (sl 1, k1) twice.

Row 9: Using A, k2, sl 1, k1, sl 1, *k5,
(sl 1, k1) 3 times, sl 1; rep from * to last
10 sts; end row with k5, sl 1, k1, sl 1, k2.
Row 11: Using B, (k1, sl 1) 3 times, *k3,
(sl 1, k1) 4 times, sl 1; rep from * to last
9 sts; end row k3, (sl 1, k1) 3 times.
Row 13: Using A, k2, *sl 1, k1; rep from
* to last st, k1.
Rows 15, 17, 19, 21, 23, and 25:
Rep Rows 11, 9, 7, 5, 3, and 1.

Knit this dramatic mosaic jacket with richly textured bouclé yarn and simple garter-stitch edgings.

Row 27: Using B, k7, *sl 1, k11; rep from * across row, end last rep with k7.

Row 29: Using A, k6, *sl 1, k1, sl 1, k9; rep from * across row; end last rep with k6.

Row 31: Using B, k5, *(sl 1, k1) twice, sl 1, k7; rep from * across row; end last rep with k5.

Row 33: Using A, k4, *(sl 1, k1) 3 times, sl 1, k5; rep from * across row; end last rep with k4.

Row 35: Using B, k3, *(sl 1, k1) 4 times, sl 1, k3; rep from * to end of row.

Row 37: Using A, rep Row 13.

Rows 39, 41, 43, 45, and 47: Rep rows 35, 33, 31, 29, and 27.

Row 48: Rep Row 4.

Rep Rows 1–48 for pat.

BACK

Using smaller needles and A, cast on 63 sts. Beg with WS row, k 3 rows. Change to larger needles and beg pat with Row 1 (RS).

Shape sides

When work measures 2" from cast-on, dec 1 st each side as foll:

Dec row: K1, k2tog, work across in est pat to last 3 sts, ssk, k1. Maintaining pat, rep Dec row every 8th row twice more—57 sts rem. Work even until piece measures 11" from cast-on.

On next RS row, work **Inc row:** K1, make 1 (M1), work in pat to last st, M1, k1. Rep the Inc row every 8th row twice more—63 sts. Work even until piece measures 15" from cast-on; end with WS row.

Shape armholes

Bind off 3 sts at beg of next 2 rows. Work Dec row same as for "Shape Sides" on next RS row, then every other row 4 times— 47 sts rem. Work even in pat until armholes measure 8" from bind-off; end with WS row.

Shape shoulders

Shape shoulders using short rows as foll:

Row 1 (RS): Work in pat to last 4 sts, *bring the yarn between the needles to the front of work, sl next st pwise from left to right needle, bring the yarn between the needles to back of work, return slipped st to left needle, turn work.

Row 2: Work in pat to last 4 sts, *bring yarn between the needles to back of work, sl next st pwise from left to right needle, bring yarn between the needles to front of work, return slipped st to left needle, turn work.

Row 3: Work in pat to 4 sts before the turning point, work same as Row 1 from *.

Row 4: Work in pat to 4 sts before the turning point, work same as Row 2 from *.

Row 5: Work in pat to 5 sts before turning point, work same as Row 1 from * (13 shoulder sts).

Row 6: Work in pat to 5 sts before turning point, work same as Row 2 from * (13 shoulder sts).

Next 2 rows: Work across row in pat, hiding the wraps as foll: On RS row, work to first wrapped st, insert the right needle tip under the wrap, then kwise into the st and k them tog; rep the process with each wrap and st as you work to end of row. On WS row, work to first wrapped st, insert the right needle tip under the wrap from the back, lift wrap onto the left needle, and p wrap and st tog; rep process with each wrap and st to end of row.

Place each set of 13 shoulder sts onto a holder. Place rem 21 sts on separate holder for back neck. Cut yarn, leaving a 6" tail.

LEFT FRONT

Using smaller needles and A, cast on 33 sts. K 3 rows. Change to larger needles and beg Mosaic pat with Row 1.

Shape sides

When work measures 2" from cast-on, dec 1 st at armhole-side edge as foll:
Dec row (RS): K1, k2tog, work across in est pat to end of row. Maintaining pat, rep Dec row on every 8th row twice more—30 sts rem. Work even until piece measures 11" from cast-on; ending with WS row.
Inc row (RS): K1, M1, work in pat to end of row. Rep Inc row on every 8th row twice more—33 sts. Work even until piece measures 14" from cast-on, ending with a WS row.
V-neck Dec row (RS): Work in pat to last 3 sts, ssk, k1. Rep V-neck Dec row on every 4th row 13 times. AT THE SAME TIME, when work measures 15" from cast-on, on next RS row, beg armhole shaping. Bind off 3 sts, work in pat to end of row.
Armhole Dec row: Work 1 st, dec 1 st, work to end of row. Rep Armhole Dec row on every 8th row twice more. Work in pat until piece measures same as Back and 13 sts rem. Shape shoulder with short rows to correspond with Back. Place shoulder sts on holder.

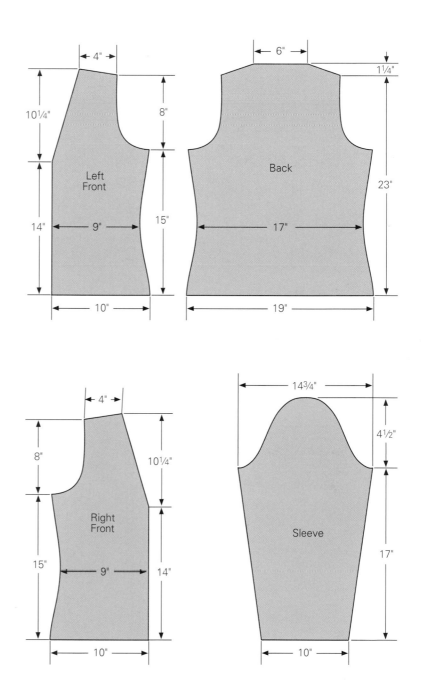

RIGHT FRONT

Work same as for Left Front, reversing shaping.

SLEEVE (MAKE 2)

Using smaller needles and A, cast on 33 sts. K 12 rows. Change to larger needles and work in pat for 8 rows. Inc row: Work 1 st, M1, cont in pat to last st, M1, work 1 st. Rep Inc row every 12th row 7 more times—49 sts. Work even until piece measures 17" from cast-on or desired length to sleeve cap.

Shape cap

Bind off 3 sts at beg of next 2 rows. Dec 1 st inside the first and last sts (same as for Back) on every 4th row 3 times, then every 2nd row 7 times. Bind off 3 sts at the beg of next 2 rows. Bind off rem 17 sts.

FINISHING

Join shoulders tog using the 3-needle bind-off as foll: Place 13 front shoulder sts onto one needle and matching 13 back shoulder sts onto 2nd needle. With WS facing, hold both needles parallel in left hand with points facing to the right. Join yarn, *insert 3rd needle into first st on both needles held in left hand and k2tog (1 st on right needle); *work next 2 sts same (2 sts on right needle), bind off 1 st as usual. Rep from * across row. Join other set of shoulder sts the same way. Seam Jacket sides tog.

Shape front band

Using circular needle and with RS facing, join A at lower edge of Right Front. Pick up and k about 1 st every 2nd row along Right Front edge and neckline, k21 Back neck sts from holder, then pick up and k same number of sts along Left Front edge same as for Right—161 sts total. Adjust this number if necessary. Beg with WS row, k 3 rows.

Buttonhole row (RS): K2, *k2tog, yo, k7; rep from * 4 more times, end k2tog, yo, just below beg of V-neck; k to end of row. K 3 more rows. Bind off loosely. Sew sleeve seams tog and then sew Sleeves to armholes. Align front bands and sew buttons on Left Front to correspond with buttonholes. Weave in loose ends to WS.

BELT

Using circular needle and A, cast on 200 sts. Work in Garter st (k every row) for 8 rows. Bind off loosely.

Mosaic Chart

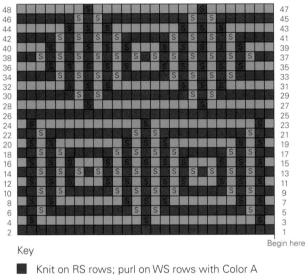

Key

■ Knit on RS rows; purl on WS rows with Color A
Ⓢ Slip purlwise on RS and WS rows (color A)
▨ Knit on RS rows; purl on WS rows with Color B
Ⓢ Slip purlwise on RS and WS rows (color B)

This variation on
a classic results in
a sleek, hip-length
mock turtle with a
feminine, shaped
waist. Detailing
at the neck, cuffs,
and hem plays up
the pattern in the
midsection to put
the sweater in
a class by itself.

fair isle
PULLOVER

Designed by **Valerie Kurita**
Photographed by **Tony Lattari**

Sizes

S (M, L, 1X, 2X, 3X)

Instructions are written for the smallest size with changes for larger sizes given in parentheses. When only one number is given, it applies to all sizes.

Notes: For ease in working, circle all numbers pertaining to the size you're knitting. When working the charted portion of the collar and cuffs, be careful not to pull yarn carried along back of work too tightly. Collar needs to stretch.

Finished Measurements

Bust = 34 (40, 44, 49, 52, 56)"
Length (Back) = 23 (23½, 24, 24½, 25, 25½)"

Materials

Yarns

Worsted weight wool blend, 860 (1,075, 1,290, 1,505, 1,720, 1,835) yds. [800, (1,000, 1,200, 1,400, 1,600, 1,800) m] in tan (MC)

Worsted weight wool blend, 860 yds. (800 m) *each* in dark brown (A), orange (B), and light green (C)

4 MEDIUM

Needles & Extras

- Size 8 (5 mm) needles OR SIZE NEEDED TO OBTAIN GAUGE
- Size 8 (5 mm) 12" circular needle
- Size F/5 (3.75 mm) crochet hook
- Three ¾"-diameter buttons
- Blunt-end yarn needle

Notes

Gauge

20 sts and 26 rows = 4" (10 cm) in St st (knit all RS rows, purl all WS rows). TAKE TIME TO CHECK YOUR GAUGE.

Knit

BACK

Using A, cast on 87 (105, 115, 125, 135, 145) sts. Work in St st (k every RS row, p every WS row) for 2 rows. Beg to work from Fair Isle Pullover Chart, *opposite*.

Chart row 1: Work sts 9–23 (17–23, 11–23, 7–23, 2–5, 15–23) once, work 18-st rep 4 (5, 5, 6, 7, 7) times, then work sts 0–0 (6–13, 6–17, 0–0, 24–28, 6–15). Work through Row 14.

Next row (RS): Change to MC. Dec 1 st at each edge of next row, then every other row 6 more times—73 (91, 101, 111, 121, 131) sts. Work even with MC until piece measures 6" from beg.

Next row: Inc 1 st at each edge on next row, then every 10th row 4 more times —83 (101, 111, 121, 131, 141) sts, and AT THE SAME TIME, when piece measures 7½" above last row of A, work Rows 1–33 of Chart once, then Rows 1–14 once more, being sure to line up sts with charted design at lower edge. Work Chart until piece measures 15" from beg, ending with a WS row.

Shape armholes

Cont Chart pat and AT THE SAME TIME bind off 3 sts at beg of next 2 (2, 2, 4, 6, 6) rows, 2 sts at beg of next 2 (2, 4, 4, 4, 6) rows, then dec 1 st each side every other row 1 (3, 3, 5, 5, 8) times—71 (85, 91, 91, 95, 95) sts. When Chart has been completed, change to MC for rem of piece and work even until armholes measure 7 (7½, 8, 8½, 9, 9½)", ending with a WS row.

Split neck

K35 (42, 45, 45, 47, 47), join a 2nd ball of yarn, and bind off next (center) st; k to end.

Shape shoulders

Note: When directions read "work both sides at the same time," that means you knit across both sides (using separate balls of yarn) to complete one row. Cont to work both sides at the same time and bind off 8 (9, 10, 9, 10, 10) sts at beg of next 6 (2, 6, 2, 4, 6) rows, 0 (10, 0, 10, 11, 0) sts at beg of next 0 (4, 0, 4, 2, 0) rows. Bind off rem 11 (13, 15, 16, 16, 17) sts at each side for Back neck.

FRONT

Work same as for Back until armhole measures 4 (4½, 5, 5½, 6, 6½)", ending with a WS row.

Shape neck

Work 30 (35, 36, 35, 37, 36) sts; join a 2nd ball of yarn, bind off center 11 (15, 19, 21, 21, 23) sts, work to end. Working both sides at the same time, bind off at each neck edge 3 sts once, then dec 1 st every other row 3 times—24 (29, 30, 29, 31, 30) sts each side. Work even until piece measures same as Back to shoulder and armholes measure 6 (6½, 7, 7½, 8, 8½)", ending with a WS row. Shape shoulders as foll: Working both sides at the same time, bind off 6 (7, 7, 7, 7, 7) sts at beg of next 6 rows. Bind off rem 6 (8, 9, 8, 10, 9) sts.

SLEEVE (MAKE 2)

Using A, cast on 40 (40, 40, 46, 46, 46) sts. Work in St st for 2 rows. Beg Chart.

Chart row 1: Work sts 13–23 (13–23, 13–23, 10–23, 10–23, 10–23) once, work 18-st rep once, then work sts 6–16 (6–16, 6–16, 6–19, 6–19, 6–19). Work through Row 14.

Change to MC, inc 1 st each side every 4th row 0 (0, 3, 3, 9, 18) times, every 6th row 0 (10, 12, 12, 8, 2) times, every 8th row 8 (3, 0, 0, 0, 0) times, every 10th row 2 (0, 0, 0, 0, 0) times—60 (66, 70, 76, 80, 86) sts. Work even with MC until piece measures 18" from beg.

Shape cap
Bind off 3 sts at beg of next 2 (2, 2, 4, 6, 6) rows, 2 sts at beg of next 2 (2, 4, 4, 4, 6) rows, dec 1 st at each edge every other row 6 (7, 7, 9, 10, 11) times, then every row 10 (12, 12, 10, 8, 8) times; bind off 2 sts at beg of next 4 rows. Bind off rem 10 sts.

FINISHING
Block pieces to measurements. Sew shoulder seams. Set in Sleeves. Sew side and sleeve seams.

Collar
With RS facing, using MC and circular needle, and beg at left Back neck, pick up and k73 (81, 89, 93, 93, 97) sts around neck. Do not join. Purl 1 row.
Chart row 1: Work sts 5–23 (1–23, 1–23, 3–23, 3–23, 1–23) once, work 18 st rep 3 (3, 3, 4, 4, 4) times, then work sts 0-0 (24–27, 6–17, 0-0, 0-0, 24–25). Work through row 14 of Chart. With A, work 2 more rows in St st. Bind off.

Button loops
With RS facing and using crochet hook, join A at top right corner of open edge of collar and work 1 row of sc along this edge of Back opening, evenly spacing three ch-3 button loops; cont to work 1 row of sc along opposite open edge. Fasten off. Sew buttons opposite button loops.

Fair Isle Pullover Chart

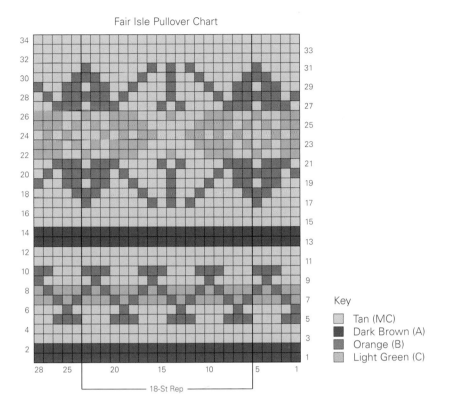

Key
- Tan (MC)
- Dark Brown (A)
- Orange (B)
- Light Green (C)

18-St Rep

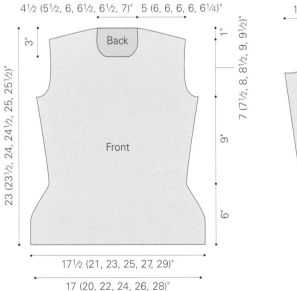

4½ (5½, 6, 6½, 6½, 7)"   5 (6, 6, 6, 6, 6¼)"

Back

3"   1"

7 (7½, 8, 8½, 9, 9½)"

23 (23½, 24, 24½, 25, 25½)"

9"

Front

6"

17½ (21, 23, 25, 27, 29)"

17 (20, 22, 24, 26, 28)"

12 (13, 14, 15, 16, 17)"

Sleeve

4½ (5¼, 5½, 6, 6½, 7)"

18"

8 (8, 8, 9, 9, 9)"

shawl-collar
COAT

This hip-length cardigan doubles as a coat just heavy enough for cool autumn days or mild winters. Basically a ribbing stitch, the main pattern only looks complex. The wide button band folds over naturally to form a shawl collar, while large graphic buttons jazz up the front.

Designed by **Cathie Hammatt**   Photographed by **Akin Girav**

■ ■ ■ ▢ ▭ Intermediate

Sizes
S (M, L)
Instructions are written for the smallest size with changes for larger sizes given in parentheses. When only one number is given, it applies to all sizes.
Note: For ease in working, circle all numbers pertaining to the size you're knitting.

Finished Measurements
Bust = 41½ (46½, 51)", with closed front band
Length (Back) = 23½ (24½, 25½)"

Materials
Yarns
Bulky weight, 1,242 (1,350, 1,512) yds. [1,127 (1,225, 1,372) m] in red

Needles & Extras
- Size 8 (5 mm) needles OR SIZE NEEDED TO OBTAIN GAUGE
- Size 6 (4 mm) needles
- Blunt-end yarn needle
- Three buttons about 1½" in diameter
- Markers for buttons

Notes
Gauge
20 sts and 20 rows = 4" (10 cm) in Main pat st on larger needles. TAKE TIME TO CHECK YOUR GAUGE.

Knit

PATTERN STITCHES

Main Pattern Stitch
(multiple of 6 sts + 2)
Rows 1 and 3: P2, *k4, p2; rep from *.
Rows 2 and 4: K2, *p4, k2; rep from *.
Rows 5 and 7: K3, p2, *k4, p2; rep
from * across row, end k3.
Rows 6 and 8: P3, k2, *p4, k2; rep
from * across row, end p3.
  Rep Rows 1–8 for pat.

Seed Stitch
(over even number of sts)
Row 1: *K1, p1; rep from *.
Row 2: *P1, k1; rep from *.
  Rep Rows 1 and 2 for pat.

BACK

Using smaller needles, cast on 98 (110,
122) sts and work in Seed st for 2½".
Change to larger needles. Keeping the
first 6 sts at each edge in Seed st (for
side slit), work in pat beg with Row 1
of Main pat st until piece measures 4"
from cast-on edge. Keeping the Main

pat lined up, discontinue Seed st
edges and work all sts in pat until piece
measures 15 (15½, 16)", or desired
length to underarm.

Shape armholes

Bind off 8 (10, 11) sts at the beg of next
2 rows—82 (90, 100) sts rem. Dec 1
st each side every other row 7 (9, 10)
times—68 (72, 80) sts rem.
  Work even in pat until piece measures
23½ (24½, 25½)" from cast-on.

Shape shoulders
and Back neck

Work across 19 (19, 22) sts, attach
another ball of yarn, and bind off center
30 (34, 36) sts; work rem sts in pat to
end of row—19 (19, 22) sts on each
shoulder.
  Working both shoulders at the same
time and using both yarn balls, dec 1 st
at each neck edge one time—18 (18, 21)
sts each shoulder. Work 1 row even.
Bind off all sts.

RIGHT FRONT

Using smaller needles, cast on 49 (55,
61) sts and work in Seed st for 2½".
Change to larger needles and work as
for Back (maintain 4" in Seed st along
the armhole edge only for the side slit),
until piece measures 15 (15½, 16)" from
cast-on.

Shape armhole

At beg on next armhole-edge row, bind
off 8 (10, 11) sts; work across row. Dec
1 st at every other armhole-edge row 7
(9, 10) times—34 (36, 40) sts rem. Work
even until piece measures 21½ (22½,
23½)" from cast-on edge.

Shape neck

At neck edge, bind off 12 (14, 15) sts,
work to end of row—22 (22, 25) sts rem.
Then, at neck edge, dec 1 st every other
row 4 times—18 (18, 21) sts rem. Work
in pat until piece measures same as
Back. Bind off all sts.

LEFT FRONT

Work same as Right Front, reversing all shaping.

SLEEVE (MAKE 2)

With smaller needles, cast on 48 (50, 52) sts. Work in Seed st for cuff for 2½". Change to larger needles and work one row in Main pat st. Beg Sleeve inc as foll:

Sizes S and M only: On next row, inc 1 st at each side, then rep inc every 4th row 15 (18) more times, then every 6th row 3 (1) more times —86 (90) sts.

Size L only: On next row, inc 1 st at each side, then every 2nd row twice more, then every 4th row 19 times—96 sts.

All sizes: Cont working in pat until piece measures 16 (17, 17)" from beg of Main pat or desired length to underarm.

Note: The 2½" cuff is folded back when worn and is not included in this measurement.

Shape cap

Bind off 8 (10, 11) st at beg of next 2 rows—70 (70, 74) sts rem. Dec 1 st each side every other row 7 (9, 10) times— 56 (52, 54) sts rem. Dec 1 st each side every row 7 (5, 5) times—42 (42, 44) sts rem. Bind off 3 (3, 4) sts at the beg of next 4 rows. Bind off rem 30 (30, 28) sts.

FINISHING

Sew shoulder seams tog. Leaving 4" open at lower side edge (side slits), sew side seams tog. Set Sleeves into armhole openings and sew in place. Sew sleeve seams.

Button band (Left Front): With smaller needle and RS facing, join yarn and pick up and k90 (96, 97) sts along front edge. Adjust these numbers if necessary. It's more important to pick up the number of sts that best fits along the front edges. The left and right bands, however, must be worked on the same number of sts. Work in Seed st for 2½". Bind off in Seed st, maintaining the same elasticity as the rest of the band.

Buttonhole band (Right Front): Rep as for Left Front until you've worked 1¼".

Buttonhole Row: The coat has 3 buttons. The middle button is at the midpoint of the band, and the other two are spaced evenly from that point. Mark the left Front band for the spacing and then refer to these markers when working the buttonholes on the right Front band. Buttonholes are worked as foll: Work in Seed st to the position marked for the first button, bind off 3 sts; *work in Seed st to the next position, bind off 3 sts; rep from * for the next buttonhole, complete the row in Seed st.

Next row: Work in Seed st and cast on 3 sts over each set of bound-off sts; work to end of row. Complete the right band same as for left. Align bands and sew buttons on Left Front at marked areas to match buttonholes.

Collar

With smaller needles, pick up and k30 (34, 36) from the bound-off Back neck sts. *Working in Seed st, cast on 2 sts at the beg of every row, then work to end of row. Rep from * until collar reaches around the coat neck to the front edge of each band. Work 1 more row. Bind off loosely in Seed st. Sew unattached collar ends to neckline and front bands. Weave in ends.

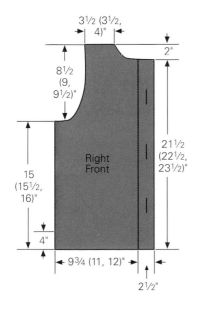

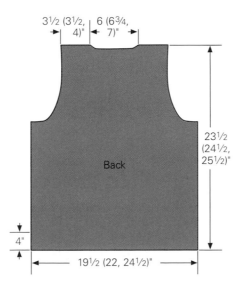

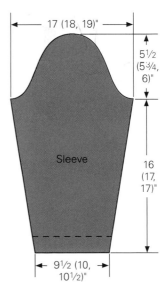

peplum CARDIGAN

A feminine twist to an ordinary cardigan, this peplum design alternates vertical "waves" with bands of stockinette stitch. The gaps are an intentional style statement, but you can make the sweater in a slightly larger size for an easier fit if you choose.

Designed by **Elena Malo**   Photographed by **Tony Lattari**

■■■■□ Intermediate

Sizes
XS (S, M, L, 1X, 2X)
Instructions are written for the smallest size with changes for larger sizes given in parentheses. When only one number is given, it applies to all sizes.
Note: For ease in working, circle all numbers pertaining to the size you're knitting.

Finished Measurements
Bust (buttoned) = 32 (34, 38, 40, 46, 50)"
Length (Back with band)= 23½ (23½, 24, 24½, 25, 25½)"

Materials
Yarns
Worsted weight wool blend, 924 (1,092, 1,176, 1,260, 1,344, 1,428) yds. [781 (923, 994, 1,065, 1,136, 1207) m] in tan

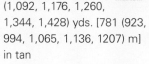

Needles & Extras
- Scrap yarn in contrast color (CC)
- Size 10 (6 mm) needles OR SIZE NEEDED TO OBTAIN GAUGE
- Size 8 (5 mm) needles
- Size 5 (3.75 mm) needles
- Size 8 (5 mm) 29" circular needle
- Five ⅝"-diameter buttons
- Blunt-end yarn needle

Notes
Gauge
16 sts and 24 rows = 4" (10 cm) in St st (knit all RS rows, purl all WS rows) using largest needles. TAKE TIME TO CHECK YOUR GAUGE.

Special Abbreviations
RT = Knit into the front of the 2nd st on needle, then knit the first st, slipping both sts off needle together.
LT = Knit into the back of the 2nd st on needle, then knit the first st, slipping both sts off needle together.
Scrap Yarn Cast-On = With Contrasting Color (CC/scrap) yarn, cast on the required number of stitches using the single cast-on method (just twist the loops onto the needle). Cut the yarn, leaving an 8" tail.
Row 1 (WS): Change to size 5 needles and MC and knit across.
Row 2: Change to size 8 needles, *k1; with yarn in front (wyif), sl 1 purlwise (pwise); rep from * across, end k1.
Row 3: *Wyif, sl 1 pwise; k1; rep from * to last st, sl last st. The CC/scrap yarn can be removed after several more rows in pat have been completed.

Knit

PATTERN STITCHES

Little Wave Pattern

(worked over 3 sts; a 12-row rep)

Row 1 (RS): Knit.

Row 2: K2, p1.

Row 3: LT, k1.

Row 4: K1, p1, k1.

Row 5: K1, LT.

Row 6: P1, k2.

Row 7: Knit.

Row 8: Rep Row 6.

Row 9: K1, RT.

Row 10: Rep Row 4.

Row 11: RT, k1.

Row 12: Rep Row 2. Rep Rows 1–12 for Little Wave pat.

Note: Refer to Special Abbreviations section, *page 26*, for instructions on Scrap Yarn Cast-On.

BACK

Using size 8 straight needles, scrap yarn, and the Scrap Yarn Cast-On, cast on 103 (107, 115, 119, 127, 135) sts and work 3 rows as directed. Change to largest needles and begin Little Wave pat.

Row 1 (RS): Knit.

Row 2 (Setup Row and Row 2 of Little Wave pat): P8 (10, 7, 9, 6, 10), *(k2, p1—Little Wave pat sts), p9 (9, 11, 11, 13, 13); rep from * 6 more times, end (k2, p1—Little Wave pat sts), p8 (10, 7, 9, 6, 10). Cont working Little Wave pat sts through Row 8 as est and remainder of sts in St st (k every RS row, p every WS row).

Row 9—Dec row: K6 (8, 5, 7, 4, 8), k2tog *k1, RT, k7 (7, 9, 9, 11, 11), k2tog; rep from * 6 times more, end k1, RT, k6 (8, 5, 7, 4, 8), k2tog—94 (98, 106, 110, 118, 126) sts. Cont as est, rep Dec row (working dec at end of each St st panel) every 10th row 4 more times—58 (62, 70, 74, 82, 90) sts. Work even until piece measures 12 (12, 12, 12, 10, 10)" from beg.

Next row—Inc row: Cont in pat and inc 1 st each side every 6th row 3 (3, 3, 3, 5, 5) times—64 (68, 76, 80, 92, 100) sts. Piece should measure approx 15" from beg, ending with a WS row.

Shape armholes

Keeping to pat, bind off 2 (2, 3, 3, 3, 3) sts at beg of next 2 rows, 0 (0, 0, 0, 2, 3) sts at beg of next 2 rows.

Next row—Dec row (RS): K1, ssk, work to last 3 sts, k2tog, k1. Rep Dec row 1 (1, 2, 2, 2, 3) more times—56 (60, 64, 68, 76, 80) sts. Work even until armholes measure 7 (7, 7½, 8, 8½, 9)".

Shape shoulders

Bind off 4 (4, 5, 5, 6, 6) sts at the beg of next 8 (6, 8, 8, 8, 6) rows, 0 (6, 0, 0, 0, 8) sts at the beg of next 0 (2, 0, 0, 0, 2) rows. Bind off rem 24 (24, 24, 28, 28, 28) sts for Back neck.

RIGHT FRONT

Working 3 rows of Scrap Yarn Cast-On as before, cast on 50 (52, 56, 58, 62, 66) sts. Change to largest needles and beg Little Wave pat.

Row 1: Knit.

Row 2 (Setup Row and Row 2 of Little Wave pat): P3 (3, 4, 4, 5, 5), *k2, p1, p9 (9, 11, 11, 13, 13); rep from * twice more, end (k2, p1, p8 (10, 7, 9, 6, 10). Cont in pat as est through Row 8.

Row 9—Dec row: K6 (8, 5, 7, 4, 8), k2tog; *k1, RT, k7 (7, 9, 9, 11, 11), k2tog; rep from * twice more, end k1, RT, k3 (3, 4, 4, 5, 5)—46 (48, 52, 54, 58, 62) sts. Cont as est, rep Dec row (working dec at end of each of first 4 St st panels) every 10th row 4 more times—30 (32, 36, 38, 42, 46) sts. Work even until piece measures 12 (12, 12, 12, 10, 10)" from beg. Cont as est and work incs at side edge only as for Back. Work even until piece measures 15" from beg, end with a WS row—33 (35, 39, 41, 45, 51) sts.

Shape neck

Next row—Dec row (RS): K1, ssk, work to end. Rep Dec row at neck edge every 4th row 12 (12, 12, 14, 14, 14) more times and AT THE SAME TIME, when piece measures same as Back to armhole, work armhole shaping same as Back at side edge. Work even until piece measures same as Back to shoulder, ending with a RS row—16 (18, 20, 20, 22, 24) sts.

Shape shoulder

At armhole edge only, bind off 4 (4, 5, 5, 5, 6) sts on every other row 4 (3, 4, 4, 4, 4) times; bind off 0 (6, 0, 0, 2, 0) sts at the beg of next WS row.

LEFT FRONT

Work as for Right Front, reversing all shaping and set up as foll:

Row 1 (RS): Knit.

Row 2 (Setup Row and Row 2 of Little Wave pat): P8 (10, 7, 9, 6, 10), *k2, p1, p9 (9, 11, 11, 13, 13); rep from * twice more, end k2, p1, p3 (3, 4, 4, 5, 5). Cont in pat as est through Row 8. Work Dec rows as for Right Front, working dec st at end of each of last 4 St st panels.

SLEEVE (MAKE 2)

Working 3 rows of Scrap Yarn Cast-On as before, cast on 37 sts. Change to largest needles and begin Little Wave pat.

Row 1: Knit.

Row 2 (Setup Row and Row 2 of Little Wave pat): P3, *k2, p1, p4; rep from * to last 6 sts, end k2, p1, p3. Cont in pat as est until piece measures 3". Inc 1 st at each side, working incs into pat, on next row then every 6th row 0 (0, 0, 0, 5, 7) times, every 8th row 0 (0, 0, 7, 6, 5) times, every 10th row 0 (0, 5, 2, 0, 0) times, every 12th row 4 (5, 2, 0, 0, 0) times—47 (49, 53, 57, 61, 63) sts. Work even until piece measures 16 (17, 18, 18, 18, 18½)" from beg, ending with a WS row.

Shape cap

Bind off 3 sts at beg of next 2 rows, 2 (2, 2, 3, 3, 3) sts at beg of next 2 rows—37 (39, 43, 45, 49, 51) sts.

Next row—Dec row: K1, ssk, work to last 3 sts, k2tog, k1.

Rep Dec row every other row 10 (11, 13, 14, 16, 17) more times. Bind off rem 15 sts.

FINISHING

Block pieces to measurements. Sew shoulder seams. Set in Sleeves. Sew side and sleeve seams.

Front band

With RS facing and circular needle, beg at lower edge of Right Front, pick up 1 st for each row to shoulder; 24 (24, 24, 28, 28, 28) sts across Back neck and 1 st for each row to lower edge of Left Front. K 1 row. Place markers for buttons on Right Front as foll: the first one 3½" from lower edge, the last one 3½" above beg of neck shaping, the one below that at beg of neck shaping and the other 2 spaced evenly between first marker and marker at neck shaping.

Row 2—Buttonhole Row: *Knit to marker, bind off 2 sts; rep from * 4 more times, knit to end. K 1 row, casting on 2 sts over bound-off sts.

Bind off. Sew on buttons opposite buttonholes.

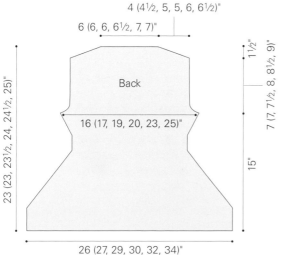

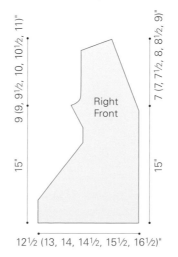

knee-length DOT COAT

When autumn's chill fills the air, reach for this chunky-knit coat that's crafted with thick double crochet stitches—it'll keep you cozy. The rich brown color creates a strong contrast for decorative cream-color circles that are crocheted separately and appliquéd in place.

Designed by **Ann E. Smith**
Photographed by **Greg Scheidemann**

▆▆ ▆ ▭ ▭ **Easy**

Sizes

S (M, L, XL)
Instructions are written for the smallest size with changes for larger sizes given in parentheses. When only one number is given, it applies to all sizes.
Note: For ease in working, circle all numbers pertaining to the size you're crocheting.

Finished Measurements
Bust (closed) = 42 (45, 49, 52¼)"
Length (Back) = 33 (34½, 34½, 36¼)"

Materials

Yarns
Bulky weight, 1,224 (1,377, 1,530, 1,683) yds. [1,120 (1,260, 1,400, 1,540) m] in dark brown (MC)

Worsted weight, approximately 400 yds. (360 m) in cream (CC)

Hooks & Extras
- Size K/10½ (6.5 mm) crochet hook OR SIZE NEEDED TO OBTAIN GAUGE
- Size G/6 (4 mm) crochet hook
- Blunt-end yarn needle

Notes
Gauge
Worked in dc on larger hook with MC, 14 sts = 6" and 4 rows = 5". TAKE TIME TO CHECK YOUR GAUGE.

Crochet

PATTERN STITCHES

Dc2tog (double-crochet two together): (Yo and draw up a lp in next st, yo and draw through 2 lps on hook) twice, yo and draw through all 3 lps on hook.

Dc3tog (double-crochet three together): (Yo and draw up a lp in next st, yo and draw through 2 lps on hook) 3 times, yo and draw through all 4 lps on hook.

BACK
Using larger hook and MC, ch 54 (58, 62, 66).
Row 1: Dc in 4th ch from hook—counts as dc; dc in each ch across—52 (56, 60, 64) sts; turn.
Row 2 (WS): Ch 3—counts as dc; dc in each dc across; turn.
Row 3: Ch 3—counts as dc; dc2tog, dc in each dc across to last 3 sts, dc2tog, dc in last dc—50 (54, 58, 62) sts; turn.

Rep last 2 rows once more—48 (52, 56, 60) sts. Work even to approx 24 (24¾, 24, 24¾)" from beg.

Shape armholes
Sl st in first 5 sts, ch 3—counts as dc; dc2tog, dc in each dc across to last 7 sts, dc2tog, dc in next dc, leave last 4 sts unworked—38 (42, 46, 50) sts.

Dec row: Ch 3—counts as dc; dc2tog, dc in each dc across to last 3 sts, dc2tog, dc in last dc—36 (40, 44, 48) sts; turn. Rep Dec row 2 (3, 3, 4) more times.

Work even on rem 32 (34, 38, 40) sts to approx 32 (33½, 33½, 35)" from beg. Fasten off.

RIGHT FRONT

Using larger hook and MC, ch 28 (30, 32, 34).

Row 1: Dc in 4th ch from hook and in each ch across—26 (28, 30, 32) sts; turn.
Row 2: Ch 3—counts as dc; dc in each dc across; turn.
Row 3: Ch 3—counts as dc; dc in each dc across to last 3 sts, dc2tog, dc in last dc; turn. Rep last 2 rows once more—24 (26, 28, 30) sts. Work even to approx 24 (24¾, 24, 24¾)" from beg.

Shape armhole

Dec row 1: Ch 3—counts as dc; dc in each dc across to last 7 sts; work dc2tog, dc in next dc, leave last 4 sts unworked—19 (21, 23, 25) sts.

Dec row 2: Ch 3—counts as dc; dc2tog, dc in each dc across; turn.
Dec row 3: Ch 3—counts as dc; dc in each dc across, ending dc2tog, dc in last dc; turn.

Rep last 2 rows until 16 (17, 19, 20) sts rem. Work even to approx 29½ (31, 31, 32¾)" from beg or 2 rows less than Back.

Shape neck

Next row: Sl st in first 6 sts, sc in next st, hdc in next st, dc in last 8 (9, 11, 12) sts; turn.
Next row: Ch 3—counts as dc; dc in each of next 7 (8, 10, 11) dc. Fasten off.

LEFT FRONT

Using larger hook and MC, ch 28 (30, 32, 34).

Row 1: Dc in 4th ch from hook and in each ch across—26 (28, 30, 32) sts; turn.
Row 2: Ch 3—counts as dc; dc in each dc across; turn.
Row 3: Ch 3—counts as dc; dc2tog, dc in each dc across; turn.

Rep last 2 rows once more—24 (26, 28, 30) sts. Work even to approx 24 (24¾, 24, 24¾)" from beg.

Shape armhole

Dec row 1: Sl st in first 5 sts, ch 3—counts as dc; dc2tog, dc in each dc across—19 (21, 23, 25) sts.
Dec row 2: Ch 3—counts as dc; dc in each dc across to last 3 sts, dc2tog, dc in last dc; turn.
Dec row 3: Ch 3—counts as dc; dc2tog, dc in each dc across; turn.

Rep last 2 rows until 16 (17, 19, 20) sts rem. Work even to approx 29½ (31, 31, 32¾)" from beg or 2 rows less than Back.
Next row—shape neck: Ch 3—counts as dc; dc in next 7 (8, 10, 11) sts, hdc in next st, sc in next st; turn.
Next row: Sl st in next sc, hdc, and dc; ch 3—counts as dc; dc in last 7 (8,10,11) dc. Fasten off.

SLEEVE (MAKE 2)

Using larger hook and MC, ch 31 (31, 33, 33).

Row 1: Dc in 4th ch from hook and in each ch across—29 (29, 31, 31) sts; turn.

Row 2: Ch 3—counts as dc; dc in each dc across; turn. Rep Row 2 for 8 (8, 8, 6) more times.

Inc row: Ch 3—counts as dc; 2 dc in next dc, dc in each dc across to last 2 sts, 2 dc in next dc, dc in last dc—31 (31, 33, 33) sts. Rep Inc row every 3 (2, 2, 2) rows 3 (4, 4, 5) more times. Work even on 37 (39, 41, 43) sts to approx 18½" from beg.

Shape cap

Row 1: Sl st in first 5 sts; ch 3—counts as dc; dc2tog, dc in each dc across to last 7 sts, dc2tog, dc in next dc, leave last 4 sts unworked—27 (29, 31, 33) sts. Dec 1 st each edge every row 6 (7, 8, 9) times—15 sts.

Last row: Ch 3—counts as dc; dc3tog, dc in each dc across to last 4 sts, dc3tog, dc in last dc—11 sts. Fasten off.

CIRCLES

Note: Leave a long tail for joining Circles to garment on last rnd of each Circle. Using CC and smaller hook, ch 4; work 12 dc in 4th ch from hook—13 dc; join in 3rd ch of beg ch-4.

Rnd 2: Ch 3—counts as dc; dc in same st as join, 2 dc in each dc around—26 sts; join.

Rnd 3: Ch 3—counts as dc; (2 dc in next dc, dc in next dc) around; end with 2 dc in last dc—39 sts; join.

Rnd 4: Ch 3—counts as dc; dc in next dc; (2 dc in next dc, dc in next 2 dc) around; end with 2 dc in last dc—52 sts; join. Fasten off.

Work Rnds 1–4 for large Circles, Rnds 1–3 for medium ones and Rnds 1 and 2 for small ones. Make 4 large, 5 medium, and 6 small circles.

FINISHING

Pin Circles onto coat. Sew in place with saved tail. Join shoulder seams. Set in Sleeves. Join underarm and side seams.

Collar

With RS facing, larger hook, and MC, work 42 (44, 48, 50) sc evenly along neck edge; turn. Work 3 more sc rows. Fasten off.

Body edging

With RS facing and larger hook, join MC at lower edge in seam.

Ch 1, sc in each ch to corner, 3 sc in corner, 2 sc over each dc post, sc in each collar row, 2 sc over each dc post, 3 sc in corner, sc in each rem ch along lower edge; join with sl st in first sc.

Rnd 2: Join a 2nd strand of MC to work border with 2 strands held tog. Working left to right for reverse sc, sc in each sc to one st past corner; sc in each sc along front edge and at same time, sk 8 sts evenly spaced before collar; sc in each sc around collar and at same time, sk 6 sts evenly spaced. Sc in each sc along next front and at same time, sk 8 sts evenly spaced; sc in each rem sc along lower edge. Fasten off. Weave in loose ends.

Button

With CC and smaller hook, work Rnds 1 and 2 of Circle. Do not fasten off.

Rnd 3: Ch 1, (sc in dc, sk next dc) around—13 sts. Make a small ball using approx ½ yd. of CC; stuff into center of button.

Last rnd: *Sl st in every other st around; rep from * until the opening is closed. Leaving a long tail, fasten off. Use tail to sew button to Left Front in first dc row below collar so that it fits next to the reverse sc border.

Button loop

With WS facing and larger hook, join MC with sl st in border sc bet last 2 dc rows on Left Front.

Ch 15, sl st in same sp as joining. Leaving a tail, fasten off. Wrap tail several times around lp and secure in place.

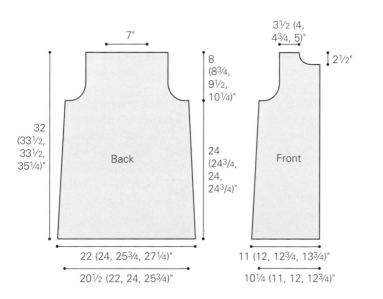

The striking snowflake pattern and the white-trim edges on this irresistible turtleneck set it apart from the usual lodge look.

FAIR ISLE
turtleneck

Designed by **Gayle Bunn**   Photographed by **Tony Lattari**

■■ ■■ ■■ ■■ ■■ **Experienced**

Sizes

S (M, L, 1X, 2X)

Instructions are written for the smallest size with changes for larger sizes given in parentheses. When only one number is given, it applies to all sizes.

Note: For ease in working, circle all numbers pertaining to the size you're knitting.

Finished Measurements

Bust = 36 (40, 44, 48, 52)"
Length (Back without turtleneck) = 23 (23½, 24, 24½, 24½)"

Materials

Yarns

Worsted weight 100% wool, 1,100 (1,210 , 1,320, 1,430, 1,540) yds. [1,000 (1,100, 1,200, 1,300, 1,400) m] in green (MC)

Worsted weight 100% wool, 330 (330, 440, 440, 550) yds. [300 (300, 400, 400, 500) m] in white (CC)

Needles & Extras

- Size 7 (4.5 mm) needles OR SIZE NEEDED TO OBTAIN GAUGE
- Size 6 (4 mm) needles
- Blunt-end yarn needle
- Two stitch holders

Notes

Gauge

20 sts and 24 rows = 4" (10 cm) in Fair Isle pat with larger needles. TAKE TIME TO CHECK YOUR GAUGE.

Chart Explanation

On right side (RS) rows, read chart from right to left and knit; on wrong side (WS) rows, read chart from left to right and purl. To begin a new row, be sure to start where you ended the previous row. For example, to follow instructions for size S, work Chart 1 as follows: beg with Row 1 (RS row), work from A to B 7 times (reading right to left), then work from B to C once to finish row. For Row 2 (WS row), read chart from left to right. Because last st knitted on Row 1 was at C, beg by purling from C to B sts, then purl sts B to A, then purl sts B to A repeatedly to finish row.

Knit

BACK

With smaller needles and CC, cast on 90 (98, 106, 118, 126) sts.
Row 1 (RS): *K2, p2; rep from * to last 2 sts, k2. Fasten off CC; attach MC.
Row 2: *P2, k2, rep from * to last 2 sts, p2.
Rep these 2 rows until piece measures 2½", inc 0 (4, 8, 2, 6) sts evenly across last rep of Row 2—90 (102, 114, 120, 132) sts. Change to larger needles.

Chart 1

Work Rows 1–19 of Chart 1, *page 37*, as foll for odd-numbered rows: work from A to B 7 (8, 9, 9, 10) times, B to C once, C to D 0 (0, 0, 1, 1) time(s). When reading chart from left to right for even-numbered rows, work from D to C 0 (0, 0, 1, 1) time(s); C to B once; B to A 7 (8, 9, 9, 10) times.

Chart 2

Beg with a purl row, work Rows 1–6 of Chart 2, *page 37*, as foll: work from D to C 0 (0, 0, 1, 1) time, from C to B once, B to A 7 (8, 9, 9, 10) times. Continue to work in pat from chart.
   Rep Rows 1–6 six more times.
Next row (WS): Using CC, p across.

Chart 3

Beg with a knit row, work Chart 3, *opposite*, as foll:

Size S: Work from C to D 5 times.

Size M: Work from A to C once, C to D 5 times, D to F once.

Size L: Work from B to C once, C to D 6 times, D to E once.

Size 1X: Work from A to C once, C to D 6 times, D to F once.

Size 2X: Work from B to C once, C to D 7 times, D to E once.

Work through Row 17 and keeping to pat, beg armhole shaping.

Shape armholes

Keeping to pat, bind off 6 (8, 10, 12, 13) sts at beg of next 2 rows—78 (86, 94, 96, 106) sts. Dec 1 st at each edge every RS row 5 (7, 9, 10, 12) times—68 (72, 76, 76, 82) sts and AT THE SAME TIME, when Chart 3 is completed, cont dot pat as est by rep Rows 31–36 until armholes measure 7¾ (8¼, 9, 9½, 9½)", ending with a WS row.

Shape shoulders

Cont dot pat, bind off 8 (8, 8, 8, 10) sts at beg of next 2 rows—52 (56, 60, 60, 62) sts. Bind off 8 (9, 9, 9, 10) sts at beg of next 2 rows; sl rem 36 (38, 42, 42, 42) sts onto holder for neck.

FRONT

Work same as Back until armholes measure 16 rows less than Back, ending with a WS row (count Back rows from armhole shaping to neck; subtract 16; difference is number of rows to work from Front armhole shaping).

Shape neck

Next row (RS): Keeping to pat, k25 (29, 29, 29, 31) sts; sl rem sts to spare needle. Dec 1 st at neck edge every row until 16 (17, 17, 17, 20) sts rem.

Work even in pat until armholes measure same as Back to beg of shoulder shaping, ending with a WS row.

Shape shoulders

Next row (RS): Keeping to pat, bind off 8 (8, 8, 8, 10) sts, work to end of row. Work 1 row even. Bind off rem 8 (9, 9, 9, 10) sts.

With RS facing, sl center 18 (18, 18, 18, 20) sts onto holder for neck. Work shoulder shaping on rem sts, reversing all shaping.

SLEEVE (MAKE 2)

Using smaller needles and CC, cast on 46 (46, 46, 50, 50) sts. Work ribbing same as Back and inc 2 (2, 8, 4, 4) sts evenly across last row—48 (48, 54, 54, 54) sts. Change to larger needles.

Chart 1

Rows 1–19 as foll: Work from A to B 4 times, B to C 0 (0, 1, 1, 1) time(s) and AT THE SAME TIME inc 1 st at each edge of rows 5, 11, and 17—54 (54, 60, 60, 60) sts.

Chart 2

Rows 1–6: Beg with a purl row, work C to B 1 (1, 0, 0, 0) time(s), B to A 4 (4, 5, 5, 5) times; inc 1 st at each edge on Row 6—56 (56, 62, 62, 62) sts. Work 6 rows of Chart 2 ten more times, inc 1 st at each edge every 6th row 5 times and then every 8th row 3 times—72 (72, 78, 78, 78) sts.

Next row (WS): With A, p across.

Chart 3

Work Rows 1–18 as follows:

Sizes S and M only: Work from C to D 4 times.

Sizes L, 1X, 2X only: Work from B to C once, C to D 4 times, D to E once.

Shape cap

Cont to work Chart 3 and beg with Row 19, bind off 3 (3, 5, 5, 5) sts at beg of next 2 rows—66 (66, 68, 68, 68) sts. Dec 1 st each edge every other row 8 (12, 15, 20, 20) times, then on every row 18 (14, 12, 6, 6) times—14 (14, 14, 16, 16) sts rem and AT THE SAME TIME, when Chart 3 is completed, cont dot pattern as est by rep Rows 31–36. Bind off.

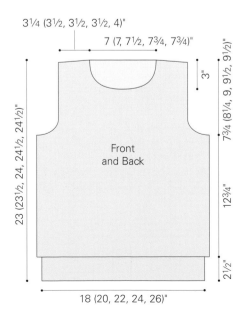

3¼ (3½, 3½, 3½, 4)"

7 (7, 7½, 7¾, 7¾)"

3"

7¾ (8¼, 9, 9½, 9½)"

23 (23½, 24, 24½, 24½)"

12¾"

Front and Back

2½"

18 (20, 22, 24, 26)"

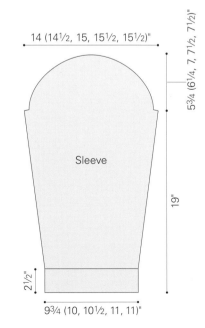

14 (14½, 15, 15½, 15½)"

5¾ (6¼, 7, 7½, 7½)"

Sleeve

19"

2½"

9¾ (10, 10½, 11, 11)"

FINISHING

Sew right shoulder seam.

Turtleneck

With RS facing and using smaller needles and MC, pick up and knit 24 sts down left Front neck edge, 18 (18, 18, 18, 20) sts from Front st holder, 24 sts up right Front neck edge, and 36 (38, 42, 42, 42) sts from Back st holder—102 (104, 108, 108, 110) sts.

Next row (WS): Work in k2, p2 ribbing for 5½", end with a WS row. Using CC, work 2 rows ribbing, then bind off in ribbing.

Sew Sleeves to armhole edges. Sew side and sleeve seams.

■ Green (MC)
□ White (CC)

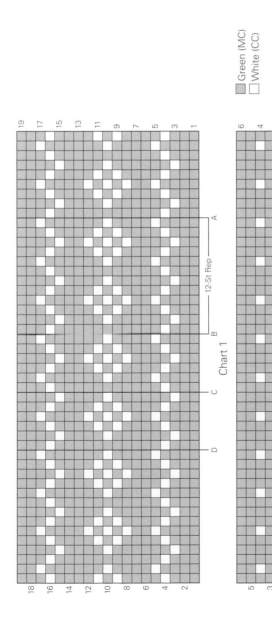

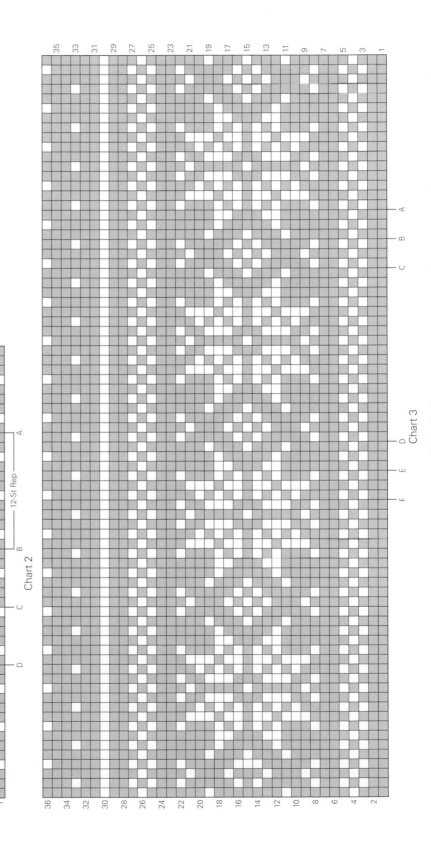

WHITE cabled PULLOVER

Designed by **Melissa Leapman**
Photographed by **Tony Lattari**

■■ ■■ ■■ ■■ ■■ **Experienced**

Sizes
S (M, L, 1X, 2X, 3X)
Instructions are written for the smallest size with changes for larger sizes given in parentheses. When only one number is given, it applies to all sizes.
Note: For ease in working, circle all numbers pertaining to the size you're knitting.

Finished Measurements
Bust = 36 (40, 44, 48, 52, 56)"
Length (Back) = 22 (23, 24, 25, 26, 27)"

Materials
Yarns
Bulky weight 100% wool, 1,100 (1,240, 1,310, 1,450, 1,520, 1,660) yds. [1,000 (1,125, 1,190, 1,315, 1,380, 1,505) m] in cream
OR
(2 strands held tog) Worsted weight cashmere blend, 2,200 (2,420, 2,640, 2,860, 3,080, 3,300) yds. [2,000 (2,200, 2,400, 2,600, 2,800, 3,000) m] in cream

Needles & Extras
• Size 11 (8 mm) needles OR SIZE NEEDED TO OBTAIN GAUGE
• Size 13 (9 mm) needles
• Cable needle (cn)
• Two stitch holders
• Stitch markers
• Blunt-end yarn needle

Notes
Gauge
16 sts and 20 rows = 4" (10 cm) in Reverse St st (knit all WS rows, purl all RS rows) with larger needles. TAKE TIME TO CHECK YOUR GAUGE.

Special Abbreviations
6-st RC (RIGHT CROSS) = Slip 3 sts onto cn and hold in back of work; k3, k3 from cn.
6-st LC (LEFT CROSS) = Slip 3 sts onto cn and hold in front of work; k3, k3 from cn.
4-st RC (RIGHT CROSS) = Slip 1 st onto cn and hold in back of work; k3, p1 from cn.
4-st LC (LEFT CROSS) = Slip 3 sts onto cn and hold in front of work; p1, k3 from cn.

This stunner
with intertwined
cables is a welcome
challenge for
an experienced
knitter. Knit it in
100 percent wool
yarn or, if your
budget can bear it,
pick a cashmere-
and-silk blend.

Knit

PATTERN STITCHES

Cable Panel A (worked over 20 sts; 12-row rep)

Row 1 (RS): K3, p4; work 6-st RC over next 6 sts; p4, k3.

Row 2 and all WS rows: K the knit sts and p the purl sts.

Row 3: K3, p3; work 4-st RC; work 4-st LC; p3, k3.

Row 5: K3, p2; work 4-st RC, p2, work 4-st LC, p2, k3.

Row 7: K3, p2, k3, p4, k3, p2, k3.

Row 9: K3, p2, work 4-st LC, p2, work 4-st RC, p2, k3.

Row 11: K3, p3, work 4-st LC, work 4-st RC, p3, k3.

Row 12: Rep Row 2.

Rep Rows 1–12 for Cable Panel A.

Cable Panel B (worked over 24 sts; 24-row rep)

Row 1 (RS): P2, k3, p4, work 6-st LC, p4, k3, p2.

Row 2 and all WS rows: Knit the knit sts and purl the purl sts.

Row 3: P2, (work 4-st LC, p2, work 4-st RC) twice, p2.

Row 5: P3, (work 4-st LC, work 4-st RC, p2) twice, p1.

Row 7: P4, work 6-st RC, p4, work 6-st LC, p4.

Row 9: P3, (work 4-st RC, work 4-st LC, p2) twice, p1.

Row 11: P2, (work 4-st RC, p2, work 4-st LC) twice, p2.

Row 13: P2, k3, p4, work 6-st RC, p4, k3, p2.

Row 15: Rep Row 3.

Row 17: Rep Row 5.

Row 19: P4, work 6-st LC, p4, work 6-st RC, p4.

Row 21: Rep Row 9.

Row 23: Rep Row 11.

Row 24: Rep Row 2.

Rep Rows 1–24 for Cable Panel B.

BACK

Using smaller needles, cast on 72 (80, 88, 96, 104, 112) sts.

Next row (RS): (K2, p2) 1 (2, 3, 4, 5, 6) time(s); k3; (p2, k2) 3 times; p2; (k3, p2) twice; (k2, p2) 3 times; (k3, p2) twice; (k2, p2) 3 times; k3; (p2, k2) 1 (2, 3, 4, 5, 6) times.

Next row: K the knit sts and p the purl sts. Rep these 2 rows until piece measures 2½" from beg, ending with a WS row. Change to larger needles.

Setup row (RS): Purl across 4 (8, 12, 16, 20, 24) sts for Reverse St st, place marker (pm), work Row 1 of Cable Panel A across next 20 sts, pm, work Row 1 of Cable Panel B across next 24 sts, pm, work Row 1 of Cable Panel A across next 20 sts, pm, purl to end of row for Reverse St st.

Work even in Reverse St st and Cable Panels until piece measures 13½ (14, 14½, 15, 15½, 16)", ending with a WS row.

Shape armholes

Keeping to pat, bind off 4 sts at beg of next 2 rows—64 (72, 80, 88, 96, 104) sts. Dec 1 st each edge of next row once, then every other row 3 times—56 (64, 72, 80, 88, 96) sts. Work even in pat until piece measures 22 (23, 24, 25, 26, 27)" from beg, ending with a WS row.

Shape shoulders

Keeping to pat, bind off 7 (9, 11, 13, 15, 17) sts at beg of next 2 rows—42 (46, 50, 54, 58, 62) sts. Bind off 8 (9, 10, 11, 12, 13) sts at beg of next 2 rows—sl rem 26 (28, 30, 32, 34, 36) sts onto holder for neck.

FRONT

Work same as Back until piece measures 19 (20, 21, 22, 23, 24)" from beg, ending with a WS row.

Shape neck

Next row (RS): Work across first 20 (23, 26, 29, 32, 35) sts; join another ball of yarn, bind off next 16 (18, 20, 22, 24, 26) sts, work rem 20 (23, 26, 29, 32, 35) sts. Working both sides at once with separate balls of yarn, bind off 2 sts at each neck edge once, then dec 1 st each neck edge every row 3 times—15 (18, 21, 24, 27, 30) sts each side. Continue, if necessary, until piece measures same as Back to shoulders.

Shape shoulders

Working both sides at once with separate balls of yarn, shape shoulders same as for Back.

SLEEVE (MAKE 2)

Using smaller needles, cast on 36 (36, 36, 44, 44, 44) sts.

Next row (RS): (K2, p2) 2 (2, 2, 3, 3, 3) times; k3; (p2, k2) 3 times; p2, k3; (p2, k2) 2 (2, 2, 3, 3, 3) times.

Next row: K the knit sts and p the purl sts. Rep last 2 rows until piece measures 2½" from beg, ending with a WS row. Change to larger needles.

Set-up row (RS): P across 8 (8, 8, 12, 12, 12) sts for Reverse St st, pm, work Row 1 of Cable Panel A across next 20 sts, p across rem 8 (8, 8, 12, 12, 12) sts for Reverse St st.

Work in Reverse St st and Cable Panel A as established, inc 1 st each edge every 7 (6, 6, 8, 7, 7) rows 8 (1, 8, 7, 4, 9) times, then every 8 (7, 7, 9, 8, 8) rows 4 (12, 6, 4, 8, 4) times—60 (62, 64, 66, 68, 70) sts.

Work even until Sleeve measures 17½ (18, 18, 18½, 18½, 19)" from beg, ending with a WS row.

Shape cap
Bind off 4 sts at beg of next 2 rows—
52 (54, 56, 58, 60, 62) sts. Dec 1 st each
edge every other row 10 (11, 12, 13, 14,
15) times—32 sts (all sizes). Dec 1 st
each edge every row until 16 sts rem.
Bind off 3 sts at beg of next 4 rows; bind
off rem 4 sts.

FINISHING
Sew left shoulder seam.

Neckband
With RS facing and using smaller
needles, pick up and k66 (70, 74, 78, 82,
86) sts evenly spaced along neck edge.
Next row (RS): P1, *k2, p2, rep from *
across, ending p1.
Next row: K the knit sts and p the purl
sts. Rep these 2 rows until neckband
measures 4" from beg. Bind off loosely
in pattern. Sew right shoulder and
neckband seam.

 Sew Sleeves to Front and Back
armholes. Sew side and sleeve seams.

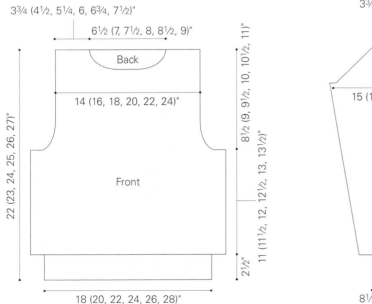

3¾ (4½, 5¼, 6, 6¾, 7½)"

6½ (7, 7½, 8, 8½, 9)"

Back

14 (16, 18, 20, 22, 24)"

22 (23, 24, 25, 26, 27)"

Front

8½ (9, 9½, 10, 10½, 11)"

11 (11½, 12, 12½, 13, 13½)"

2½"

18 (20, 22, 24, 26, 28)"

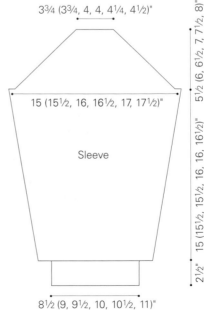

3¾ (3¾, 4, 4, 4¼, 4½)"

15 (15½, 16, 16½, 17, 17½)"

Sleeve

5½ (6, 6½, 7, 7½, 8)"

15 (15½, 15½, 16, 16, 16½)"

2½"

8½ (9, 9½, 10, 10½, 11)"

lace-front
PULLOVER

Flower-and-leaf motifs grace the lacy front
of this artsy sweater. Crochet the motifs individually,
then maneuver them into a pleasing composition
on a paper pattern. Trace around them, pencil in the
positions for the connecting chains, and finish
the front using your pattern as a guide.

Designed by **Lidia Karabinech**   Photographed by **Greg Scheidemann**

■■■■■■ Experienced

Sizes
S (M, L, XL)
Instructions are written for the
smallest size with changes for
larger sizes given in parentheses.
When only one number is given,
it applies to all sizes.
Note: For ease in working, circle
all numbers pertaining to the size
you're crocheting.

Finished Measurements
Chest = 38 (40, 42, 45)"
Length (Back) = 22 (22½, 22½, 23)"

Materials
Yarns
Bulky weight acrylic, 740
(740, 925, 925) yds. [668
(668, 835, 835) m] in
variegated brown (MC)

5 BULKY

Bulky weight 100% polyester,
244 yds. (220 m)—all sizes—
in rust (CC)

Hooks & Extras
• Size K/10½ (6.5 mm) crochet hook
  OR SIZE NEEDED TO OBTAIN
  GAUGE
• Blunt-end yarn needle

Notes
Gauge
Using hook and MC, 10 hdc and
8 rows = 4" (10 cm). TAKE TIME TO
CHECK YOUR GAUGE.

Crochet
PATTERN STITCHES

Hdc2tog: Yo and draw up a lp in each of next 2 sts, yo and draw through all 5 lps on hook.

Note: The flowers and leaves that make up the pullover Front are joined by a series of chain lengths. The instructions for doing this are not specific to any of the sizes; you must create your own assembly, following a basic diagram and the photo.

BACK

Using MC, ch 49 (51, 53, 56). Sc in 2nd ch from hook and in each ch across—48 (50, 52, 55) sts; turn.

Row 2: Ch 1, sc in each sc across; turn.

Rows 3 and 4: Rep Row 2.

Row 5: Ch 2—counts as hdc; hdc in each st across; turn.

Rep Row 5 until piece measures 14 (14, 13, 13)" from beg.

Shape armholes

Sl st in first 5 sts, ch 2, hdc in next 39 (41, 43, 46) sts; leave rem 4 sts unworked; turn.

Dec row: Ch 2—counts as hdc; hdc2tog, hdc in each hdc across to last 3 sts; hdc2tog, hdc in last hdc; turn.

Rep Dec row 2 (2, 2, 3) more times—34 (36, 38, 39) sts.

Work even until piece from beg measures 22 (22½, 22½, 23)" from beg.

Shape shoulders

Sl st in first 6 (6, 7, 7) sts, ch 2, hdc in next 23 (25, 25, 26) sts; leave last 5 (5, 6, 6) sts unworked; turn. Ch 1, sl st in first 6 (7, 7, 7) sts, ch 2, hdc in next 13 (13, 13, 14) sts for Back neck; leave last 5 (6, 6, 6) sts unworked. Fasten off.

SLEEVE (MAKE 2)

Using MC, ch 21 (21, 23, 23). Sc in 2nd ch from hook and in each ch across—20 (20, 22, 22) sts; turn. Work 3 more sc rows.

Next Row: Ch 2—counts as hdc; hdc in each sc across; turn.

Inc Row: Ch 2, hdc in same st; hdc in each hdc across; end with 2 hdc in last hdc; turn.

Cont in hdc, inc 1 st each edge every 4th row 6 (5, 5, 3) more times, then every 2nd row 0 (2, 3, 6) times. Work even on 34 (36, 40, 42) sts until piece measures 18" from beg.

Shape cap

Ch 1, sl st in first 5 sts, ch 2, hdc in next 25 (27, 31, 33) sts; leave last 4 sts unworked; turn. Dec 1 st each edge every row 10 (11, 12, 13) times—6 (6, 8, 8) sts rem. Fasten off.

FRONT

Border

Using MC, ch 49 (51, 53, 56). Sc in 2nd ch from hook and in each ch across—48 (50, 52, 55) sts; turn. Work 3 more sc rows. Fasten off and set aside.

Flowers and leaves

Using CC, make 9 small flowers, 7 big flowers, and 9 leaves.

Small flower (3" across widest portion): Ch 6; join with sl st to form a ring.

Rnd 1: Ch 3—counts as dc; work 9 dc in ring; join with sl st in 3rd ch of beg ch-3.

Rnd 2: Ch 1, sc in same st as join; (ch 4, sk dc, sc in next dc) 4 times, ch 4, sk dc; join with sl st in first sc—5 ch-4 lps.

Rnd 3: In each ch-4 lp around work sc, hdc, 3 dc, hdc, and sc; join and fasten off—5 petals.

Large flower (4½" across widest portion): Work as for small flower but do not fasten off.

Rnd 4: Ch 1; * sc in sc, hdc in hdc, dc in dc, 2 dc in next dc, dc in next dc, hdc in hdc, sc in sc; rep from * around; join and fasten off.

Leaf (4½" long): Ch 15. Sc in 2nd ch from hook and in next 3 ch, hdc in 3 ch, dc in 5 ch, hdc in next ch; in last ch work 2 sc, ch 2, and 2 sc.

Working along opposite edge of foundation ch, hdc in next ch, dc in 5 ch, hdc in 3 ch, sc in last 4 ch; join with sl st in first ch and fasten off.

FINISHING

Collar

Using MC, ch 26 (26, 28, 28). Hdc in 2nd ch from hook and in each ch across. With RS of back facing, hdc in each of the 14 (14, 14, 15) rem hdc for back neck; join with sl st in first hdc.

Rnd 2: Ch 2—counts as hdc; hdc in each hdc around; join with sl st in 2nd ch of beg ch-2. Rep Rnd 2 until collar measures 5" from beg. Join and fasten off.

Sew sides of front border to sides of back border. Join sleeve seams.

Referring to Front/Back diagram, *below*, draw and cut out a paper pattern measuring 19 (20, 21, 22½)" wide and 20½ (21, 21, 21½)" long.

Place the crocheted Back onto this pattern and draw armhole openings in place; cut out pattern—shoulders measure 13½ (14½, 15¼, 15½)" across.

Using the photo, *opposite*, as a guide, lay out flowers and leaves on the pattern. Begin at the top and place one small flower in the center of the Front neck and two large flowers at the shoulders. Draw around the shapes.

Continue placing and drawing shapes onto the pattern until the Front is similar to the photo. Remove flowers and leaves. Next, determine locations for chains; draw lines on the pattern. Now you have a guide for connecting the leaves and flowers.

After the Front is assembled with chain-stitch lengths, join the side motifs to the Back from border to armhole (about 12½, 12½, 11½, 11½"). Join motifs to border, collar, and shoulders. Set in Sleeves, joining motifs to sleeve cap.

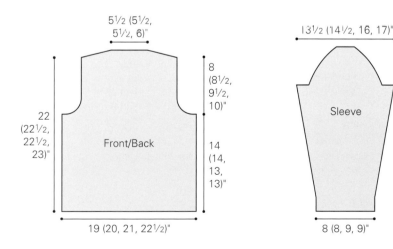

long fitted cardigan

Designed by **Svetlana Avrakh**   Photographed by **Tony Lattari**

■■■□□ Easy

Sizes

S (M, L, 1X, 2X, 3X)

Instructions are written for the smallest size with changes for larger sizes given in parentheses. When only one number is given, it applies to all sizes.
Note: For ease in working, circle all numbers pertaining to the size you're knitting.

Finished Measurements

Bust = 38 (42, 46, 50, 54, 58)"
Length = 34½ (35, 36, 37½, 38, 38½)"

Materials

Yarns

Worsted weight 100% wool, 1,784 (1,784, 2,007, 2,007, 2,230, 2,453) yds. [1,624 (1,624, 1,827, 1827, 2,030, 2,233) m] in rust

4 MEDIUM

Needles & Extras

- Size 7 (4.5 mm) needles OR SIZE NEEDED TO OBTAIN GAUGE
- Size 6 (4 mm) needles
- Size 6 (4 mm) 40" or longer circular needle
- Blunt-end yarn needle

Notes

Gauge

20 sts and 26 rows = 4" (10 cm) in St st (knit all RS rows, purl all WS rows) with larger needles.
TAKE TIME TO CHECK YOUR GAUGE.

Knit

BACK

Using larger needles, cast on 99 (105, 117, 129, 135, 147) sts.
Row 1 (RS): *K3, p3, rep from * to last 3 sts, k3.
Row 2: *P3, k3, rep from * to last 3 sts, p3.
   Rep these 2 rows until piece measures 2" from beg, ending with a RS row.

Dec row (WS): Purl across, decreasing 4 (0, 2, 4, 0, 2) sts evenly across row—95 (105, 115, 125, 135, 145) sts.
Next row: Knit across. Work in St st (knit every RS row, purl every WS row) until piece measures 7 (7, 7, 8, 8, 8)", ending with a WS row.

Shape sides

K2, k2tog; knit to last 4 sts, ssk, k2—93 (103, 113, 123, 133, 143) sts. Work St st for 13 rows even. Rep last 14 rows 5 times more—83 (93, 103, 113, 123, 133) sts. Work even until piece measures 22 (22, 22, 23, 23, 23)" from beg, ending with a WS row.

Designed to be worn with a belt, this dress-it-up-or-down cardigan is a cinch to make; the stitches are either stockinette or 3×3 rib.

Next row: K2, make 1 (M1); k to last 2 sts, M1, k2—85 (95, 105, 115, 125, 135) sts. Work 11 rows even. Rep last 12 rows once more—87 (97, 107, 117, 127, 137) sts.
Next row: K2, M1; k to last 2 sts, M1, k2—89 (99, 109, 119, 129, 139) sts.

Work even until pieces measures 27 (27, 27, 28, 28, 28)" from beg, ending with a WS row.

Shape armholes

Bind off 5 sts at beg of next 2 rows—79 (89, 99, 109, 119, 129) sts.
Next row (RS): K2, k2tog; k to last 4 sts, ssk, k2—77 (87, 97, 107, 117, 127) sts.
Next row: P2, p2tog; p to last 4 sts, p2tog through back loop (tbl), p2—75 (85, 95, 105, 115, 125) sts.

Rep last 2 rows twice—67 (77, 87, 97, 107, 117) sts. P1 row.

Next row: K2, k2tog; k to last 4 sts, ssk, k2—65 (75, 85, 95, 105, 115) sts. P1 row. Rep last 2 rows 0 (2, 4, 6, 8, 10) times more—65 (71, 77, 83, 89, 95) sts.

Work even until armhole measures 7½ (8, 9, 9½, 10, 10½)", ending with a WS row.

Shape neck

Next row (RS): Bind off 6 (6, 7, 8, 8, 9) sts. K6 (7, 7, 7, 8, 8) sts (including st on right needle after binding off), turn. Leave rem sts on spare needle. P 1 row. Bind off rem sts.

With RS facing, join yarn to sts on spare needle. Bind off 41 (45, 49, 53, 57, 61) sts for Neck, k to end of row.
Next row (WS): Bind off 6 (6, 7, 8, 8, 9) sts. P6 (7, 7, 7, 8, 8) sts (including st on right needle after binding off). K 1 row. Bind off rem sts.

LEFT FRONT

With larger needles, cast on 51 (57, 63, 69, 75, 75) sts. Work k3, p3 ribbing same as Back for 2", decreasing 1 (2, 3, 4, 5, 0) st(s) evenly spaced across last row—50 (55, 60, 65, 70, 75) sts. Work even in St st until piece measures 7 (7, 7, 8, 8, 8)" from beg, ending with a WS row.

Shape side

Next row: K2, k2tog, k to end of row—49 (54, 59, 64, 69, 74) sts. Work 13 rows even. Rep last 14 rows 5 more times—44 (49, 54, 59, 64, 69) sts. Work even until piece measures 22 (22, 22, 23, 23, 23)" from beg, ending with a WS row.
Next row: K2, M1, k to end of row—45 (50, 55, 60, 65, 70) sts. Work 11 rows even. Rep last 12 rows once—46 (51, 56, 61, 66, 71) sts.
Next row: K2, M1, k to end of row—47 (52, 57, 62, 67, 72) sts. Work even until piece measures 14 rows before beg of Back armhole shaping, ending with a WS row.

Shape neck

Next row (RS): K to last 4 sts, ssk, k2—46 (51, 56, 61, 66, 71) sts. P 1 row. Rep last 2 rows 3 more times—43 (48, 53, 58, 63, 68) sts.
Next row: K to last 4 sts, ssk, k2—42 (47, 52, 57, 62, 67) sts. Work 3 rows even.
Next row: K to last 4 sts, ssk, k2—41 (46, 51, 56, 61, 66) sts. P1 row.

Shape armhole

Row 1 (RS): Bind off 5 sts, k to end of row—36 (41, 46, 51, 56, 61) sts.
Row 2: Purl.
Row 3: K2, k2tog, k to last 4 sts, ssk, k2—34 (39, 44, 49, 54, 59) sts.
Row 4: P to last 4 sts, p2tog tbl, p2—33 (38, 43, 48, 53, 58) sts.
Row 5: K2, k2tog, k to end of row—32 (37, 42, 47, 52, 57) sts.
Row 6: Rep Row 4—31 (36, 41, 46, 51, 56) sts.
Row 7: Rep Row 3—29 (34, 39, 44, 49, 54) sts.

Row 8: Rep Row 4—28 (33, 38, 43, 48, 53) sts.

Row 9: Rep Row 3—26 (31, 36, 41, 46, 51) sts.

Row 10: Purl.

Row 11: Rep Row 3—24 (29, 34, 39, 44, 49) sts.

Row 12: Purl.

Row 13: Rep Row 5—23 (28, 33, 38, 43, 48) sts.

Row 14: Purl. Cont in St st, decreasing 1 st at neck edge every 4th row until 12 (13, 14, 15, 16, 17) sts rem.

Work even until armhole measures same as Back, ending with a WS row. Bind off all sts.

RIGHT FRONT

Work same as Left Front, reversing all shaping.

SLEEVE (MAKE 2)

With smaller needles, cast on 51 (51, 51, 57, 57, 57) sts. Work k3, p3 ribbing same as Back until piece measures 7" from beg.

Next row (RS): Change to larger needles and knit, increasing 1 st each edge—53 (53, 53, 59, 59, 59) sts. Purl 1 row. Cont in St st, increasing 1 st at each edge every 4th row until there are 55 (57, 61, 77, 87, 93) sts, then every 6th row until there are 71 (73, 75, 81, 89, 95) sts. Work even until Sleeve measures 17 (17, 18, 18, 18½, 18½)" from beg, ending with a WS row.

Shape cap

Bind off 5 sts at beg of next 2 rows—61 (63, 65, 71, 79, 85) sts.

Next row (RS): K2, k2tog, k to last 4 sts, ssk, k2—59 (61, 63, 69, 77, 83) sts. P1 row. Rep these 2 rows 10 (10, 10, 11, 13, 14) times—39 (41, 43, 47, 51, 55) sts.

Next row: K2, k2tog, k to last 4 sts, ssk, k2—37 (39, 41, 45, 49, 53) sts.

Next row: P2, p2tog tbl, p to last 4 sts, p2tog, p2—35 (37, 39, 43, 47, 51) sts.

Rep last 2 rows until 13 (13, 15, 15, 17, 17) sts rem. Bind off all sts.

FINISHING

Sew shoulder seams.

Front edges and collar

With RS facing, using circular needle, and beg at bottom edge of Right Front, pick up and k134 (134, 134, 140, 140, 140) sts to beg of V-neck shaping, 48 (55, 59, 60, 61, 62) sts to shoulder, 41 (45, 49, 53, 57, 61) sts across Back, 48 (55, 59, 60, 61, 62) sts down to end of V-neck shaping, 134 (134, 134, 140, 140, 140) sts down Left Front to bottom edge—405 (423, 435, 453, 459, 465) sts.

Row 1 (WS): *K3, p3, rep from * to last 3 sts, k3.

Row 2: *P3, k3, rep from * to last 3 sts, p3. Rep these 2 rows for 4", ending with RS row. Bind off all sts.

Sew Sleeves to Front and Back armholes. Sew side and sleeve seams.

Tie belt (not shown)

With smaller needles, cast on 9 sts.

Row 1: K1, p to last st, k1.

Row 2: Sl first st as if to knit, k1, p to end.

Row 3: Sl first st as if to purl, p1, k to end.

Rep Rows 2 and 3 until belt measures 54" or as long as desired. Bind off all sts.

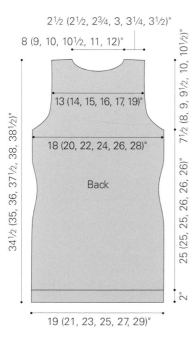

2½ (2½, 2¾, 3, 3¼, 3½)"

8 (9, 10, 10½, 11, 12)"

13 (14, 15, 16, 17, 19)"

18 (20, 22, 24, 26, 28)"

Back

7½ (8, 9, 9½, 10, 10½)"

25 (25, 25, 26, 26, 26)"

2"

34½ (35, 36, 37½, 38, 38½)"

19 (21, 23, 25, 27, 29)"

2½ (2½, 2¾, 3, 3¼, 3½)"

7½ (8, 9, 9½, 10)"

9½ (10, 11, 11½, 12, 12½)"

Left Front

25 (25, 25, 26, 26, 26)"

2"

10 (11, 12, 13, 14, 15)"

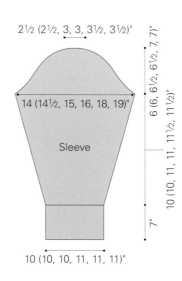

2½ (2½, 3, 3, 3½, 3½)"

6 (6, 6½, 6½, 7, 7)"

14 (14½, 15, 16, 18, 19)"

Sleeve

10 (10, 11, 11, 11½, 11½)"

7"

10 (10, 10, 11, 11, 11)"

VIOLET FAIR ISLE
twin set

Designed by **Shirley Paden**   Photographed by **Tony Lattari**

 **Experienced**

Sizes

S (M, L, 1X, 2X)

Instructions are written for the smallest size with changes for larger sizes given in parentheses. When only one number is given, it applies to all sizes.

Note: For ease in working, circle all numbers pertaining to the size you're knitting.

Finished Measurements

Pullover

Bust = 35 (38, 40, 43, 45)"
Length (Back) = 20½ (21, 21½, 22, 22½)"

Vest

Bust = 36 (38½, 40¾, 43¼, 45¾)"
Length = 25 (25, 26, 26, 27)"

Materials

Yarns

Pullover

Worsted weight 100% wool, 1,090 (1,090, 1,308, 1,526, 1,744) yds. [1,000 (1,000, 1,200, 1,400, 1,600) m] in violet (A)

Worsted weight 100% wool, 218 yds. (200 m) *each* in plum (B) and cocoa heather (C)

Vest

Worsted weight 100% wool, 654 (654, 872, 872, 1,090) yds. [600 (600, 800, 800, 1,000) m] in violet (A)

Worsted weight 100% wool, 436 (436, 436, 654, 654) yds. [400 (400, 400, 600, 600) m] in plum (B)

Worsted weight 100% wool, 218 (218, 218, 436, 436) yds. [200 (200, 200, 400, 400) m]
each in cocoa heather (C), ecru (D), and wine (E)

Needles & Extras

- Size 6 (4 mm) needles (for Pullover) OR SIZE NEEDED TO OBTAIN GAUGE
- Size 4 (3.5 mm) needles (for Pullover)
- Size 4 (3.5 mm) 16" circular needle (for Pullover)
- Size 6 (4 mm) 16" circular needle (for Pullover)
- Size 8 (5 mm) 32"–36" circular needle (for Vest)
- Size D/3 (3 mm) crochet hook (for Vest edging)
- Three sets of hook-and-eye fasteners (for Vest)
- Stitch markers
- Stitch holders
- Blunt-end yarn needle

Notes

Gauge

Pullover

20 sts and 27 rows = 4" (10 cm) in St st (knit all RS rows, purl all WS rows) with larger needles.

Vest

20 sts and 20 rows = 4" (10 cm) in Fair Isle pat. TAKE TIME TO CHECK YOUR GAUGE.

A dazzling vest over a terrific turtleneck takes the classic twin set from demure to divine. Today's duo dares to be different, with racer-back styling and stunning colors.

Knit

PATTERN STITCHES

1×1 Rib Pattern (over odd number of sts; a multiple of 2 sts + 1)

Row 1 (RS): *K1, p1; rep from * to last st, k1.

Row 2: *P1, k1; rep from * to last st, p1.

These 2 rows form 1×1 Rib pat.

PULLOVER
BACK

Using smaller needles and A, cast on 95 (101, 107, 113, 119) sts. Work 1½" in 1×1 Rib ending on a WS row and dec 6 sts evenly across last row—89 (95, 101, 107, 113) sts.

Change to larger needles and work in St st (knit every RS row, purl every WS row) for 4 rows.

Shape sides

Dec 1 st at each end of next row and every foll 4th row 5 more times—77 (83, 89, 95, 101) sts.

Work even until piece measures 6½" from beg, ending with a WS row. Inc 1 st at each end of next row and every foll 4th row twice more, then on every foll 6th row 3 more times—89 (95, 101, 107, 113) sts. Work even until piece measures 12½" from beg, ending with a WS row.

Shape armholes

Bind off 3 (3, 3, 3, 4) sts at the beg of next 2 (2, 4, 4, 2) rows, 2 (2, 2, 2, 3) sts at the beg of foll 4 (6, 4, 6, 4) rows and 1 (1, 1, 1, 2) st(s) at the beg of next 6 (4, 6, 4, 6) rows—69 (73, 75, 79, 81) sts. Work even until piece measures 18 (18½, 19, 19½, 20)" from beg, ending with a WS row.

Shape neck

Next row (RS): K28 (30, 31, 33, 34), join a new ball of yarn and bind off center 13 sts; k28 (30, 31, 33, 34). Working each side separately, bind off at neck edge 3 sts twice, 2 sts 1 (1, 1, 2, 2) time(s) and 1 st 4 (4, 4, 3, 3) times—16 (18, 19, 20, 21) sts.

Work even until piece measures 20½ (21, 21½, 22, 22½)" from beg, ending with a WS row. Bind off.

FRONT

Work same as Back.

SLEEVE (MAKE 2)

Using smaller needles and A, cast on 43 (43, 43, 51, 51) sts. Work 2½" in 1×1 Rib, ending with a WS row. Change to larger needles and work Rows 1–11 in St st, following Cuff Chart, *opposite*, using Fair Isle technique and noting 8-st rep will be worked 5 (5, 5, 6, 6) times.

Note: When working from charts, read odd-numbered rows from right to left and even-numbered rows from left to right. Inc 1 st at each end of every foll 6th (6th, 5th, 6th, 6th) row 4 (11, 4, 4, 11) times, then at each end of every foll 7th (7th, 6th, 7th, 7th) row 8 (2, 10, 8, 2) times—67 (69, 71, 75, 77) sts. Work even until piece measures 18" from beg, ending with a WS row.

Shape cap
Bind off 3 sts at beg of next 2 (4, 4, 4, 4) rows, 2 sts at beg of foll 6 (6, 6, 6, 6) rows and 1 st at beg of foll 6 (6, 20, 22, 24) rows—37 (39, 27, 29, 29) sts.
Sizes S and M only: (Bind off 2 sts at beg of next 2 rows followed by 1 st at beg of next 2 rows) 3 (4) times, then bind off 3 sts at beg of foll 4 rows. Bind off rem 15 sts.
Sizes L, 1X, and 2X only: Bind off 3 sts at beg of foll 4 rows. Bind off rem 15 (17, 17) sts.

FINISHING
Block pieces to measurements. Sew shoulder and side seams.

Neckband
With RS facing and using larger 16" circular needle and A, pick up sts around neck edge as foll: 24 (24, 24, 26, 26) sts from left shoulder to center Front neck; 24 (24, 24, 26, 26) sts from center Front neck to right shoulder; 24 (24, 24, 26, 26) sts from right shoulder to center Back neck; 24 (24, 24, 26, 26) sts from center Back neck to left shoulder—96 (96, 96, 104, 104) sts. Place marker to indicate beg of rnd and work Rows 1–4 of Neckband Chart, *below* (reading rnds from right to left), in Fair Isle, noting 4-st rep will be worked 24 (24, 24, 26, 26) times. Break off B. Using A, k 1 rnd. Change to smaller circular needle and work 3½" in 1×1 Rib. Bind off in rib.
Sew sleeve seams. Set in sleeves.

VEST
Note: Body is worked in one piece to armholes.
Using A, work 1 selvedge st at each end of row in Garter st (k every row) throughout.

BODY
Using A, cast on 183 (195, 207, 219, 231) sts onto size 8 circular needle. Do not join, working back and forth across needle in rows as foll:
Row 1 (RS): With A, k1 for selvedge st; work Row 1 of Vest Chart 1, *page 54,* in Fair Isle, noting 12-st rep will be worked 15 (16, 17, 18, 19) times; with A, k1 for selvedge st.
Row 2: With A, k1; work Row 2 of Vest Chart 1 in Fair Isle, noting 12-st rep will be worked 15 (16, 17, 18, 19) times; with A, k1.
Vest Chart 1 is now in position. Cont working Vest Chart 1 in Fair Isle until Row 53 of Chart is complete, then work Vest Chart 2, *page 54,* until Row 10 (10, 14, 14, 20) is complete.

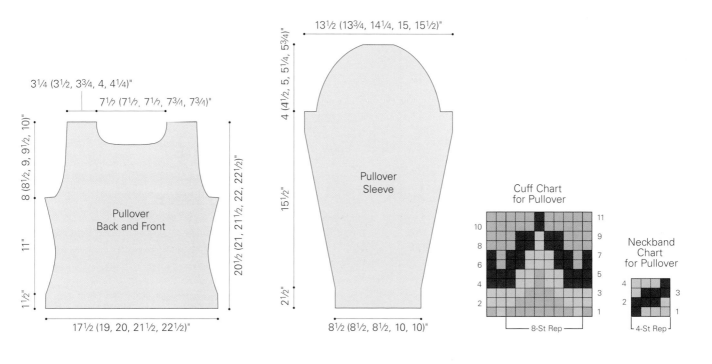

3¼ (3½, 3¾, 4, 4¼)"

7½ (7½, 7½, 7¾, 7¾)"

8 (8½, 9, 9½, 10)"

11"

1½"

Pullover
Back and Front

17½ (19, 20, 21½, 22½)"

20½ (21, 21½, 22, 22½)"

13½ (13¾, 14¼, 15, 15½)"

4 (4½, 5, 5¼, 5¾)"

15½"

2½"

Pullover
Sleeve

8½ (8½, 8½, 10, 10)"

Cuff Chart
for Pullover

8-St Rep

Neckband
Chart
for Pullover

4-St Rep

Shape V-neck

Working Chart pat as est, dec 1 st at each end of next row and foll RS rows 3 (3, 5, 5, 4) more times—175 (187, 195, 207, 221) sts.

Sizes S and M only: Dec 1 st at each end of foll 4th row, then work 3 rows even.

All sizes: Ensure that all sizes have Row 24 (24, 26, 26, 30) of Chart 2 completed. Piece should measure approx 16 (16, 16½, 16½, 17)" from beg—173 (185, 195, 207, 221) sts rem.

Divide and shape armholes

Next row (RS): K2tog, work pat across 35 (38, 40, 43, 47) sts (Right Front), bind off 8 sts, work pat across until there are 83 (89, 95, 101, 107) sts on RH needle (Back); bind off 8 sts, work pat across until there are 35 (38, 40, 43, 47) sts on RH needle; k2tog (Left Front).

LEFT FRONT

Cont on last 36 (39, 41, 44, 48) sts for Left Front. Leave rem sts on holders.
Note: When Chart 2 is complete, beg working Chart 1 at Row 31.

Dec 1 st at neck edge on foll RS row(s) 0 (0, 1, 1, 2) more times; then on every foll 4th row 10 more times and, AT THE SAME TIME on RS rows, bind off at armhole edge 3 sts 2 (3, 2, 3, 3) times; then 2 sts 5 (6, 5, 6, 6) times and 1 st 4 (2, 6, 4, 5) times—6 (6, 8, 8, 10) sts rem. Cont working Chart 1 as est until piece measures 25 (25, 26, 26, 27)" from beg, ending with a WS row. Bind off.

RIGHT FRONT

With WS facing, join yarn to 36 (39, 41, 44, 48) sts for Right Front and work as for Left Front, reversing all shapings.

BACK

With WS facing, join yarn to 83 (89, 95, 101, 107) sts. Shape racer back by binding off at each edge 6 sts 1 (1, 2) time(s); 5 sts 1 (2, 1, 2, 2) time(s);

4 sts 3 (3, 3, 2, 3) times; 3 sts 1 (1, 1, 2, 1) times; 2 sts 2 (1, 1, 1, 1) time(s); and 1 st 1 (1, 1, 0, 0) time(s)—21 (21, 25, 25, 29) sts. Work even in pat on rem sts for 3½ (3½, 3½, 3½, 4½)", ending on a WS row.
Note: When Chart 2 is complete, beg working Chart 1 at row 31.

Beg with next RS row, cast on 3 (3, 3, 3, 4) sts at beg of next 2 rows, then 3 (3, 4, 4, 5) sts at beg of foll 4 rows—39 (39, 47, 47, 57) sts.

Shape Back neck

Next row (RS): Work pat across first 12 (12, 15, 15, 19) sts, join new balls of yarn to rem sts and bind off center 15 (15, 17, 17, 19) sts, pat across rem 12 (12, 15, 15, 19) sts.

Working each side separately, bind off at neck edge 6 (6, 7, 7, 9) sts—6 (6, 8, 8, 10) sts. Cont working Chart 1 as est until piece measures 25 (25, 26, 26, 27)" from beg. Bind off.

Key

■ Violet (A)
■ Plum (B)
■ Cocoa Heather (C)
□ Ecru (D)
■ Wine (E)

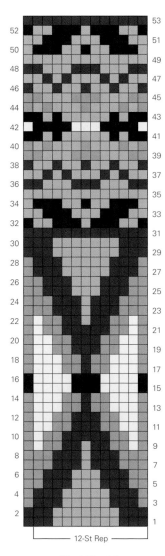

Vest Chart 1

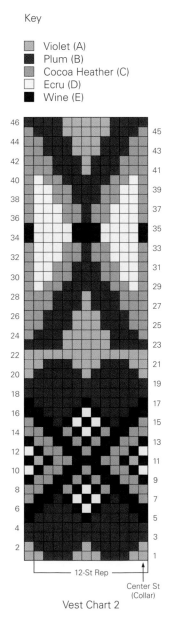

Vest Chart 2

FINISHING
Sew shoulder seams.

Right Vest collar
Note: Work 1 st at each side as a selvedge st, make inc 1 st inside of selvedge sts.

Using size 8 circular needle and A, cast on 3 sts.

Row 1 (WS): P3.

Beg on Row 11 (11, 15, 15, 21) of Vest Chart 2, *opposite;* inc 1 st at beg and end of next row (noting center st is aligned with center st of chart)—5 sts.

Working inc sts into chart pat, inc 1 st at beg (inner edge) of every foll 4th row 14 more times and AT THE SAME TIME inc 1 st at end (outer edge) of every foll 4th row twice more, then every foll 6th row 8 more times—29 sts.

Note: When Vest Chart 2 has been completed, beg working Vest Chart 1 from Rows 31–52, then rep Rows 31–52 as needed to complete the following instruction.

Work 12 (12, 14, 14, 16) rows even in Chart pat.

Shape center Back
Bind off 10 sts at beg of foll 2 RS rows, then 9 sts at beg of next RS row.

Left Vest collar
Work as for Right Vest collar, reversing all shapings.

Block pieces to measurements. Sew center Back collar seam. Sew inner edge of collar to neck with RS of collar facing WS of Body. Using A and crochet hook, work 1 row of sc and 1 row of reverse sc (work sc from left to right) around entire Vest edge, beg and ending at the center Back collar. Work same edging around armholes. Sew 3 sets of hooks and eyes to Fronts, placing the first at the base of the V-neck shaping and the rem 2 spaced 2" apart.

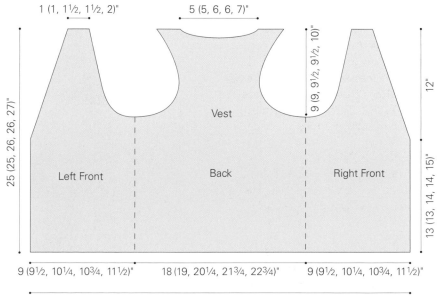

Soft green mohair forms the main body of this sweater, which is complemented by warm earth tones at the neck, wrists, and hem. The bands of distinctive cable ribbing turn what might be a basic V-neck into something simply stunning.

mohair V-NECK

Designed by **Lisa Carnahan**   Photographed by **Greg Scheidemann**

■■■■☐ Intermediate

Sizes

S (M/L, L/XL, XXL/XXXL)
Instructions are written for the smallest size with changes for larger sizes given in parentheses. When only one number is given, it applies to all sizes.
Note: For ease in working, circle all numbers pertaining to the size you're knitting.

Finished Measurements
Bust = 36 (42½, 49, 55½)"
Length (hem to shoulder) = 21 (22, 24, 26)"

Materials

Yarns
Bulky weight mohair blend, 492 (656, 820, 1066) yds. [450 (600, 750, 900) m] in moss green (MC)

Bulky weight mohair blend, 328 (410, 410, 410) yds. [300 (375, 375, 375) m] in rusty brown (CC)

Needles & Extras
- Size 10½ (6.5 mm) knitting needles OR SIZE NEEDED TO OBTAIN GAUGE
- Size 9 (5.5 mm) 16" circular needle
- Cable needle (cn)
- Ring-type stitch marker
- Blunt-end yarn needle

Notes

Gauge
13 sts and 19 rows = 4" (10 cm) in St st (knit RS rows, purl WS rows). TAKE TIME TO CHECK YOUR GAUGE.

Special Abbreviations
3×3RC = Slip next 3 stitches to cn and leave at back of work; knit 3, then knit 3 from cn.

Note: The first stitch along each edge is a selvedge stitch used for seaming. It is not reflected on schematics *(page 58)* or in finished measurements.

Knit

BACK
Using larger needles and CC, cast on 90 (106, 122, 138) sts.
Rows 1, 3, and 5 (WS): K2; * p6, k2; rep from * to end.
Rows 2 and 6: P2; * k6, p2; rep from * to end.
Row 4: P2; * 3×3RC, p2; rep from * to end.
   Rep Rows 1–6 until piece measures approx 6" from beg, ending with WS row. Change to MC yarn.

Dec row (RS): *K1, k2tog; rep from * to last 0 (1, 2, 0) sts, k0 (1, 2, 0)—60 (71, 82, 92) sts.
   Cont working in St st until piece measures approx 13½ (13½, 14½, 16)", ending with a WS row.

Shape armholes
Bind off 3 (3, 4, 5) sts at beg of next 2 rows. Bind off 2 sts at beg of next 2 rows. Dec rows—Next 3 (4, 5, 6) rows: K1, ssk, k to last 3 sts, k2tog, k1.
   Work even on 44 (53, 60, 66) sts until armhole measures 6½ (7½, 8½, 9)".

Shape Back neck and shoulders
Next row: Work across 14 (17, 19, 21) sts; join 2nd ball of yarn and bind off center 16 (19, 22, 24) sts; work rem 14 (17, 19, 21) sts. Working both shoulders at the same time with separate balls of yarn, dec 1 st at each neck edge on next 3 rows. Work even on rem 11 (14, 16, 18) sts until armhole measures 7½ (8½, 9½, 10)". Bind off.

FRONT

Work as for Back to armhole shaping, ending with WS row.

Shape armholes and neck

Bind off 3 (3, 4, 5) sts at beg of next 2 rows.

Bind off 2 sts at beg of next 2 rows. **Next row:** K1, ssk, k19 (24, 29, 33), k2tog, k1; attach a 2nd ball of yarn and bind off 0 (1, 0, 0) st, k1, ssk, k19 (24, 29, 33), k2tog, k1. Working both sides at the same time with separate balls of yarn, dec 1 st each armhole edge on next 2 (3, 4, 5) RS rows for fully fashioned shaping. AT THE SAME TIME, dec 1 st each neck edge as est every 2nd row 10 (11, 13, 14) more times—11 (14, 16, 18) sts. Work even until armhole measures same as Back, ending with WS row. Bind off.

SLEEVE (MAKE 2)

Using larger needles and CC, cast on 42 (42, 50, 50) sts. Work as for Back until piece measures 6", ending with WS row. Change to MC yarn.

Dec row (RS): *K1, k2tog; rep from * to last 0 (0, 2, 2) sts, k0 (0, 2, 2)—28 (28, 34, 34) sts. P 1 row. Cont in St st, inc 1 st each side edge every 2nd row 0 (0, 2, 4) times, every 4th row 4 (10, 5, 10) times, then every 6th row 6 (2, 4, 0) times—48 (52, 56, 62) sts. Work even until piece measures approx 18 (18, 17½, 17)" from beg.

Shape cap

Bind off 3 (3, 4, 5) sts at beg of next 2 rows. Bind off 2 sts at beg of next 2 rows. Dec 1 st each side edge every other row 3 (3, 2, 2) times.

Dec 1 st each side edge every 4th row 0 (1, 2, 3) times. Dec 1 st each side edge every other row twice. Over next 6 rows, bind off 2 sts twice, 3 sts twice, and 4 sts twice. Bind off rem 10 (12, 14, 16) sts.

FINISHING

Seam shoulders. Set in Sleeves. Sew side and underarm seams.

Neckband

With RS facing and using circular needle and CC, beg at left shoulder seam, pick up and k29 (33, 37, 41) sts along left front neck, place marker on needle; pick up and k29 (33, 37, 41) sts along right front neck to shoulder seam; pick up and k 22 (26, 30, 30) sts along back neck—80 (92, 104, 112) sts. Join and work in rnds as foll:
Rnd 1: *K2, p2; rep from * to end of rnd.
Rnds 2 and 4: Cont in rib as est to 2 sts before marker, k2tog, slip marker, ssk, cont in rib to end of rnd.
Rnds 3 and 5: Cont in rib as est.

Bind off all sts, working dec at V shaping.

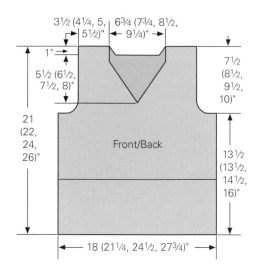

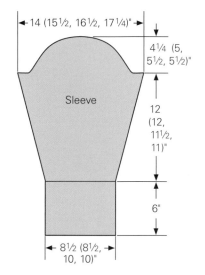

Cropped short, with big buttons and a charming Peter Pan collar, this boxy jacket is a versatile addition to your cool-weather wardrobe.

Designed by **Charlotte Parry**
Photographed by **Tony Lattari**

BOXY
JACKET

Sizes

S (M, L, 1X, 2X, 3X)

Instructions are written for the smallest size with changes for larger sizes given in parentheses. When only one number is given, it applies to all sizes.
Note: For ease in working, circle all numbers pertaining to the size you're knitting.

Finished Measurements

Bust = 36 (40, 44, 48, 52, 56)"
Length (Back) = 19 (19, 21, 21, 23)"

Materials

Yarns

Worsted weight blend, 826 (944, 1,062, 1,180, 1,298, 1,416) yds. [756 (864, 972, 1,080, 1,198, 1,316) m] in burnt orange

Needles & Extras

- Size 8 (5 mm) needles OR SIZE NEEDED TO OBTAIN GAUGE
- Size G/6 (4 mm) crochet hook
- Four 2¼"-diameter buttons
- Blunt-end yarn needle

Notes

Gauge

16 sts and 24 rows = 4" (10 cm) in St st (knit all RS rows, purl all WS rows). TAKE TIME TO CHECK YOUR GAUGE.

Knit

BACK

Beg at lower edge, cast on 72 (80, 88, 96, 104, 112) sts. Work in St st (k every RS row, p every WS row) for 1", ending with a RS row.
Next row (WS): K across to create turning ridge for hem.
Next row (RS): K across. Cont in St st until piece measures 11 (11, 12, 12, 13, 13)" from beg, ending with a WS row.

Shape armholes

Bind off 3 sts at beg of next 2 rows—66 (74, 82, 90, 98, 106) sts.
Bind off 2 sts at beg of next 2 rows—62 (70, 78, 86, 94, 102) sts.
Dec 1 st at each edge every other row twice—58 (66, 74, 82, 90, 98) sts. Cont in St st until armholes measure 8 (8, 9, 9, 10, 10)". Bind off all sts.

LEFT FRONT

Beg at lower edge, cast on 36 (40, 44, 48, 52, 56) sts. Work same as for Back to armhole, ending with a WS row.

Shape armhole

Bind off 3 sts at beg of row, k to end—33 (37, 41, 45, 49, 53) sts. P 1 row. Bind off 2 sts at beg of row, k to end—31 (35, 39, 43, 47, 51) sts. P 1 row. Dec 1 st at armhole edge every RS row twice—29 (33, 37, 41, 45, 49) sts. Cont in St st until armhole measures 5 (5, 6, 6, 7, 7)", ending with a RS row.

Shape neck

Next row (WS): Bind off 5 (5, 5, 6, 6, 6) sts, p to end—24 (28, 32, 35, 39, 43) sts. Cont in St st, binding off at neck edge 3 (4, 4, 5, 5, 6) sts once, 2 (3, 4, 4, 5, 6) sts once—19 (21, 24, 26, 29, 31) sts. Dec 1 st on next 3 (3, 4, 4, 5, 5) WS rows—16 (18, 20, 22, 24, 26) sts. Work even until piece measures same as Back to shoulder. Bind off all sts.

RIGHT FRONT

Work same as Left Front, reversing all shaping.

SLEEVE (MAKE 2)

Beg at lower edge, cast on 36 (38, 40, 42, 44, 46) sts. Work in St st for 1½", ending with a RS row.

Next row (WS): K across to create turning ridge for hem. Work in St st for 1½", ending with a WS row.

Next row (RS): Inc 1 st at each edge on this row, then every 6th row once and every 9th row 8 times—56 (58, 60, 62, 64, 66) sts. Work even until piece measures 15½ (15½, 16, 16, 16½, 16½)" above turning ridge, ending with a WS row.

Shape cap

Bind off 3 sts at beg of next 2 rows—50 (52, 54, 56, 58, 60) sts.

Bind off 2 sts at beg of next 2 rows—46 (48, 50, 52, 54, 56) sts.

Dec 1 st at each edge every other row 14 (14, 15, 15, 16, 16) times—18 (20, 20, 22, 22, 24) sts.

Bind off 2 sts at beg of next 2 rows—14 (16, 16, 18, 18, 20) sts.

Bind off 3 sts at beg of next 2 rows—8 (10, 10, 12, 12, 14) sts. Bind off all sts.

FINISHING

Fold all lower-edge hems to WS along turning ridge and sew into place. Sew shoulder seams.

Right Front edge hem

With RS facing and beg at top of lower-edge hem and working up to neck edge, pick up and k62 (62, 70, 70, 76, 76) sts. Work in St st for 1". Bind off all sts. Fold hem to WS and sew into place.

Left Front edge hem

Work as for Right Front edge hem, beg at neck and working down to top of lower-edge hem.

Collar

With WS facing, pick up and k19 (19, 20, 20, 21, 21) sts along Left Front neck edge, 26 (30, 34, 38, 42, 46) sts along Back neck edge, and 19 (19, 20, 20, 21, 21) sts along Right Front neck edge—64 (68, 74, 78, 84, 88) sts. Work in St st for 2½", ending with a WS row.

Dec row: K1, ssk; k to last 3 sts, k2tog, k1—62 (66, 72, 76, 82, 86) sts.

Dec row: P1, p2tog; p to last 3 sts, p2tog through back loop, p1—60 (64, 70, 74, 80, 84) sts. Bind off all sts purlwise.

Button loop (make 4)

Using crochet hook, ch 15; fasten off, leaving an 8" tail.

Working on Right Front, mark four loop positions 2 sts in from Front edge, placing one 2 rows down from collar, another 3½" up from lower edge, and the rem 2 evenly spaced bet first two markings.

Fold loop in half; with RS facing and holding folded loop on wrong side of marker, insert crochet hook at marker and pull fold of loop to right side, keeping ends on wrong side. Knot ends to secure button loop.

Sew Sleeves to Front and Back pieces along underarm. Sew side and sleeve seams. Sew buttons opposite button loops.

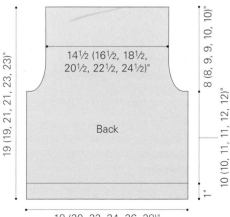

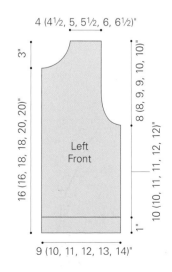

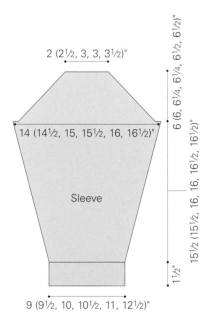

asymmetrical JACKET

Designed by **Anna Mishka**
Photographed by **Greg Scheidemann**

■■■■□ **Intermediate**

Sizes
S (M, L, XL)
Instructions are written for the smallest size with changes for larger sizes given in parentheses. When only one number is given, it applies to all sizes.
Note: For ease in working, circle all numbers pertaining to the size you're crocheting.

Finished Measurements
Bust (buttoned) = 36 (40, 44, 48)"
Length (Right Back) = 18½ (18½, 20½, 20½)"

Materials
Yarns
Worsted weight metallic blend, 920 (1,035, 1,035, 1,150) yds. [840 (945, 945, 1,050) m] in bronze

4 MEDIUM

Hooks & Extras
- Size I/9 (5.5 mm) crochet hook OR SIZE NEEDED TO OBTAIN GAUGE
- Five ⅜"-diameter buttons
- Blunt-end yarn needle

Notes
Gauge
5 tr2tog and 7½ rows = 4" (10 cm) in Lace pat.18 sts and 18 rows = 4" (10 cm) in Seed st. TAKE TIME TO CHECK YOUR GAUGE.

Crochet
PATTERN STITCHES
Seed Stitch (multiple of 2 sts + 1 st; a rep of 2 rows)
Row 1 (WS): Ch 1, sc in first sc; * sc in next ch-1 sp, ch 1, sk next sc; rep from * across, ending sc in last ch-1 sp, sc in last sc; turn.
Row 2: Ch 1, sc in first sc; * ch 1, sk next sc, sc in next ch-1 sp; rep from * across, ending ch 1, sk next sc, sc in last sc; turn.
  Rep Rows 1 and 2 for Seed st.
Sc2tog: Draw up a lp in next 2 sts, yo and draw through all 3 lps on hook.

Notes: Back is made in two separate pieces and then joined together. Each chain-1 space counts as one stitch, and each chain-2 space counts as two stitches.

RIGHT BACK
Beg at lower edge, ch 43 (43, 49, 49).

Lace Pattern
Row 1 (RS): Sc in 2nd ch from hook and in each ch across—42 (42, 48, 48) sts; turn.
Row 2: Ch 5—counts as tr and ch-1; yo twice and draw up a lp in next st, (yo and draw through 2 lps on hook) twice, sk next 2 sc; yo twice and draw up a lp in next st, (yo and draw through 2 lps on hook) twice, yo and draw through all 3 lps on hook—beg tr2tog made, ch 2. * Yo twice and draw up a lp in same sc as last st, (yo and draw through 2 lps on hook) twice, sk next 2 sc, yo twice and draw up a lp in next sc; (yo and draw through 2 lps on hook) twice, yo and draw through all 3 lps on hook—tr2tog made, ch 2; rep from * across, ending tr in last sc—13 (13, 15, 15) tr2tog; turn.

You'll love the exceptional styling on this asymmetrical sweater jacket. Stitched in metallic yarn, the sweater front, back, and cuffs are designed with a decorative treble-crochet stitch. A tighter-weave stitch adorns the sleeves and left side.

Row 3: Ch 1, sc in first tr; * 2 sc in next ch-2 sp, sc in next st; rep from * across to last ch-5, sc in 5th and 4th ch of ch-5—42 (42, 48, 48) sc; turn.

Rep Rows 2 and 3 for Lace pat until piece measures 11" from beg, ending with Row 2.

Shape armhole

Row 1 (RS): Sl st in first 6 sts, ch 1, sc in same st as last sl st, work in pat to end of row—37 (37, 43, 43) sc; turn.

Row 2: Work in pat across to last 2 sc, ch 1 (instead of ch 2), sk next sc, tr in last sc—11 (11, 13, 13) tr2tog; turn.

Row 3: Ch 1, work in pat across—35 (35, 41, 41) sc; turn.

Row 4: Work in pat to last 3 sc, ch 2, sk 2 sc, tr in last sc—10 (10, 12, 12) tr2tog; turn.

Row 5: Ch 1, work in pat to end of row—33 (33, 39, 39) sc; turn. Work even in pat until armhole measures approx 7½ (7½, 8½, 8½)", ending with a WS row; fasten off.

LEFT BACK

Ch 36 (42, 42, 52).

Foundation Row (RS): Sc in 2nd ch from hook; * ch 1, sk next ch, sc in next ch; rep from * across—35 (41, 41, 51) sts; turn. Work Seed st until work from beg measures 7½", ending with a WS row.

Shape armhole

Row 1 (RS): work in pat across, leaving last 5 sts unworked—30 (36, 36, 46) sts; turn.

Row 2: Ch 1, sc in first sc, sc2tog over next 2 sts, pat to end of row; turn.

Row 3: Ch 1, pat to end of row; turn. Rep last 2 rows 4 (4, 4, 6) more times—25 (31, 31, 39) sts; turn. Work even in pat until armhole measures same length as Right Back, ending with a WS row; fasten off.

Sew backs tog, leaving 3½" at lower edge of Right Back free to form asymmetrical bottom edge.

RIGHT FRONT

Ch 52 (58, 61, 67).

Row 1 (RS): Sc in 2nd ch from hook and in each ch across—51 (57, 60, 66) sts; turn. Rep Row 2 of Lace pat—16 (18, 19, 21) tr2tog.

Row 3 of Lace pat. Rep last 2 rows of pat for 11", ending with a WS row.

Shape armhole

Work in pat across, leaving last 5 sts unworked—46 (52, 55, 61) sc.

Row 2: Ch 5—counts as tr and ch-1; sk next sc, tr2tog over next 4 sts, work in pat to end of row—14 (16, 17, 19) tr2tog; turn.

Row 3: Ch 1, work in pat to last ch-5, sk 5th ch, sc in 4th ch of ch-5—44 (50, 53, 59) sc; turn.

Row 4: Ch 5—counts as tr and ch-1; sc next 2 sc, tr2tog over next 4 sts, work in pat to end of row—13 (15, 16, 18) tr2tog; turn.

Row 5: Ch 1, work in pat to end of row—42 (48, 51, 57) sc; turn.

Work even in pat until armhole measures approx 4½ (4½, 5½, 5½)", ending with a RS row.

Shape neck

Ch 5—counts as tr and ch-1; work 4 (5, 6, 7) tr2tog, ending ch 2, tr in last sc; leave rem 27 (30, 30, 33) sc unworked; turn.

Rep Row 3—15 (18, 21, 24) sc; turn.

Work even in pat until armhole measures same length as on Back; end with a WS row. Fasten off.

LEFT FRONT

Ch 24 (28, 32, 34).

Row 1 (RS): Sc in 2nd ch from hook; * sk next ch, sc in next ch; rep from * across—23 (27, 31, 33) sts; turn.

Rep Rows 1 and 2 of Seed st until work measures 7½" from beg, ending with a WS row.

Shape armhole

Sl st in first 6 sts, ch 1, sc in same st as last sl st, work in pat to end of row—18 (22, 26, 28) sts; turn.

Row 2. Ch 1, sc in first sc, sc2tog over next 2 sts, work in pat to end of row; turn.

Row 3: Ch 1, work in pat to end of row; turn. Rep last 2 rows 4 (4, 4, 6) more times—13 (17, 21, 21) sts. Cont even in pat until armhole measures same length as on Right Front. Fasten off.

SLEEVE (MAKE 2)

Ch 34 (34, 40, 40).

Row 1 (RS): Sc in 2nd ch from hook, and in each ch across—33 (33, 39, 39) sc; turn.

Rep Row 2 of Lace pat—10 (10, 12, 12) tr2tog. Rep Row 3 of Lace pat—33 (33, 39, 39) sc. Rep last 2 rows of pat for 6", ending with Row 2.

Next row (RS): Ch 1, sc in first tr; * 2 sc in next ch-2 sp, sc in next st, 3 sc in next ch-2 sp, sc in next st; rep from * to last ch-5, 2 sc in 5th ch, sc in 4th ch of ch-5—39 (39, 45, 45) sc; turn.

Next row: Ch 1, sc in first sc; * sc in next sc, ch 1, sk sc; rep from * across, end with sc in next sc, ch 1, sk next sc, sc in last 2 sc; turn.

Next row: Ch 1, sc in first sc; * ch 1, sk next sc, sc in next sc; rep from * to last 2 sc; ch 1, sk sc, sc in last sc, turn. Rep last 2 rows of pat, working 2 sc in first and last st on next and every foll 4th row to 45 (45, 51, 51) sts, then every foll 6th row to 57 (57, 63, 63) sts, taking inc sts into pat. Work even until Sleeve measures 17½"; end with a WS row.

Shape cap

Sl st in first 4 sts, ch 1, sc in same st as last sl st, work in pat to last 3 sts and leave last 3 sts unworked—51 (51, 57, 57) sts; turn.

Next row: Ch 1, sc in first sc, sc2tog over next 2 sts, work in pat to last 3 sts, sc2tog over next 2 sts, sc in last st; turn.

Next row: Ch 1, pat to end of row; turn. Rep last 2 rows 3 (3, 5, 5) more times—43 (43, 45, 45) sc; turn.

Next row: Ch1, sc in first sc, sc2tog over next 2 sts, work in pat to last 3 sts, sc2tog over next 2 sts, sc in last st; turn. Rep last row until 9 sts rem.

Note: In order to have 9 sts rem, you need to work this dec row 17 times for sizes S and M and 18 times for sizes L and XL.

Fasten off.

FINISHING

Sew shoulder seams. Set in Sleeves; sew side and sleeve seams. With RS facing, join yarn at bottom right corner of Front, ch 1, 3 sc in same sp; sc, evenly around, working 3 sc in each corner; join with sl st in first sc. Do not turn.

Working left to right for reverse sc, ch 1, sc in each sc around. Fasten off.

Mark Left Front for placement of 5 buttons. First button is ½" from lower edge, last button is 4½" from shoulder seam, and rem 3 buttons are spaced evenly between them. Use holes of first round of sc as buttonholes. Sew on buttons.

Sleeve edging

With RS facing, join yarn at underarm seam, ch 1, sc in same sp; sc evenly around; join with sl st in first sc.

Ch 1, work reverse sc around. Fasten off.

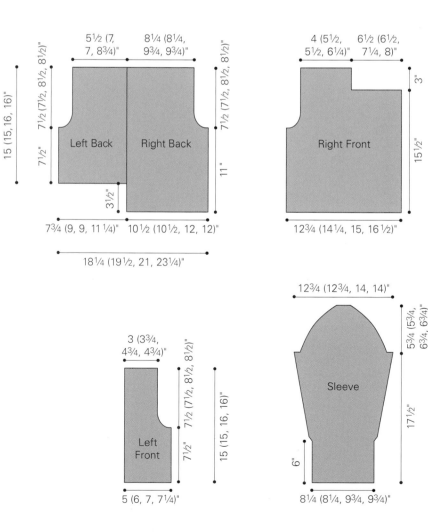

mandarin
COLLAR JACKET

This striking mandarin collar jacket with an asymmetrical closure and modified basket-weave stitch pattern adds a touch of sophistication to your wardrobe. Knitted with an elegant yarn, the soft robin's-egg-blue sweater is edged with a rich chocolate trim of single and reverse single crochet.

Designed by **Ann E. Smith**   Photographed by **Greg Scheidemann**

■■ ■■ ■■ ▢ **Intermediate**

Sizes

S (M, L, XL)

Instructions are written for the smallest size with changes for larger sizes given in parentheses. When only one number is given, it applies to all sizes.

Note: For ease in working, circle all numbers pertaining to the size you're knitting.

Finished Measurements

Bust (closed) = 36 (39½, 42½, 46)"
Length (Back without collar) = 21½ (22, 22½, 23)"

Materials

Yarns

Worsted weight, 762 (889, 889, 1,016) yds. [696 (812, 812, 928) m] in soft blue (MC)

4 MEDIUM

Worsted weight, 127 yds. (116 m)—all sizes—in brown (CC)

Needles & Extras

- Size 9 (5.5 mm) knitting needles OR SIZE NEEDED TO OBTAIN GAUGE
- Size 8 (5 mm) knitting needles
- Size G/6 (4 mm) crochet hook
- Blunt-end yarn needle
- Two sets of snap fasteners

Notes

Gauge

22 sts and 34 rows = 6" (15 cm) in Body pat with larger needles. TAKE TIME TO CHECK YOUR GAUGE.

Special Abbreviations

ssk (sl, sl, knit) = Slip next 2 stitches (sts) to right-hand needle singly and knitwise; insert tip of left-hand needle through front loops of both sts and knit them together.

Knit

PATTERN STITCHES

Body Pattern (a multiple of 6 sts; 8-row rep)

Row 1 (WS): Purl.

Row 2: Knit.

Row 3: (P3, k3) across.

Row 4: *P1, k into st one row below next st; p1, k3; rep from * across.

Rows 5 and 6: Rep Rows 1 and 2.

Row 7: (K3, p3) across.

Row 8: *K3, p1, k into one row below next st, p1; rep from * across.

Rep Rows 1–8 for Body pat.

Note: Jacket trim is crocheted in 2 rounds: 1 round of single crochet and one round of reverse single crochet.

BACK

Beg at lower edge and using larger needle and MC, cast on 66 (72, 78, 84) sts. Work even in Body pat until piece measures approx 13½" from beg, ending with a WS row.

Shape armhole

Bind off 4 (4, 5, 5) sts at beg of next 2 rows—58 (64, 68, 74) sts.

Dec row (RS): K1, ssk, work Body pat to last 3 sts, k2tog, k1. Work Body pat across next row. Rep last 2 rows 4 times more—48 (54, 58, 64) sts. Cont in est pat until piece measures approx 21 (21½, 22, 22½)" from beg, ending with a WS row.

Shape shoulders and Back neck

Bind off 13 (15, 16, 18) sts at beg of next 2 rows. Bind off rem 22 (24, 26, 28) sts.

RIGHT FRONT

Beg at lower edge and using larger needles and MC, cast on 24 (27, 30, 33) sts.

Row 1 (WS): P (first row of Body pat).

Row 2 (RS): K1, make 1 (M1) (see Make 1 directions, *page 269*), k to end.

Row 3: (P3, k3) across, ending with p1 (4, 1, 4). Including new sts in Body pat as they accumulate, inc 1 st at front edge every RS row until there are 48 (51, 54, 57) sts. Work even on next WS row.

Dec row: K1, ssk, work Body pat across. Rep Dec row every RS row 7 (6, 5, 4) more times, then every 4th row 10 (11, 12, 13) times. AT THE SAME TIME, when piece measures approx 13½" from beg, ending with a RS row, shape armhole.

Shape armhole

Next row (WS): Bind off 4 (4, 5, 5) sts, work Body pat to end.

Next row (RS): Work Body pat to last 3 sts, k2tog, k1. Dec 1 st at armhole edge every RS row 3 more times. Work even to approx 19 (19½, 20, 20½)" from beg, ending with a WS row—22 (25, 27, 30) sts.

Shape neck

On RS rows, bind off 5 (6, 7, 8) sts once, 2 sts once, and 1 st twice. Work even on rem 13 (15, 16, 18) sts to same length as Back, ending with a WS row. Bind off.

LEFT FRONT

Beg at lower edge and using larger needles and MC, cast on 24 (27, 30, 33) sts.

Row 1 (WS): P (first row of Body pat).

Row 2 (RS): K to last st, M1, k1.

Row 3: K1 (4, 1, 4), (p3, k3) across. Working new sts into Body pat as they accumulate, inc 1 st at front edge every RS row until there are 48 (51, 54, 57) sts. Work even on next WS row.

Dec row: Work Body pat to last 3 sts, k2tog, k1. Rep Dec row every RS row 7 (6, 5, 4) times more, then every 4th row 10 (11, 12, 13) times until piece measures approx 13½" from beg, ending with a WS row.

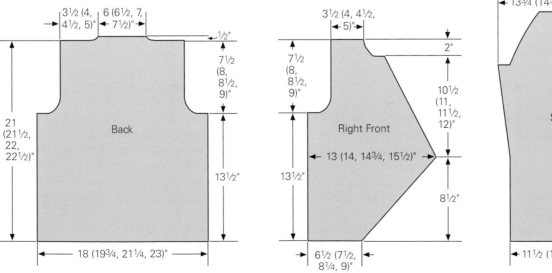

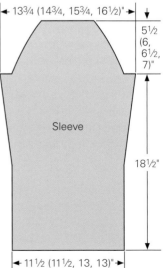

Shape armhole

Next row (RS): Bind off 4 (4, 5, 5) sts, work Body pat to end. Work 1 row even.
Next row (RS): K1, ssk, work Body pat to end. Dec 1 st at armhole edge every RS row 3 more times. Complete as for Right Front, reversing neck shaping.

SLEEVE (MAKE 2)

Beg at lower edge and using larger needles and MC, cast on 42 (42, 48, 48) sts. Work Body pat to 9" from beg, ending with a WS row.
Next row: Including new sts in Body pat as they accumulate, inc 1 st each edge in this row and in every 10th (8th, 10th, 8th) row 3 (5, 4, 5) more times. Work even on 50 (54, 58, 60) sts until piece measures approx 18½" from beg, ending with a WS row.

Shape cap

Bind off 4 (4, 5, 5) sts at beg of next 2 rows—42 (46, 48, 50) sts. Work 3 rows even in Body pat.
Dec row (RS): K1, ssk, work Body pat to last 3 sts, k2tog, k1. Rep last 4 rows 3 times more—34 (38, 40, 42) sts. Rep

Dec row every other row until 26 sts rem. Bind off 3 sts at beg of next 2 rows. Bind off rem 20 sts.

FINISHING

Without pressing iron directly on fabric, block pieces to measurements. Sew shoulder seams.

Shape collar

With RS facing and using smaller needles and MC, pick up and k51 (55, 59, 63) sts evenly spaced around neck. Beg with a p row, work 8 rows in St st. K next row on WS for turning ridge. K 1 more row.
Next row: (P1, k1) across, ending with p1.
Next row: (K1, p1) across, ending with k1.
Next 5 rows: Cont in rib pat as est. Bind off loosely. Fold collar in half to WS, and sew collar edge to pickup row.

Set in sleeves. Join underarm and side seams.

Make Body trim

With RS facing and using crochet hook, join CC at left side seam with sl st, ch 1,

sc in same st as sl st. Work sc evenly along lower edge of Back and Right Front, 3 sc in corner, 34 sc evenly spaced up shaped edge of Right Front to next corner, 3 sc in corner, 47 (49, 51, 53) sc evenly spaced to collar. Working through both thicknesses, work 5 sc along collar edge, 3 sc in corner, sc in each st across top of collar to next corner, 3 sc in corner. Working through both thicknesses, work 5 sc along edge, 47 (49, 51, 53) sc to next corner, 3 sc in corner, 34 sc evenly spaced down shaped edge of Left Front to next corner, 3 sc in corner, sc in each st along lower edge of Left Front; join with sl st in first sc. Ch 1, working left to right for reverse sc, sc in each sc around. Fasten off.

Make Sleeve trim

With RS facing and using crochet hook, join CC at seam with sl st, ch 1, sc in same st. Sc in each st around; join. Work reverse sc in each sc around; fasten off.

Sew snaps to each point of fronts, near crochet edging. Sew second halves of snaps to line up.

bags & purses

Stand out from the crowd with a one-of-a-kind carryall that expresses your unique personality.

felted
tapestry
bag

Voluptuous vines and leaves, fanciful flowers—clearly
Mother Nature inspired this classy felted carryall.
The floral pattern is duplicate-stitched after the bag front
is knitted. The I-cord handles, closure, and knotted
button are added before the entire bag is felted.

Designed by **Nicky Epstein**   Photographed by **Tony Lattari**

■■■□ Intermediate

Sizes
Finished Measurements
Before felting: 14×18"
After felting: 13¾×14"

Note: Floral design is worked in
Duplicate Stitch embroidery after
Front piece has been knitted.
Duplicate Stitch embroidery causes
minimal width shrinkage.

Materials
Yarns
Worsted weight 100%
(feltable) wool, approx
500 yds. (460 m) in
brown (MC)

DK weight 100%
(feltable) wool, approx
80 yds. (73 m) *each* in
gold, light pink, light blue-green, dark
pink, and dark blue-green

Needles & Extras
- Size 9 (5.5 mm) needles OR SIZE
  NEEDED TO OBTAIN GAUGE
- Size 8 (5 mm) double-pointed
  needles (dpn)
- Four stitch holders
- Blunt-end yarn needle

Notes
Gauge
14 sts and 22 rows = 4" (10 cm) in St
st (knit all RS rows, purl all WS rows)
with MC and larger needles. TAKE
TIME TO CHECK YOUR GAUGE.

Knit

FRONT

Using larger needles and MC, cast on 40 sts. K 1 row, p 1 row. Cont in St st (k every RS row, p every WS row), casting on 2 sts at beg of next 6 rows—52 sts. Inc 1 st at beg of next 8 rows—60 sts. Work even until there are 78 rows from beg, ending with a WS row.

Shape top

Next row (RS): Bind off 8 sts, k14 (counting sts on RH needle), attach another ball of yarn, bind off next 16 sts, k to end.
Next row: Bind off 8 sts, p to end—14 sts each side.
Next row: Working each side separately, ssk, k to last 2 sts, k2tog—12 sts each side.
Next row: P all sts. Rep these last 2 rows until 4 sts rem on each side.
   Place sts on holders.

BACK

Work same as Front.

HANDLE (MAKE 2)

Slide sts from one Front holder onto larger needle. Work St st for 24", ending with a WS row.

Next row (RS): Insert right needle into first st on LH needle, then into first st on rem Front holder; k the 2 sts tog. Rep with rem 3 sts. Bind off all sts. Knit Handles for Back in same manner.

Embroidery

Following Tapestry Bag Chart, *opposite*, and working on knit side of Front, embroider the design using DK-weight yarns and Duplicate st, *page 268*.

POCKET (MAKE 2)

Using larger needles and MC, cast on 25 sts. Work St st until piece measures 5", ending with a RS row. K 3 rows for top edge. Bind off all sts. Sew Pocket to purl side of Front 2½" down from center of top edge. Sew second Pocket to Back in same manner.

GUSSET

Using larger needles and MC, cast on 18 sts. Work in St st until piece measures 50" or length needed to fit along side and bottom edges of Front piece. When correct length has been obtained, bind off all sts.
   With knit sides tog, sew one long edge of Gusset to Front along side and bottom edges. Sew rem long side to Back in same manner.

CORDS

Top I-cord edging

Measure circumference of top edge of bag. Using dpn and MC, cast on 5 sts. *K5, do not turn work, slide sts to opposite end of needle, rep from * until cord measures same as circumference of Bag. Bind off all sts. Beg at center of Back, sew cord along top edge of Bag.

Cord closure loop

Work same as top I-cord edging until cord measures 7". Leave sts on needle, pick up the 5 cast-on sts (there are now 10 sts on needle and the cord has formed a loop). Work 10 sts even in St st (do not slide sts to form a cord) for ½". Bind off all sts. Working on knit side of Back, center bound-off edge of cord closure loop 1" down from top edge so loop extends upward; sew 10-st portion of cord closure loop to Bag.

Cord button

Work same as top I-cord edging until cord measures 2". Bind off all sts. Tie it into a knot. Thread cast-on tail and bind-off tail through yarn needle and sew knot to center of top edge of Front just below top I-cord edging.

FELTING

Follow felting instructions on *page 270*.

Felting Tips

Make a swatch.

If you're new to felting, make a swatch, wash it, and observe how the swatch transforms itself to become something totally new. Note how the swatch changes in appearance and size with each successive washing.

Keep a felting journal.

Write down the needle size and the yarn you've felted. Be sure to include information such as the number of stitches, size of the swatch before felting, and number of washings. Next time you'll have a felting record for that yarn.

Add felted embellishments.

To make felted embellishments of a contrasting color, knit a straight piece of stockinette stitching, felt it by washing it at least twice, cut out the shapes you want, and then wash them once more to soften the blunt cut edges. Or consider buying secondhand wool sweaters at thrift sales for the same purpose. Wash them twice and then cut them into the desired shapes.

Felted Tapestry Bag Chart

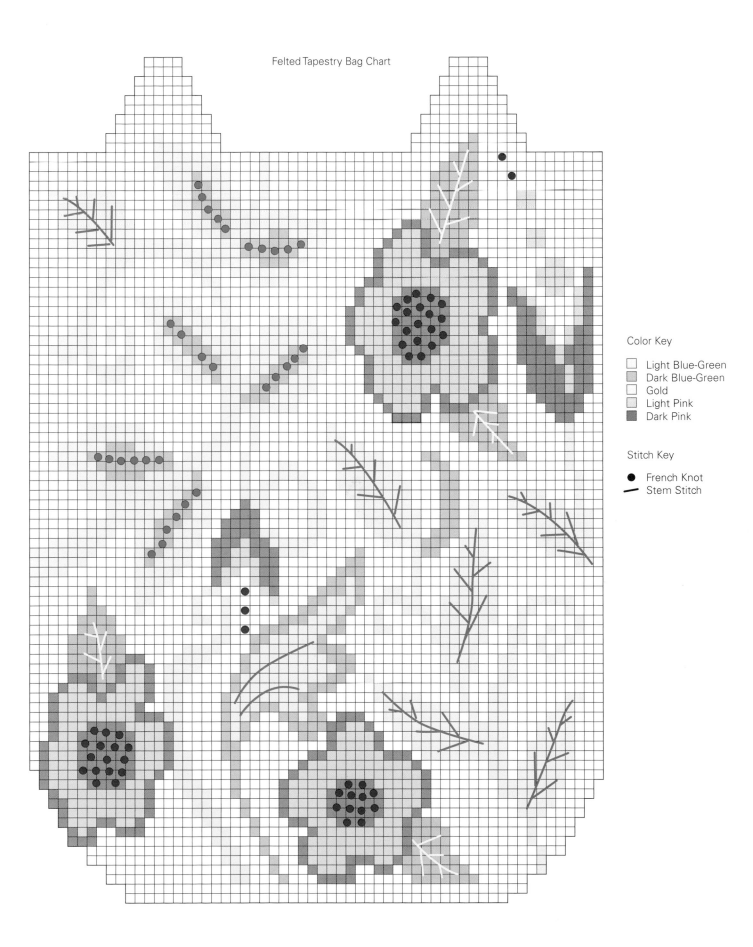

Color Key

☐ Light Blue-Green
▨ Dark Blue-Green
☐ Gold
▨ Light Pink
▨ Dark Pink

Stitch Key

● French Knot
— Stem Stitch

BUTTON clutch

Designed by **Gabrielle Hamill**
Photographed by **Akin Girav**

■■■■■ Experienced

Sizes
Finished Measurements
11×5¾×4"

Materials
Super bulky weight ribbon, 220 yds. (200 m) in rainbow

6 SUPER BULKY

Needles & Extras
- Size 7 (4.5 mm) 16" circular needle OR SIZE NEEDED TO OBTAIN GAUGE
- Size 7 (4.5 mm) double-pointed needles (dpns) OR SIZE NEEDED TO OBTAIN GAUGE
- Size 9 (5.5 mm) needles OR SIZE NEEDED TO OBTAIN GAUGE
- Three ⅞"-diameter buttons
- Blunt-end yarn needle
- 24" of ½"-diameter corded rope for handles
- Two small stitch holders
- Four coil-type stitch markers

Notes
Gauge
22 sts and 28 rows = 4" (10 cm) in St st (knit all RS rows, purl all WS rows) on smallest needles. TAKE TIME TO CHECK YOUR GAUGE.

Knit
PATTERN STITCHES
Stockinette Stitch (St st)
When knitting in rows (back and forth), k the RS rows and p the WS rows. When knitting in the round, k all rnds.

CLUTCH
Beg at the base, cast on 42 sts on size 9 (5.5 mm) needles.

Row 1: K into the front and back of every stitch—84 stitches. Every st knitted into the front will be a st A, and every st knitted into the back will be a st B.

Transfer sts to size 7 (4.5 mm) dpns and arrange sts so that every A is on one side of the cast-on ridge and every B is on the other.

Turn work inside out so that cast-on ridge is on the inside of the Clutch (WS).
Rnd 2: (K1, make 1 [M1], k38, M1, k1, place marker [pm], k1, double inc *(see page 78)*, k1, pm) twice—92 sts.
Rnd 3: Knit.
Rnd 4: (K1, M1, k40, M1, k2, M1, k2, M1, k1) twice—100 sts.
Rnds 5–10: Switch to circular needle. Knit.

Rnd 11: (K1, M1, k42, M1, k2, M1, k4, M1, k1) twice—108 sts.
Rnds 12–17: Knit.
Rnd 18: (K1, M1, k44, M1, k2, M1, k6, M1, k1) twice—116 sts.
Rnds 19–24: Knit.
Rnd 25: (K1, M1, k46, M1, k2, M1, k8, M1, k1) twice—124 sts.
Rnds 26–27: Knit.

BACK TOP
Row 28: K across the first 49 sts. Wrap yarn *(see page 78)* around the 50th st. Place the next 12 sts between the st markers onto a holder.

Color and technique combine to fashion this smart clutch suitable for day or night. Featuring a wrapped stitch that helps prevent gaps, the pattern uses ribbon yarn for a truly elegant look.

Row 29: P 48 sts, wrapping yarn on the 49th st. Sl the 12 sts between the next set of markers onto another st holder. Cont wrapping in this manner through Row 39 and until 6 sts are wrapped on each edge of the Back Top.

Handle Base A

Rows 40–43: K across next 6 sts, wrapping yarn on the 7th. P across 5 sts, wrapping yarn on the 6th. K across 4 sts, wrapping yarn on the 5th. P across 3 sts, wrapping yarn on the 4th.
Row 44: K across 3 unwrapped sts. (K next st and its wrap tog) twice; bind off. Bind off center 24 sts so that 13 sts rem before holder. This leaves 3 unwrapped sts for Handle and 8 wrapped sts on right edge.

Handle Base B

Rep Rows 40–43 on the rem 7 unwrapped sts on the back. Note that there are 2 wrapped sts to the right and 8 wrapped sts to the left of the 3 unwrapped sts. K3 for strap; (k next st and its wrap tog) twice, cont as est to bind off all of the rem 8 wrapped sts.

Bind off the 12 sts from holder. This leaves 3 unwrapped sts and 2 wrapped sts on left edge.

FRONT TOP

With 50 sts to work on this side, pm after st 24 and 26 to mark buttonhole. Rep Rows 28–39 of Back Top, creating Handle Bases C and D. AT THE SAME TIME, on Row 38, bind off center 2 sts; then on the next row, cast on 2 sts over the buttonhole. Rep Rows 40–43 of Handle Bases A and B. AT THE SAME TIME, on Row 42 of both Handle Bases, bind off the center 2 sts. On Row 43, cast on 2 sts over each buttonhole. This will create the buttonholes for the two outside buttons.

HANDLE (MAKE 2)

Join yarn and bind off the first 8 wrapped sts as est on right edge of Back Top and Handle Base A. With dpn, k3 unwrapped sts and cast on 2 additional sts. Make a 12" I-cord (*see below*) on the 5 sts. Leaving a 6" tail, cut yarn. Insert 12" of corded rope into I-cord strap.

Join yarn and bind off the first 2 wrapped sts as est on left edge of Back Top and Handle Base B. Graft I-cord strap end to Handle Base B (see "Grafting Stockinette Stitches" on *page 270*). Join the first 3 sts of the I-cord strap to the unwrapped 3 sts of the Handle Base. Sew remaining 2 sts to the WS of the base. Repeat on Handle Bases C and D.
Note: When sewing the second I-cord strap to Handle Base D, be careful not to sew up the buttonholes.

FINISHING

Sew buttons to WS of Back, opposite the buttonholes. Weave in any rem ends along WS.

Techniques

Wrapping

On a purl side of the work, purl to the last stitch indicated. With yarn in front, slip the next stitch to the right needle as if to purl. Turn the work so that the yarn is now in the back. Bring the yarn forward around the slipped stitch. Slip the slipped stitch again as if to purl. Bring the yarn to the back between the slipped stitch and the next stitch. Knit the rest of the row. When picking up the wrapped stitch to work later, insert the needle into the wrap (it looks like a little bead below the stitch) and the stitch itself, knitting or purling the two together. This helps to prevent gaps that can show up when rows are partially fastened off (as on the shoulders of a sweater).

On a knit side of the work, knit to the last stitch indicated. With yarn in back, slip the next stitch to the right needle as if to knit. Turn the work so that the yarn is now in the front. Bring the yarn around the slipped stitch to the back. Slip the slipped stitch again as if to knit. Bring the yarn to the front between the slipped stitch and the next stitch. Purl the rest of the row. When picking up the wrapped stitch to work later, insert the needle into the wrap and the stitch, knitting or purling the two together.

Increase

M1 (make one): With the right-hand needle, lift the horizontal thread lying between the needles and place it onto the left-hand needle. Knit the new stitch through the back loop.
Double Inc (make two): Knit in front, then back, then front again.

I-cord (use two double-pointed needles)

Cast on number of stitches indicated. *Slide stitches to opposite end of double-pointed needle and knit them, pulling yarn snugly across back of the work. DO NOT TURN.* Repeat from * to * to desired length. Bind off.

This perfectly proportioned purse puts paisley in a whole new light. All the individual pieces are felted, and then the whole bag is felted again for an especially dense fabric.

paisley
FELTED BAG

Designed by **Linda Cyr**
Photographed by **Tony Lattari**

Sizes

Finished Measurements

After felting: 14×8×4"

Materials

Yarns

Worsted weight 100% (feltable) wool, 330 yds. (approx 300 m) in salmon (MC)

Worsted weight 100% (feltable) wool, approx 110 yds. (100 m) *each* in copper (A), brown (B), ivory (C), khaki (D), light blue-green (E), and dark blue-green (F)

Needles & Extras

- Size 9 (5.5 mm) 24" (60 cm) circular needle OR SIZE NEEDED TO OBTAIN GAUGE
- ½ yd. of lining fabric
- Magnetic purse fastener
- 13½×3½" piece of ¼"-thick crafts foam for base
- Blunt-end yarn needle
- One pair ¾" metal purse-handle loops
- Sewing needle and thread
- Man's 1"-wide leather belt for strap

Notes

Gauge

16 sts and 22 rows = 4" (10 cm) in St st (knit all RS rows, purl all WS rows; knit every row when knitting in the round) before felting. TAKE TIME TO CHECK YOUR GAUGE.

Special Abbreviations

sl1-k = slip next stitch knitwise

wyib = with yarn in back of work

Knit

BASE

Using MC, cast on 75 sts and work back and forth across needle in rows.

Row 1: Sl1-k, wyib, k across.

Rep Row 1 for 41 more times.

SIDES

Pick up and k21 sts along left side of Base, 75 sts along cast-on edge, and 21 sts along right side of Base—192 sts. Place marker between first and last sts to designate beg of rnd. Work in St st (k every rnd) until sides measure 12" long. Bind off all sts loosely.

Small Felt Piece

(make 1 each using A, B, C, and D) Cast on 48 sts and work in St st (k every RS row, p every WS row) until piece measures 9" long. Bind off all sts loosely.

Large Felt Piece

(make 1 each using E and F) Cast on 48 sts and work in St st until piece measures 18" from beg. Bind off all sts loosely.

Felting

Felt purse, small felt pieces, and large felt pieces following instructions on *page 270.* Allow pieces to dry before proceeding.

FINISHING

Using actual-size pattern pieces, *opposite,* and sharp scissors, cut 2 each of the foll:

Fig. 1 (Large Flower) in E; Fig. 2 (Large Circle) in F; Fig. 3 (Small Flower) in A; Fig. 4 (Medium Circle) in C; Fig. 5 (Large Paisley) in F and B; Fig. 6 (Small Paisley) in B and F; Fig. 7 (Small Circle) in C and D. Cut 24 Fig. 8 (Leaf) in D.

Using photo on *page 79* as a guide and matching yarns, sew appliqué pieces of flowers and paisleys together and to Bag, noting design is the same on back and front of Bag. Embroider vine in Chain st using B around front and back of entire Bag. Sew Leaves in position.

Lightly refelt Bag to smooth cut edges. Dry Bag and trim any stray pieces of yarn.

Cut 2 pieces of lining fabric 15×11". Sew side and bottom seams with a ½" seam allowance. Turn under ½" at top edge, press, and stitch. Attach magnetic closure to center top of lining. Place crafts foam in bottom of Bag. Stitch lining in place around top edge of Bag. Pinch corners at each side to make 4"-deep pleats (2" of fabric on each side); position purse-handle loops in place, and secure pleats through all thicknesses.

Thread belt through loops, doubling it so the buckle is to the outside and on top.

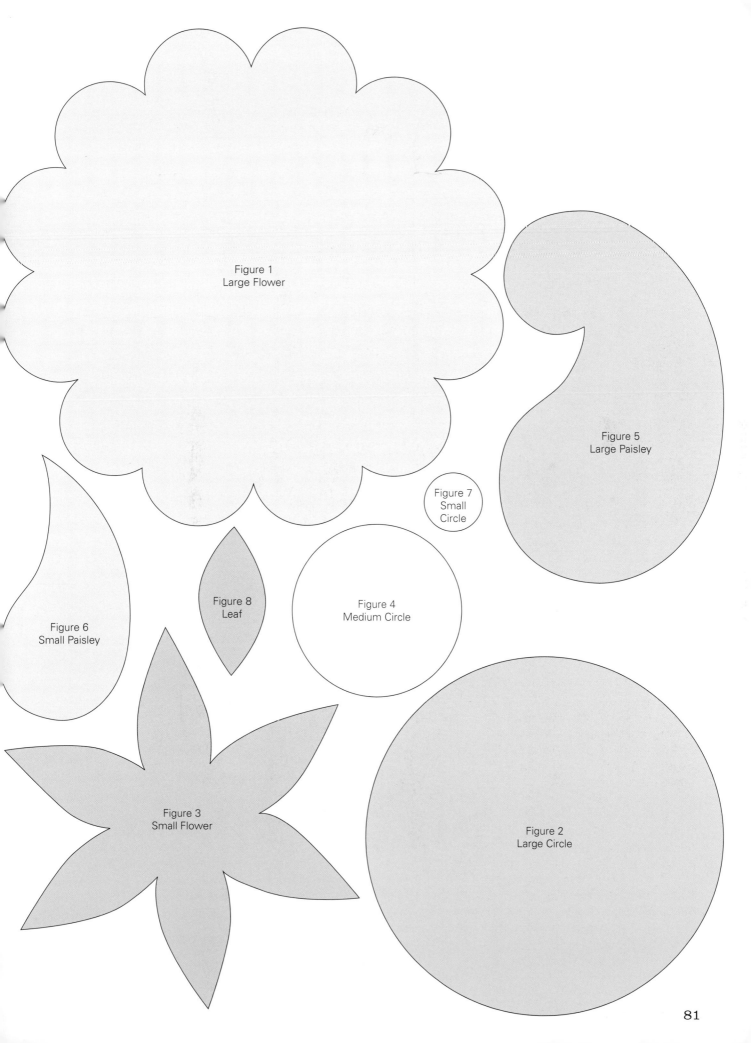

Figure 1
Large Flower

Figure 5
Large Paisley

Figure 7
Small
Circle

Figure 6
Small Paisley

Figure 8
Leaf

Figure 4
Medium Circle

Figure 3
Small Flower

Figure 2
Large Circle

felted blue DOTTED bag

Designed by **Sara Jane Treinen**   Photographed by **Akin Girav**

■■■■□ Intermediate

Sizes
Finished Measurements
Before felting: 20×11×3¾"
After felting: 13¾×6¼×1½"

Materials
Yarns
Worsted weight 100% (feltable) wool, 400 yds. (366 m) in light blue (MC)

Worsted weight 100% (feltable) wool, approx 220 yds. (188 m) in dark blue (CC)

Needles & Extras
- Size 10½ (7 mm) 24" circular needle OR SIZE NEEDED TO OBTAIN GAUGE
- Size 10½ (7 mm) double-pointed needles (dpns)
- Size H/8 (5 mm) crochet hook
- Four stitch holders
- Four stitch markers (one of a different color)
- Blunt-end yarn needle
- Sewing thread to match CC yarn
- Sewing needle

Notes
Gauge
13 sts and 17 rows = 4" (10 cm) before felting. TAKE TIME TO CHECK YOUR GAUGE.

Special Abbreviations
sc-dec = Using crochet hook, draw up loop in st, draw up loop in next st, yo and draw yarn through all 3 loops on hook.

Knit
BASE
Cast on 13 sts onto dpns using MC.
Row 1: Knit.
Row 2: K1, yo, k2tog; k to end of row.
Row 3: P1, yo, p2tog; p to end of row,
Rep Rows 2 and 3 thirty-two more times (there will be 33 yo spaces on each side).
Next row: Purl.

SIDES
Using circular needle, pick up stitches around the Base.
Rnd 1 (RS): K13 sts across short end, place marker (pm) of distinct color to mark beg of rnd; pick up 66 sts along long side by picking up 2 sts in every yo space as follows: pick up and k1 st in st above the space, then pick up second st by inserting the needle into the yo space and k1 st, pm after these 66 sts are picked up. Pick up and k13 sts along next short side, pm. Pick up 66 sts along second long side; pm. K across 13 sts to beg of rnd marker—158 sts around.

After knitting the body of this bag, toss it in the washing machine and—voila!—the bag will be smaller, denser, and sturdier. After it's dry, sew the crocheted dots and button closure to the bag, and felt it a final time.

Rnd 2: *K1, yo, k2tog, k until 2 sts rem before next marker, yo, k2tog, slip marker (sm), k1, yo, k2tog, knit to 2 sts before next marker, yo, k2tog; sm; rep from * around. (Cont to slip markers as you come to them in each rnd.)

Rnds 3 and 4: Knit.

Rep Rnds 2–4 until piece measures approx 10" from top to bottom, measuring from Rnd 2 of sides.

Note: Next rnd establishes the stitches and position for handles. Count sts from beg marker to ensure accuracy.

Next rnd: *K23, sl the last 4 sts just worked onto holder, k24, place last 4 sts just worked onto holder, k19, sm; k13 across narrow side, sm; rep from * to work next 2 sides—4 openings for handles made.

Next rnd: K and AT THE SAME TIME cast on 4 sts over each of the 4 openings (above sts on holders)—158 sts.

Next 2 rnds: Knit.

Before beginning the bind-off rnd, mark the 33rd and 34th sts of one of the long sides for the position of the button loop.

I-cord bind-off rnd: Using dpn and double strand of yarn, cast on 4 sts; place these 4 sts onto LH side of circular needle. **K3, ssk (includes 4th I-cord st plus one st from bag), do not turn work; sl 4 sts from RH side of needle back to LH side; rep from ** to the marked button loop sts and bind off the first marked st.

Work the buttonloop as foll: With the 4 sts on the LH side of needle, *use a separate dpn and k4, pulling the yarn across the back of the work to work the first st; then second, third, and fourth stitches; do not turn, slide these sts to opposite end of dpn and rep from * until cord measures approx 10". Then return the 4 sts to the LH side of the circular needle and cont I-cord bind-off as before until all sts are bound off. Then sl 1, k3tog, pass slipped stitch over (psso). Fasten off, leaving an 8" tail. Use tail to join beg and end of I-cord; weave tail through cord.

HANDLE (MAKE 2)
Right side
With RS of Bag facing, sl the 4 sts on holder (on the RH side) onto dpn. Using double strand of yarn, k each of these 4 sts tog with each of the matching cast-on sts to close the opening. Work I-cord as for button loop until cord measures 12". Leave sts on needle.

Left side
Work as for right side of Handle until cord measures 2". Using Kitchener st, *page 270*, weave handle ends tog. Rep Handle instructions on opposite side of Bag.

DOT (MAKE 11)
Using crochet hook and CC, ch 4.

Rnd 1: Dc in 4th ch from hook; work 11 more dc in same ch; join with sl st to third ch of beg ch-4.

Rnd 2: Ch 1, sc in each dc around; join with sl st to first sc; fasten off. Weave in all ends.

BUTTON
Roll CC yarn into a small 1"-diameter ball to use as stuffing for shaping the Button; set aside.

Using crochet hook and CC, ch 4.

Rnd 1: Dc in 4th ch from hook; work 11 more dc in same ch; join with sl st to 3rd ch of beg ch-4.

Rnd 2: Ch 3, dc in each dc around; join with sl st to top of beg ch-3.

Rnd 3: Ch 1, insert needle into top of same st as join and draw up loop, draw up loop in next st—3 loops on hook; yo and draw yarn through all 3 loops; (work sc-dec over next 2 dc) 5 times. Before completing rnd, insert yarn ball into center of work and cont to crochet around it to secure it in place; join last sc-dec with sl st to first sc-dec; fasten off, leaving tail; weave in ends.

FELTING
Put Bag, Dots, and Button in a mesh lingerie bag; machine-wash. (See felting instructions on *page 270* and "Felting Tips" on *page 74*.) Periodically check Bag to determine stage of felting. Most items will take 2 to 3 washings; do not place items in dryer at any time.

Felt the Purse, Dots, and Button up to the point when you think they need only one more wash. Let them dry; then hand-sew the Dots and Button to the Bag (see photo, *above*, for arrangement). Use matching sewing thread to sew the buttonloop sides tog, leaving an opening large enough for the Button to pass through.

Felt the Bag once more. In the process of shaping, use the eyelets (yos) as guides to shape the front, back, and sides.

textured-squares
bag

Create the soft textured squares on this all-cotton bag
by marrying knit and purl stitches. You'll love this versatile
bag—you'll want to have several in different colors.

Designed by **Linda Medina**   Photographed by **Tony Lattari**

■ ■ □ □ **Easy**

Sizes

Finished Measurements

11½×9"

Materials

Yarns

Worsted weight
100% cotton, 236 yds.
(212 m) in turquoise

4 MEDIUM

Needles & Extras

- Size 7 (4.5 mm) needles OR SIZE NEEDED TO OBTAIN GAUGE
- Size G (4 mm) crochet hook
- Blunt-end yarn needle
- Two stitch holders
- One 1¼"-diameter button
- Basting thread

Notes

Gauge

18 sts and 22 rows = 4" (10 cm) in St st (knit all RS rows, purl all WS rows). TAKE TIME TO CHECK YOUR GAUGE.

Knit

PATTERN STITCHES

Squares Pattern (multiple of 10 sts + 2; 12-row rep)

Row 1 (RS): Knit.
Row 2: Purl.
Row 3: K2, *p8, k2; rep from * across.
Row 4: P2, *k8, p2; rep from * across.
Row 5: K2, *p2, k4, p2, k2; rep from * across.
Row 6: P2, *k2, p4, k2, p2; rep from * across.
Row 7: Rep Row 5.
Row 8: Rep Row 6.
Row 9: Rep Row 5.
Row 10: Rep Row 6.
Row 11: Rep Row 3.
Row 12: Rep Row 4.
   Repeat Rows 1–12 for Squares pat.

RIGHT HALF

Cast on 102 sts. Work Rows 1 and 2 of Squares pat.

Rows 3–12: Cont in pat, dec 1 st at each edge every row—82 sts.

   Work Rows 1–12 of pat 3 more times, dec 1 st at each edge every row—10 sts. Do not bind off.

Shape strap

Row 1: Knit 10.
Row 2: Purl 10.
   Rep Rows 1 and 2 until strap measures 11"; place sts on holder.

LEFT HALF

Cast on 102 sts.
Row 1 (RS): Knit.
Row 2: Purl.
Rows 3–48: Cont in St st and dec 1 st at each edge every row—10 sts.
   Shape strap same as for Right Half; sl sts onto holder.

BOTTOM

Cast on 51 sts. Work in St st until piece measures 2" from beg. Bind off.

FINISHING

With WS tog, pin lower edge of Left Half along front, one side, and back edges of Bottom; baste into place using thread. With WS of Right Half overlapping right side of Left Half, pin lower edge of Right Half along front, opposite side, and back edges of Bottom; baste into place. Using yarn and working through all layers, sew Right and Left Halves to Bottom.

Straps

Slip strap sts onto separate knitting needles. With RS tog, join strap using 3-needle bind-off method (see *page 268*). Fold strap in half lengthwise; using yarn, sew long edges tog.

Edging

With WS facing and using crochet hook, beg at V-point and sc along one diagonal edge of Right Half, slip st past strap, then sc along opposite diagonal edge of Right Half. Ch 1, turn. Sc in each sc and sl st back to beg sc. Fasten off.

Button Loop

Pin Right Half to Left Half along overlapping front and back diagonal edges. With WS facing and using crochet hook, sl st top edge of bag into V-point where Left and Right Halves overlap. Ch 14; sc into each ch; sl st back into V-point to form button loop. Sc along edge of Left Half to V-point on opposite side. Ch 1; turn. Work 1 sc in each sc back to button loop. Fasten off. Using yarn, sew inside and outside overlapping edges into place. Sew button to Bag.

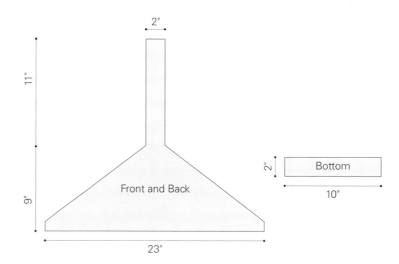

raffia
tote

Even a newbie knitter can make this stylish 12-inch square tote created with variegated raffia. It's worked in garter stitch with simple crocheted edging at the top.

Designed by **Linda Cyr** Photographed by **Tony Lattari**

■■ ■■ ☐ ☐ ☐ Easy

Sizes

Finished Measurements
12" wide top (flares to 16"); 12" high

Materials

Yarns
Worsted weight natural raffia, 600 yds. (550 m) in variegated blue-green

4 MEDIUM

Needles & Extras
- Size 10 (6 mm) 24" circular needle OR SIZE NEEDED TO OBTAIN GAUGE
- Size K/10½ (6.5 mm) crochet hook
- Stitch markers
- Blunt end yarn needle
- ½ yd. cotton canvas fabric for lining
- 1 pair ¾×25" leather purse straps
- Sewing needle and thread

Notes

Gauge
12 sts and 24 rows = 4" (10 cm) in Garter st (knit all rows; when knitting in the round, purl 1 rnd, knit 1 rnd) using 2 strands of yarn held tog.
TAKE TIME TO CHECK YOUR GAUGE.

Yarn is held doubled throughout.

Knit

BASE
Using 2 strands of yarn held together, cast on 37 sts. Work in rows.
Row 1: Sl 1 knitwise, k to end.
Repeat this row 22 more times.

SIDES
Turn and sl 1, k36, pick up and k12 sts along side edge, pick up and k36 sts along cast-on edge, pick up and k 11 sts along rem side, k sl st from beg of rnd—96 sts. Place marker (pm) for beg of rnd. Work in rnds of Garter st (p 1 rnd, k 1 rnd) for 11 rnds.

Next Dec rnd: *K2tog, pm, k34, ssk, k10; rep from * once more—92 sts.
Next 11 rnds: Work in Garter st, do not work last st of final rnd, remove beg-of-rnd marker.
Next Dec rnd: K2tog, pm, k34, ssk, k to 2 sts before marker, k2tog, sl marker, k34, ssk, k to end—88 sts.
Rep last 12 rnds 4 more times—72 sts.
Bind off, but do not fasten off.
With crochet hook, insert hook in last st. Work 2 rnds of sl st below bound-off rnd. Fasten off.

FINISHING
Steam block Tote. To make lining, cut fabric 25×17". Fold in half with WS tog so that folded piece measures 12½×17". Mark the center 13" of the 17" edge opposite the fold. The marked edge will become the lining top edge. On each side, draw a line from the outside edge at fold to the outside edge of marked 13". Trim piece along marked line. Using a ½" seam allowance, sew both sides. Fold down top ½" to WS and press in place. Insert lining into Tote and sew around top. Sew straps to outside of Tote, using photo, *opposite*, as a guide for placement.

felted
knitting
TOTE

First knitting back and forth on a circular needle and then knitting in the round, you can work up this tote quickly. After hand-sewing the handles to the body, wash it in your machine until you're happy with the results.

Designed by **Virginia Rowan Rokholt**   Photographed by **Akin Girav**

■■■□□ Easy

Sizes

Finished Measurements

Before felting: 44" circumference; 24" high (excluding handles)

After felting: 36" circumference; 13" high (excluding handles)

Materials

Yarns

Super bulky weight, 715 yds. (650 m) in variegated tan

6 SUPER BULKY

Needles & Extras

• Size 13 (9 mm) 24" circular needle
• Crochet hook
• Stitch marker
• Blunt-end yarn needle

Notes

Gauge

Before felting: 11 sts and 14 rnds= 4" (10 cm) in St st (knit all rounds). TAKE TIME TO CHECK YOUR GAUGE.

Knit

BASE

Cast on 40 sts. Knit even in Garter st (knit all rows, going back and forth) for 5".

BODY

Rnd 1: K40 sts; pick up and k20 sts across short edge of Base; pick up and k40 sts across other side; pick up and k20 sts across rem short edge; place marker to indicate beg of rnd—120 sts.

Join sts and knit in the round, working even in St st (k every row) until Body measures approx 17" from beg.
Dec rnd: (K10, k2tog) around—110 sts rem. Work even in St st until Body measures 24".

P 3 rnds. Bind off loosely.

HANDLE (MAKE 2)

Cast on 4 sts. K 4 rows; break off yarn, leaving a 6" tail. Cast on another 4 sts onto the same needle. K 4 rows.

K across all 8 sts and cont in Garter st for 12" more. K 4 rows on first 4 sts; bind off. K 4 rows on rem 4 sts; bind off. Fold Handle in half lengthwise and sew edge closed, leaving the 4 stitch tabs free.

FINISHING

Evenly position the 2 tabs at the ends of the Handles to the inside and outside of the Tote and stitch securely to edge of bag. Weave in ends.

Fringe

Cut about 80 strands of yarn approx 8" long. For each fringe, fold strand of yarn in half and use crochet hook to draw fold through top (purled) edge of Tote, forming a loop. Pull ends of fringe through this loop. Pull to tighten. Repeat evenly around bag opening. Extra fringe can be placed randomly on the Tote. Trim fringe if necessary.

Felting

Refer to felting instructions on *page 270*.

FELTED EVENING CLUTCH

A night out calls for special touches, and this small clutch is the perfect accessory. A basic stockinette stitch swatch is crocheted together at the side seams, folded into an envelope shape, then felted and trimmed. Attach an exquisite button, and you're ready to go.

Designed by **Virginia Rowan Rokholt**   Photographed by **Greg Scheidemann**

■■□□□ Easy

Sizes
Finished Measurements
Before felting: Approx 12×6"
After felting: Approx 10½×5½"

Materials
Yarns
Super bulky weight (feltable) wool or wool blend), 165 yds. (150 m), in flecked brown

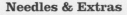

6 SUPER BULKY

Needles & Extras
- Size 13 (9 mm) knitting needles OR SIZE NEEDED TO OBTAIN GAUGE
- Size G/6 (4 mm) crochet hook
- Hook-and-loop fastener
- 1½"-diameter button

Notes
Gauge
Before felting: 8 sts = 4" (10 cm) in St st (knit all RS rows, purl all WS rows) using 2 strands of yarn held tog. TAKE TIME TO CHECK YOUR GAUGE.

Yarn is held doubled throughout.

Knit
Using 2 strands of yarn held together, cast on 23 sts. Beg with a purl row, work St st to 18" from beg. Bind off loosely.

Fold Clutch in thirds to create an envelope shape with a flap of 6" and a body height of 6". Holding RS tog, crochet side seams. Piece will measure approx 6" tall and 12" wide before felting. Turn right side out.

FELTING
Refer to felting instructions on *page 270*. When felting is complete, shape and allow to dry.

FINISHING
Cut a triangle from each side of the Clutch flap to create an envelope shape. Sew hook-and-loop fastener to bottom center of inside flap and to matching position on Clutch body. Sew button to front center of flap.

accessories

Look stunning with scarves, shawls, hats, socks, and even jewelry that you've stitched yourself.

mohair SCARF

This dramatic scarf, measuring 90 inches long including the fringe, gets its airy look from the baby mohair yarn knitted in garter stitch on big needles.

Designed by **Margarita Mejia**   Photographed by **Tony Lattari**

■□□□□ **Beginner**

Sizes

Finished Measurements

10×70" (not including fringe) (Scarf will stretch when worn.)

Note: The yarn used in the project shown, *opposite,* is a combination of several different types and colors of yarn knotted together continuously in one skein. To get the same effect, look for yarns with ribbon or self-striping luxury yarns.

Materials

Yarns

Worsted weight 100% baby mohair, 220 yds. (200 m) in orange or a mix of orange hues

Needles & Extras

- Size 35 (19 mm) needles OR SIZE NEEDED TO OBTAIN GAUGE
- Crochet hook
- Blunt-end yarn needle

Notes

Gauge

7 sts = 4" (10 cm) in Garter st (knit all rows). (Row gauge varies depending on yarn type.) TAKE TIME TO CHECK YOUR GAUGE.

Knit

Cast on 18 sts. Work even in Garter st (k every row) until piece measures 70" from beg. Bind off.

FRINGE

For each short edge, cut 48 strands of yarn, each 14" long. For each Fringe, place 4 strands together. Fold the strands in half, and using a crochet hook, knot 12 Fringes evenly spaced along each edge. Trim ends.

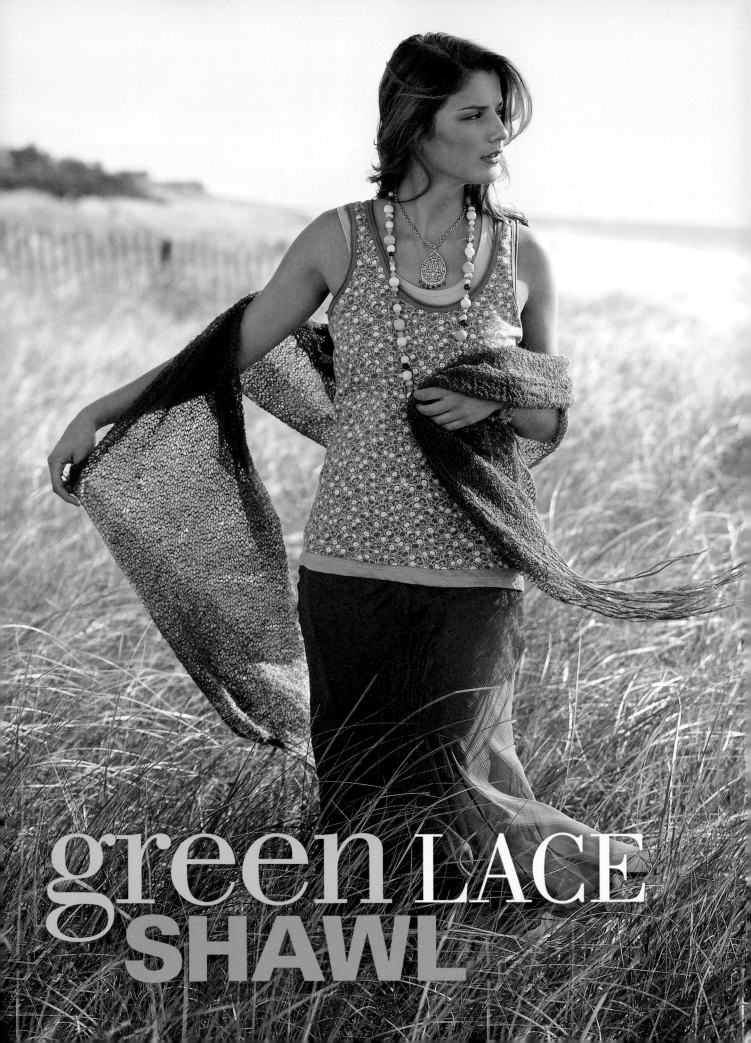

green LACE
SHAWL

Knitting this showoff-worthy shawl requires just three things: knowledge of simple garter stitch, big needles, and a supply of a super-fine linen/mohair blend yarn. When finished, the piece is blocked and shaped to form the fluted edges.

Designed by **Linda Bender**
Photographed by **Tony Lattari**

 Beginner

Sizes

Finished Measurements

24×80" (not including fringe)

Materials

Yarns

Lace weight linen-mohair blend, 1,000 yds. (910 m) in forest green

Needles & Extras

- Size 10 (6 mm) needles OR SIZE NEEDED TO OBTAIN GAUGE
- Crochet hook
- Blunt-end yarn needle

Notes

Gauge

12 sts and 22 rows = 4" (10 cm) in Garter st (knit all rows), before blocking. TAKE TIME TO CHECK YOUR GAUGE.

Knit

Measure 44 yards for fringe, set aside. Cast on 60 stitches. Work in Garter st (k every row) until Shawl reaches 80" or desired length. Bind off loosely.

FINISHING

Fringe

Cut 66 strands of yarn, each 24" long. For each fringe, fold the strand in half, and using a crochet hook, knot each fringe along the short edge of the Shawl. For even placement, knot one strand in each corner and one in the center of each short side. Space 15 strands on each side of center strand.

Blocking

Wet Shawl. Place on towel or drying rack. Fold shawl in half loosely to make it easier to work with. Block by stretching the piece to the sides, pulling the edges outward at intervals to create a fluted effect. The yarn will shrink back to about half of what was pulled, so don't be afraid to exaggerate. If, when the Shawl has dried, you wish to heighten the fluted effect, wet again and reblock.

snowflake **SET**

This cozy hat, scarf, and mittens trio, worked
in eye-catching blue and white wool, is ready for the slopes
or the lodge. The Nordic-inspired snowflake pattern is knitted
in on the hat and scarf.

Designed by **Sandi Prosser**   Photographed by **Tony Lattari**

▬▬▬▬ ▭ Intermediate

Sizes
Finished Measurements
Hat: Circumference = 22½"
Mitten: Length = 10"
Scarf: 8×60"

Materials
Yarns
Worsted weight, 525 yds.
(475 m) in bright blue (MC)

Worsted weight, 105 yd.
(95 m), in white (CC)

Needles & Extras
- Size 8 (5 mm) needles OR SIZE
  NEEDED TO OBTAIN GAUGE
- Size 7 (4.5 mm) needles for Hat
- Size 8 (5 mm) double-pointed needles
  (dpns) for Mittens
- Stitch holders
- Stitch markers

Notes
Gauge
17 sts and 22 rows = 4" (10 cm) in
St st (knit all RS rows, purl all WS
rows; when knitting in the round,
knit every row) with larger needles.
TAKE TIME TO CHECK YOUR GAUGE.

Knit
PATTERN STITCHES
Seed Stitch (over an odd number
of sts; a multiple of 2 sts + 1)
Row 1 (RS): K1, *p1, k1; rep from *
to end of row.
  Rep this row to form Seed st.

HAT
First earflap
Using smaller needles and MC, cast on
7 sts and work 2 rows in Seed st.

Row 3: K1, p1, k1, yarn over (yo), k1, yo,
k1, p1, k1—9 sts.
Row 4: K1, p1, k1, p3, k1, p1, k1.
Row 5: K1, p1, k1, yo, k3, yo, k1, p1,
k1—11 sts.
Row 6: K1, p1, k1, p5, k1, p1, k1.
Row 7: K1, p1, k1, yo, k5, yo, k1, p1,
k1—13 sts.
Row 8: K1, p1, k1, p7, k1, p1, k1.
Row 9: K1, p1, k1, yo, k7, yo, k1, p1,
k1—15 sts.

Row 10: K1, p1, k1, p9, k1, p1, k1.
Row 11: K1, p1, k1, yo, k9, yo, k1, p1,
k1—17 sts.
Row 12: K1, p1, k1, p11, k1, p1, k1.
  Leave these 17 sts on a spare needle.
Break yarn.

Second earflap
Work same as first earflap. Do not
break yarn.

Join earflaps

Cast on 11 sts. Work Seed st across these 11 sts and 17 sts of second earflap. Cast on 35 sts. Work Seed st across 17 sts of first earflap. Cast on 11 sts—91 sts. Work 5 rows in Seed st.

Change to larger needles. K3 edge sts (k on RS, p on WS, alternating MC and CC yarns to match 2 outside sts on Hat Chart, *page 103*). Work first rep beg at start Hat. Work 14-st rep 5 more times, ending last rep at end Hat. K2 edge sts at beg edge sts. Cont to work rem 12 rows of chart, keeping edge sts in St st. Using MC, work even in St st (k every RS row, p every WS row) until piece from joining row measures 4½", ending with a WS row.

Shape top

Next row (RS): K1, *k2tog, k13; rep from * to end—85 sts.

P 1 row.

Next row: K1, *k2tog, k12; rep from * to end—79 sts.

P 1 row.

Cont as est, dec 6 sts evenly across all RS rows (as est) until 43 sts rem.

Next row (WS): *P5, p2tog; rep from * to last st, p1—37 sts.

Next row: K1, *k2tog, k4; rep from * to end—31 sts.

Next row: *P3, p2tog; rep from * to last st, p1—25 sts.

Next row: K1, *k2tog, k2; rep from * to end—19 sts.

Next row: *P1, p2tog; rep from * to last st, p1—13 sts.

Next row: K1, *k2tog; rep from * to end—7 sts.

Break yarn, leaving a long end. Draw end through rem sts and fasten securely. Sew center back seam.

TWISTED CORD TIES

Using 4 lengths of MC, make two 12"-long ties. Knot ends and trim evenly. Attach one end of each tie to the point of each earflap.

MITTENS
Left Mitten

Cast on 34 sts and divide onto 3 dpn as foll: 11 sts on needle #1, 12 sts on needle #2, 11 sts on needle #3. Place marker (pm) to mark beg of rnd and join, being careful not to twist sts.

Work in k1, p1 rib for 3".

Change to St st (k every rnd) and work 4 rnds.

Shape thumb gusset

Rnd 1: K13, make 1 (M1), k2, M1, k to end.

Rnd 2 and every other rnd: Knit.

Rnd 3: K13, M1, k4, M1, k to end.

Rnd 5: K13, M1, k6, M1, k to end.

Rnd 7: K13, m1, k8, m1, k to end.

Rnd 9: K13, M1, k10, M1, k to end—44 sts.

Mitten Chart

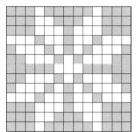

Scarf Chart

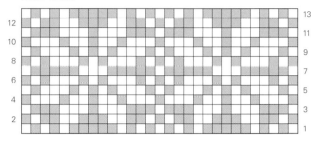

Hat Chart

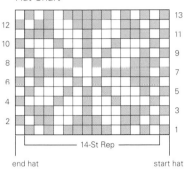

Key

☐ White (CC)
▨ Bright Blue (MC)

Next rnd: K13, place next 12 sts on holder for thumb, cast on 2 sts, k to end—34 sts.

Work even until piece measures 10" from beg.

Shape top of Mitten

Rnd 1: K1, ssk, k11, k2tog, k2, ssk, k11, k2tog, k1.

Rnd 2: K1, ssk, k9, k2tog, k2, ssk, k9, k2tog, k1.

Rnd 3: K1, ssk, k7, k2tog, k2, ssk, k7, k2tog, k1.

Rnd 4: K1, ssk, k5, k2tog, k2, ssk, k5, k2tog, k1.

Rnd 5: K1, ssk, k3, k2tog, k2, ssk, k3, k2tog, k1.

Rnd 6: K1, ssk, k1, k2tog, k2, ssk, k1, k2tog, k1—10 sts.

Break yarn, leaving a long end. Draw end through rem sts and fasten securely.

Thumb

Pick up 5 sts from 12 sts on holder with needle #1, 5 sts with needle #2, and 2 sts with needle #3, then pick up and k2 from base of thumb (the edge of 2 cast-on sts)—14 sts. Work even in St st until thumb measures 2½".

Shape top of thumb

Rnd 1: (K2tog, k1) 4 times, k2.

Rnd 2: (K2tog) 5 times.

Rnd 3: (K2tog) twice, k1—3 sts.

Break yarn, leaving a long end. Draw end through rem sts and fasten securely.

Right Mitten

Work same as Left Mitten, except position thumb gusset as follows:

Rnd 1: K19, M1, k2, M1, k to end.

Shape remainder of thumb gusset and Right Mitten the same as for Left.

Embroider snowflake motif

Using CC and following Mitten Chart, *above,* embroider snowflake motif on back of Mittens using duplicate st (*page 268*). Center design on top of palm, even with the rnd that begins palm over 34 sts.

SCARF

Note: Using the Fair Isle technique means following the chart for placement of MC and CC while knitting the odd-numbered rows and purling the even-numbered rows.

Using larger needles and MC, cast on 35 sts and work in Seed st for 6 rows.

Next row (RS): K1, p1, k1, place marker (pm), k to last 3 sts, pm, k1, p1, k1.

Next row: K1, p1, k1, slip marker (sm), p to last 3 sts, sm, k1, p1, k1.

Next row: K1, p1, k1, sm, work Row 1 of Scarf Chart, *above,* over the 29 sts between markers using Fair Isle technique, sm, k1, p1, k1.

Cont working first and last 3 sts in Seed st and center 29 sts in Fair Isle pat until chart is complete. Break off CC.

Next row (RS): K1, p1, k to last 2 sts, p1, k1.

Next row: K1, p1, k1, p to last 3 sts, k1, p1, k1.

Rep last 2 rows until Scarf measures 55", ending with a WS row. Rep entire Scarf Chart again.

Next row (RS): K1, p1, k to last 2 sts, p1, k1.

Next row: K1, p1, k1, p to last 3 sts, k1, p1, k1.

Work 6 rows in Seed st, and bind off in Seed st.

Block Scarf to finished measurements.

BIG
seed-stitch
SCARF

If you've just started knitting, this project is for you. Just knit one, purl one, using super bulky weight yarn and big needles to make this project come together quickly.

Designed by **Nancy Wyatt**   Photographed by **Greg Scheidemann**

■ ■ □ □ **Easy**

Sizes
Finished Measurements
7½×60"

Materials
Yarns
Super bulky weight, 105 yds. (96 m) in multicolor

Needles & Extras
• Size 19 (12 mm) knitting needles OR SIZE NEEDED TO OBTAIN GAUGE
• Blunt-end yarn needle

Notes
Gauge
5 sts and 8 rows = 4" (10 cm) in pat. TAKE TIME TO CHECK YOUR GAUGE.

Knit
Cast on 9 sts.
Row 1: K1, *p1, k1; rep from * to end. Rep Row 1 for pat until work from beg measures 60". Bind off in pat. Weave in loose ends.

Tip
If you find that the first and last rows of your scarf pull in too much, try using a needle one or two sizes larger on those two rows.

For instance, if you're knitting a scarf on size 11 needles, use size 13 on the cast-on and bind-off rows. Try this idea when casting on ribbing for sweaters or mittens, too. Also remember to cast on and bind off loosely.

COZY SOCKS

Once a mainstay for every knitter, handmade socks are again all the rage. These are designed to fit most women—just keep knitting them to the desired length.

Designed by **Susan Strawn**   Photographed by **Jay Wilde**

Sizes

Finished Measurements

Length from top to heel = 7½"
Circumference at top = 9"
Length of foot = knit to individual
length

Materials

Yarns

Super fine weight sock
yarn, 440 yds. (200 m)
in variegated blue

Needles & Extras

- Size 1 (2.25 mm) set of five
  double-pointed needles (dpns) OR
  SIZE NEEDED TO OBTAIN GAUGE
- Size 2 (2.75 mm) set of five dpns
- Stitch markers
- Stitch holders
- Blunt-end yarn needle

Notes

Gauge

28 sts and 48 rnds = 4" (10 cm) in St st
(knit all rows in the round) on larger needles.
TAKE TIME TO CHECK YOUR GAUGE.

Knit

Using larger dpns, cast on 60 sts. Place
marker (pm), arrange stitches onto 4
needles (15 sts on each), and join, taking
care not to twist sts.

Next 10 rnds: Knit.

Picot rnd: *K2tog, yo; rep from * to
end of rnd.

Next 10 rnds: Knit.

PATTERN STITCHES

Rnd 1: *K4, p1; repeat from * to end
of rnd.

Rnd 2: *K3, p2; repeat from * to end
of rnd.

Rnd 3: *K2, p3; repeat from * to end
of rnd.

Rnd 4: *K1, p4; repeat from * to end
of rnd.

Cont in pat (Rnds 1–4) for 56 rnds.

Change to smaller size dpns and work
in pat for another 24 rnds.

Set up Heel Flap: Needle #1: K15 sts,
turn work to WS, sl 1, p across 14 sts on
needle #1, then p15 from needle #4—turn.
These 30 sts will form the heel flap. The
sts on needles #2 and #3 (30 sts total)
are the instep sts and are not worked at
this time. Place these sts onto holders.

HEEL FLAP

Work back and forth in Heel st pat as
foll on 30 sts from #1 and #4 needles:

Rows 1 and 3 (RS): Sl 1, (k1, sl 1) to
last st, k1.

Rows 2 and 4 (WS): Sl 1, p29.

Rep Rows 1–4 until flap measures about
2" or desired length, ending with RS row.

HEEL TURN (SHORT ROWS)

Row 1 (WS): Sl 1, p16, p2tog, p1, turn.

Row 2 (RS): Sl 1, (k1, sl 1) across next
5 sts, ssk, k1, turn.

Row 3: Sl 1, p to within 1 st of turning
gap, p2tog, p1, turn.

Row 4: Sl 1, (k1, sl 1) to within 1 st of
turning gap, ssk, k1, turn.

Rep Rows 3 and 4 until all sts have been
worked; end with RS row—18 sts rem.

HEEL GUSSET

Cont with needle #1 (the needle with 18
heel sts), pick up and k15 sts along side
of Heel Flap; remove 30 instep sts from
holders and place 15 sts each on empty
needles #2 and #3, work across these
30 sts in est Triangles st pat; with empty
needle #4, pick up and k15 along other
side of Heel Flap and k9 heel sts from
needle #1. Place marker before next st
to denote beg of rnd—needle #1 has 24
sts; needles #2 and #3 each have 15 sts
in est Triangles St pat; needle #4 has 24
sts—78 sts.

INSTEP

Rnd 1: Beg with needle #1, k21 sts,
k2tog, k1; on needles #2 and #3, work
in est Triangles st pat; on needle #4, k1,
ssk, k21 sts to marker—76 sts.

Rnd 2: Work even.

Rep Rnds 1 and 2, working 1 less st on
each of needles #1 and #4 on Rnd 1 until
60 sts rem.

FOOT

Work even in St st on needles #4 and #1,
and the Triangles st pat on needles #2
and #3 until Foot measures about 2" from
desired length.

TOE

Change to St st on all needles and work
2 rnds even.

Rnd 1 (dec): On needle #1, k to last
3 sts, k2tog, k1; on needle #2, k1, ssk,
k to end of needle; on needle #3, k to
last 3 sts, k2tog, k1; on needle #4; k1,
ssk, k to end of rnd.

Rnd 2: Knit.

Rep Rnds 1 and 2 until 8 sts rem on
each needle (32 sts). Then rep Rnd 1
(dec) until 2 sts rem on each needle—
8 sts total.

FINISHING

Cut yarn, leaving a 6" tail; thread
blunt-end yarn needle and weave yarn
through all 8 sts. Pull yarn tail gently to
close Toe; weave through sts once more,
then secure yarn tail on WS of work. Fold
over top edge to WS at picot rnd to form
border and hem; using blunt-end yarn
needle, loosely whipstitch hem in place.
Weave in loose ends to WS.

nubby
WINTER TRIO

Multicolored nubby bands on the hat and mittens
of this trio take their cue from the main body of the scarf.
Tassels on the hat and scarf ends add a playful touch.

Designed by **Marilyn Losee**   Photographed by **Tony Lattari**

■■□□ **Easy**

Sizes
Finished Measurements
Hat: Circumference = 18"
Scarf: 6×51"
Mittens: Adult size M

Materials
Yarns
Bulky weight, 150 yds.
(138 m) in black (A)

Bulky weight, 100 yds.
(92 m) in dark red (B)

Bulky weight nubby 100% nylon,
110 yds. (100 m) in multicolor (C)

Worsted weight, 315 yds.
(290 m) in black (D)

Needles & Extras
- Size 13 (9 mm) needles OR SIZE NEEDED TO OBTAIN GAUGE
- Size K10.5 (6.5 mm) crochet hook
- Blunt-end yarn needle
- Two stitch holders
- Safety pin

Notes
Gauge
10 sts and 18 rows = 4" (10 cm) in
Seed st using A. TAKE TIME TO
CHECK YOUR GAUGE.

Special Abbreviations
CD = Work with the strands of
yarns C and D held together.

Knit

PATTERN STITCHES

Seed Stitch (on odd number of sts; a multiple of 2 sts + 1)

Row 1 (RS): K1, *p1, k1; rep from * to end of row.

Rep this row to form Seed st over an odd number of sts.

Seed Stitch (on even number of sts; a multiple of 2 sts)

Row 1 (RS): *K1, p1; rep from * to end of row.

Row 2 (WS): *P1, k1; rep from * to end of row.

Rep Rows 1 and 2 to form Seed st over an even number of sts.

SCARF

Using A, cast on 15 sts. Work 10 rows in Seed st. Fasten off A. Using CD, work 10 rows in Garter st (k every row). Rep these 20 rows 8 times more. Fasten off CD. Using A, work 10 rows in Seed st. Bind off all sts in Seed st.

TASSELS

Using D, make six 3" Tassels, leaving one 12" tail on each tassel. Working on short edges of Scarf, attach a Tassel to each corner and to center of edge as foll: Using crochet hook and long tail, ch 8; use yarn needle and remainder of tail to stitch Tassel to Scarf.

HAT

Using CD, cast on 40 sts. Work Garter st (k every row) for 2". Fasten off CD.

Next row (RS): Using B, k 1 row (mark this row with safety pin to indicate RS).

Next row: Beg Seed st and work until piece measures 8" from beg, ending with a WS row.

Shape crown

Row 1 (RS): *Work 4 sts in Seed st, k2tog, p2tog; rep from * across—30 sts.

Row 2: *Work 2 sts in Seed st, k2tog, p2tog; rep from * across—20 sts.

Row 3: Keeping to pat, work 2 sts tog across—10 sts.

Cut yarn, leaving a 12" tail. Using yarn needle, thread tail through rem sts and pull to gather; fasten off. Sew seam.

TASSEL

Make one Tassel same as for Scarf and attach to top of Hat.

MITTENS

Right and Left Mittens

With CD, cast on 22 sts. Work in k1, p1 rib for 2". Fasten off CD. Change to B and cont in rib for 4 rows. Change to St st (k every RS row, p every WS row) and work until piece measures 4½" from beg, ending with a WS row.

Shape thumb gusset

Row 1 (RS): K10, make 1 (M1), k2, M1, k10—24 sts.

Row 2: P10, M1, p4, M1, p10—26 sts.

Row 3: K10, M1, k6, M1, k10—28 sts.

Row 4: P10, M1, p8, M1, k10—30 sts.

Row 5: K10, M1, k10, M1, k10—32 sts.

Row 6: Purl.

Row 7: K11, place 10 sts on holder, k11—22 sts on needle. Work even in St st until piece measures 8" from beg, ending with a WS row.

Shape top

Dec 1 st each edge every other row 5 times—bind off rem 12 sts.

Thumb

Place 10 sts from holder onto needle. Pick up 1 st at base of thumb, k10 sts from needle, pick up 1 st at base of thumb—12 sts. Work in St st for 1½" or desired length, ending with a WS row.

Next row: K2tog across—6 sts.

Cut yarn, leaving a long tail. Thread tail through rem sts and pull to gather; then sew thumb seam.

FINISHING

Fold Mitten in half; sew side and top seams. Make second Mitten in same manner.

cold-weather
COZIES

Designed by **Charlotte Parry**
Photographed by **Tony Lattari**

Orange and blue play off each other perfectly in this colorful hat, scarf, and mitten set. Garter-stitch borders bring even more interest to the hat and scarf.

Sizes

Finished Measurements
Scarf: 7×66"
Hat: Circumference = 22"
Mittens: Adult size M

Materials

Yarns
Light worsted weight
Scarf: 330 yds. (300 m) in orange (MC); 110 yds. (100 m) in blue (CC)
Hat: 110 yds. (100 m) *each* in orange (MC) and blue (CC)
Mittens: 220 yds. (200 m) in orange (MC); 110 yds. (100 m) in blue (CC)

3 LIGHT

Needles & Extras
- Size 7 (4.5 mm) needles for Scarf OR SIZE NEEDED TO OBTAIN GAUGE
- Size 6 (4 mm) 16" circular needle for Hat
- Size 6 (4 mm) double-pointed needles (dpns) for Mittens
- Size 4 (3.5 mm) double-pointed needles (dpns) for Mittens
- Stitch holder
- Stitch marker
- Blunt-end yarn needle

Notes

Gauge
Scarf
20 sts and 26 rows = 4" (10 cm) in St st (k all RS rows, p all WS rows) using largest needles
Hat and Mittens
22 sts and 26 rows = 4" (10 cm) in St st (knit all rows when knitting in the round) using size 6 needles.
TAKE TIME TO CHECK YOUR GAUGE

Knit

SCARF

Using MC, cast on 37 sts. K 9 rows, p 1 row.

Next row (RS): Follow Pattern Chart, *opposite,* for next 16 rows. Note that all odd-numbered rows are knit and all even-numbered rows are purled. End all odd-numbered rows with p1; end all even-numbered rows with k1. Work 6-st pat rep on Rows 5–11; end each row as directed above.
Next row (RS): Using MC, knit.
Next row (WS): K2, purl 33 sts, k2.
  Rep these 2 rows until Scarf measures 62" from beg, ending with a WS row.
Next row (RS): Work 16 rows of Pattern Chart as before. Fasten off CC.
  Using MC, p 1 row, k 8 rows.
  Bind off all sts.

HAT

Using size 6 circular needle and MC, cast on 114 sts. Place marker (pm) to mark beg of rnd and join, taking care not to twist sts. (K 1 rnd, p 1 rnd) 4 times. K 2 rnds.
  Work 16 rnds of Pattern Chart, working 6-st rep 19 times. Fasten off CC.
  Using MC, k every rnd until piece measures 4" from beg.
  P 3 rnds. K 2 rnds.

Shape crown
Dec rnd 1: *K2tog, k15, ssk; rep from * around—102 sts. K 2 rnds.
Dec rnd 2: *K2tog, k13, ssk; rep from * around—90 sts. K 2 rnds.
Dec rnd 3: *K2tog, k11, ssk; rep from * around—78 sts. K 2 rnds.
Dec rnd 4: *K2tog, k9, ssk; rep from * around—66 sts. K 2 rnds.
Dec rnd 5: *K2tog, k7, ssk; rep from * around—54 sts. K 2 rnds.

Dec rnd 6: *K2tog, k5, ssk; rep from * around—42 sts. K 2 rnds.
Dec rnd 7: *K2tog, k3, ssk; rep from * around—30 sts. K 2 rnds.
Dec rnd 8: *K2tog, k1, ssk; rep from * around—18 sts. K 2 rnds.
Dec rnd 9: K2tog around—9 sts.
  Cut yarn and pull through rem 9 sts.

MITTENS
Left Mitten
With smaller needles and MC, cast on 42 sts. Divide sts onto 3 needles—14 sts on each needle. Place marker to mark beg of rnd and join, taking care not to twist sts.
  Work in k1, p1 rib for 3". Change to larger needles and k 4 rnds.

Shape thumb gusset

Rnd 1: K17, make 1 (M1), k2, M1, k23—44 sts.

Rnds 2, 4, 6, 8, 10, and 12: Knit.

Rnd 3: K17, M1, k4, M1, k23—46 sts.

Rnd 5: K17, M1, k6, M1, k23—48 sts.

Rnd 7: K17, M1, k8, M1, k23—50 sts.

Rnd 9: K17, M1, k10, M1, k23—52 sts.

Rnd 11: K17, M1, k12, M1, k23—54 sts.

Rnd 13: K17, M1, k14, M1, k23—56 sts.

Rnds 14–16: Knit.

Next rnd: K17, place next 16 sts on holder, cast on 2 sts, k23—42 sts.

K 5 rnds. Work 16 rnds of Pattern Chart (work 6-st rep 7 times each rnd). Fasten off B.

Shape top

Rnd 1: *K1, ssk, k15, k2tog, k1; rep from * around—38 sts.

Rnd 2: *K1, ssk, k13, k2tog, k1; rep from * around—34 sts.

Rnd 3: *K1, ssk, k11, k2tog, k1; rep from * around—30 sts.

Rnd 4: *K1, ssk, k9, k2tog, k1; rep from * around—26 sts.

Rnd 5: *K1, ssk, k7, k2tog, k1; rep from * around—22 sts.

Divide sts evenly onto 2 needles (11 sts each needle). Weave sts tog using Kitchener st, *page 270*, or bind off using 3-needle bind-off, *page 268*.

Shape thumb

Place 16 sts from holder onto 2 needles. With third needle, pick up 2 sts at base of thumb—18 sts. Divide evenly onto 3 needles (6 sts each needle). K for 2".

Next rnd: K2tog around—9 sts.

Next rnd: K1, (k2tog) 4 times—5 sts.

Pull yarn through 5 sts and fasten off.

Right Mitten

Work same as Left Mitten, reversing thumb placement as directed below.

Shape thumb gusset

Rnd 1: K 23, M1, k3, M1, k17—44 sts.

Work rem thumb gusset rnds same as for Left Mitten using this setup; then cont same as for Left Mitten.

Pattern Chart

Key
■ Blue (CC)
■ Orange (MC)

└─ 6-St Rep ─┘

silk
SCARF

A scarf this dynamic instantly elevates even the most basic outfit. Using just two 100 percent spun silk yarns—one studded with sequins—you'll look totally sophisticated!

Designed by **Margarita Mejia**
Photographed by **Tony Lattari**

Sizes

Finished Measurements

6½×63½" not including fringe

Materials

Yarns

Worsted weight 100% spun silk,
260 yds. (238 m) in tan (A)

Worsted weight 100% spun silk with sequins,
225 yds. (206 m) in burnt orange (B)

Needles & Extras

- Size 7 (4.5 mm) needles OR SIZE NEEDED TO OBTAIN GAUGE
- Blunt-end yarn needle
- Crochet hook

Notes

Gauge

18 sts and 29 rows = 4" (10 cm) in Garter st (knit all rows) with A.
18 sts and 24 rows = 4" (10 cm) in St st (knit all RS rows, purl all WS rows) with B. TAKE TIME TO CHECK YOUR GAUGE.

As designed, the long edges of this Scarf tend to roll inward. If you wish to counteract this tendency, knit the first and last 5 sts of *each* row when working in St st, creating a Garter st edge.

Knit

Using A, cast on 30 sts. *Work even in Garter st (k every row) for 18 rows. Using B, work even in St st (k RS rows, purl WS rows) for 14 rows; rep from * 10 more times. Using A, work even in Garter st for 18 rows. Bind off.

FRINGE

For each short end of Scarf, cut 20 strands of each yarn, each 16" long. For each Fringe, place 2 strands of each yarn together. Fold the strands in half, and using a crochet hook, knot 10 Fringes evenly spaced along each edge. Trim ends.

cable
WRISTLETS

Refine your cable
technique by
making these
wristlets, which
are perfect for
sporting on
chilly days.

Designed by **Darlene Hayes**
Photographed by **Tony Lattari**

Sizes

S (M, L)

Instructions are written for the smallest size with changes for larger sizes given in parentheses. When only one number is given, it applies to all sizes.

Note: For ease in working, circle all numbers pertaining to the size you're knitting.

Finished Measurements

Wrist circumference = 6 (7 ½, 9)"

Materials

Yarns

Worsted weight, 150 yds. (137 m) in cream

Needles & Extras

- Set of 5 size 8 (5 mm) double-pointed needles (dpns) OR SIZE NEEDED TO OBTAIN GAUGE
- Stitch marker
- Cable needle (cn)
- Size H/8 (5 mm) crochet hook
- Blunt-end yarn needle

Notes

Gauge

18 sts and 24 rows = 4" (10 cm) in St st (knit every row when knitting in the round). TAKE TIME TO CHECK YOUR GAUGE.

Special Abbreviations

C4F = Slip 2 stitches to cable needle (cn) and hold in front, knit 2, knit 2 from cn.

Knit

PATTERN STITCHES

1x1 Rib Pattern (a multiple of 2 sts; 1-rnd rep)
Row 1: *P1, k1; rep from * around.
Rep Rnd 1 for 1x1 Rib pat.

Cable Pattern (one cable is 6 sts; 6-rnd rep)
Rnd 1: P1, C4F, p1.
Rnds 2–6: P1, k4, p1.
Rep Rnds 1–6 for Cable pat.

WRISTLET (MAKE 2)

Cast on 32 (40, 44) sts. Divide sts onto 4 needles as foll: 10 (14, 16) sts on Needles #1 and #3; 6 sts on Needles #2 and #4. Join, taking care not to twist sts. Mark beg of rnd, placing marker bet first and last sts of rnd. Work in 1x1 Rib pat for 1".

Rnd 1: Work across Needle #1 in St st (k every RS row); work Rnd 1 of Cable pat on Needle #2; k sts on Needle #3; work Rnd 1 of Cable pat on Needle #4.
Rnds 2–6: K all sts, working Rnds 2–6 of Cable pat on Needles #2 and #4.
Rnd 7—Inc rnd: On Needle #1, k1, make 1 (M1), k to last st of Needle #1, M1, k1. Work even to end of rnd, keeping to Cable pat on Needles #2 and #4—34 (42, 46) sts.
Rnds 8–18: Work even, keeping to Cable pat on Needles #2 and #4.
Rnd 19—Inc rnd: Work even across Needles #1 and #2; on Needle #3, k1, M1, k to last st of Needle #3, M1, k1; work even to end of rnd—36 (44, 48) sts.
Rnds 20–29: Work even, keeping to Cable pat on Needles #2 and #4.

Rnd 30—Inc rnd: On Needle #1, k1, M1, k to last st of Needle #1, M1, k1, work even to end of rnd—38 (46, 50) sts. Work even until piece measures approx 8" from beg, end with Rnd 2 of Cable pat. P 1 rnd, then work 1 rnd in 1x1 Rib pat.
Next rnd—Eyelet rnd: *K2tog, yo; rep from * around.
P 1 rnd. Bind off.

TIE (MAKE 2)

With crochet hook, ch 24". Fasten off. Weave it through Eyelet rnd and tie in bow.

elegant SHAWL

This simple but elegant shawl takes you from day to evening in high style. Knit it with a fine wool mohair for a beautiful drape across your shoulders.

Designed by **Gayle Bunn**   Photographed by **Greg Scheidemann**

■■ ■■ ■■ □ Intermediate

Sizes
Finished Measurements
28×64"

Materials
Yarns
Bulky weight mohair blend, 82 yds. (75 m) in gold

Needles & Extras
• Size 9 (5.5 mm) knitting needles OR SIZE NEEDED TO OBTAIN GAUGE
• Blunt-end yarn needle

Notes
Gauge
13 sts and 23 rows = 4" (10 cm) in pattern. TAKE TIME TO CHECK YOUR GAUGE.

Special Abbreviations
psso = Pass slip stitch over last stitch made.
sl1-k = With yarn in back, slip one stitch knitwise.
sl1-p = With yarn in front, slip one stitch purlwise.

Knit
Cast on 90 sts.
Row 1 (RS): K1; *yo, sl1-k, k1, psso; rep from * across; end with k1.
Row 2: P1; *yo, sl1-p, p1, psso; rep from * across; end with p1.
   Rep Rows 1 and 2 until work measures approx 64"; end with Row 2. Bind off.

FINISHING
Tassel (MAKE 4)
Wind yarn around a 6" piece of cardboard 25 times. Break yarn, leaving a long tail, and thread it through the yarn needle. Slip needle through all loops on the cardboard, and tie tightly at one end to make the tip of the Tassel. Slip bundle off the cardboard, and wind a separate strand of yarn several times around the strands ¾" below the top of the Tassel. Draw needle through top, and sew Tassel to one corner. Cut through strands at the opposite end, and trim evenly. Attach a Tassel to each corner of Shawl.

Yes, it is possible to crochet with wire! This five-strand necklace employs a simple chain-stitch to attach beads on 26-gauge copper wire.

Designed by **Miranda Stewart**
Photographed by **Greg Scheidemann**

beads-and-wire
NECKLACE

Sizes
Finished Measurements
Length = 22"

Materials
Hooks & Extras
- Size H/8 (5 mm) crochet hook
- #26-gauge permanently coated copper wire, 15 yds.
- Beads as follows:
  25, 6 mm pyramid; 25, 8 mm matte finish;
  60, 4 mm faceted; 2, 10 mm matte finish;
  15, 6 mm teardrop; 25, 6 mm faceted;
  20, 6 mm faceted; 25, 3 mm teardrop;
  15, 6 mm pyramid; 35, 6 mm faceted;
  30, 6 mm glass
- Wire cutter
- Needle-nose pliers or combination pliers with
  built-in cutter
- Toggle closure

Crochet

Divide beads into 5 equal batches—59 total beads in each group. One batch will be used for each strand of the Necklace. Cut copper wire into five 3-yard pieces.

FIRST STRAND

Tie a knot close to one end of the copper wire to prevent beads from falling off. Randomly string 1 batch of beads onto the wire (approx 11¾" of beads).

Start at the opposite end of the wire.

Leaving a 6" tail, make a slip knot, ch 4.

* Slip bead up to hook, ch 1; rep from * across for a total of 59 beads.

Ch 4 without beads. Pull wire through the remaining lp on the hook to secure. Set aside. (The chain with beads will measure approx 22", depending on tension.)

Make 4 more strands as for First Strand.

FINISHING

To assemble the necklace, gather all strands together at one end. Twist wire ends together tightly beyond the crochet for approx 1½". Trim off excess wire. Thread twisted wire through one end of toggle closure.

To create a wrapped loop, twist excess wire around the base below the toggle. Wrap 2 to 3 times. Cut off excess wire.

Eliminate any sharp wire ends by crimping the wire ends tightly with the needle-nose pliers. Repeat for the other side of the toggle.

babies

Make something special—
a blanket, a toy, or a layette—for the
tiniest recipient on your list.

Ready for an update
on the traditional layette?
Skip the usual pastels
in favor of these newer,
richer colors for a more
contemporary layette.
The sweater, beanie, and
booties are great for a boy
or a girl (sized for 6, 12,
and 18 months).

striped layette

Designed by **Sandi Prosser**
Photographed by **Greg Scheidemann**

■■□□□ Easy

Sizes

Pullover & Hat: 6 (12, 18) months
Booties: S (M)

Instructions are written for the smallest size with changes for larger sizes given in parentheses. When only one number is given, it applies to all sizes.
Note: For ease in working, circle all numbers pertaining to the size you're knitting.

Finished Measurements
Pullover
Chest = 19 (21, 23)"
Length (Back before Neckband) = 9 (10, 11½)"
Hat
Circumference = 15 (16, 17)"
Booties
Length (toe to heel) = 4¼ (5¼)"

Materials

Yarns
DK weight, 250 yds. (230 m) *each* in blue (MC), raspberry (A), light green (B), and white (C)

Needles & Extras
- Size 6 (4 mm) needles OR SIZE NEEDED TO OBTAIN GAUGE
- Size 4 (3.5 mm) needles
- Blunt-end yarn needle
- Stitch holders
- Two ⅜"-diameter buttons

Notes

Gauge
22 sts and 28 rows = 4" (10 cm) in St st (knit all RS rows, purl all WS rows) with larger needles. TAKE TIME TO CHECK YOUR GAUGE.

Knit

PATTERN STITCHES
Stripe

Row 1 (RS): Using MC, K3; *using A, k1; using MC, k3; rep from * across.

Row 2: Using MC, p1; *using A, p1; using MC, p3; rep from * to last 2 sts, using A, p1; using MC, p1.

Rows 3–12: Using A, work in St st (knit RS rows, purl WS rows), beg with a knit row.

Row 13: *Using A, k1; using B, k1; rep from * to last st, using A, k1.

Row 14: *Using B, p1; using A, p1; rep from * to last st, using B, p1.

Rows 15–24: Using B, work in St st, beg with a knit row.

Row 25: Using B, k3; *using C, k1; using B, k3; rep from * across.

Row 26: Using B, p1; *using C, p1; using B, p3; rep from * to last 2 sts, using C, p1; with B, p1.

Rows 27–36: Using C, work in St st, beg with a knit row.

Row 37: *Using C, k1; using MC, k1; rep from * to last st, using C, k1.

Row 38: *Using MC, p1; using C, p1; rep from * to last st, using MC, p1.

Rows 39–48: Using MC, work in St st, beg with a knit row.

Repeat Rows 1–48 for Stripe pat.

PULLOVER
BACK

Using smaller needles and MC, cast on 51 (59, 63) sts. Knit 1 row (WS). Change to larger needles and work in pat as foll:

Rows 1, 3, 5, 7, 9 and 11 (RS): Knit.

Rows 2 and 8: Purl.

Rows 4 and 6: P4 (4,2), *k3, p5; rep from * to last 7 (7, 5) sts, k3, p4 (4, 2).

Rows 10 and 12: P 0 (0, 6), *k3, p5; rep from * to last 3 (3, 9) sts, k3, p 0 (0, 6).

Rep Rows 1–12 until piece measures 3 (4, 5½") from beg, ending with a WS row. Beg with Row 1, work Stripe pat until piece measures 9 (10, 11½") from beg, ending with a WS row.

Shape neck and shoulder

Next row (RS): Keeping to Stripe pat, bind off 38 (42, 44) sts, k to end of row—13 (17, 19) sts rem. Work 4 rows in St st on rem sts for button flap.

Next row (WS): *K1, p1; rep from * to last st, k1.

Bind off rem sts.

FRONT

Work same as Back until piece measures 7 (8, 9½") from beg, ending with a WS row.

Shape neck and shoulder

Next row (RS): Keeping to Stripe pat, work 18 (22, 24) sts. Sl rem 33 (37, 39) sts onto holder.

Working on 18 (22, 24) sts on needle, dec 1 st at neck edge every row 5 times—13 (17, 19) sts. Work 4 rows even.

Shape buttonholes

Next row (RS): *K4 (5, 5), k2tog, yo, rep from * twice, k to end of row. P 1 row; k 1 row.

Next row (WS): *K1, p1; rep from * to last st, k1. Bind off sts in ribbing.

Sl sts from holder onto needle and bind off center 15 sts; k rem 18 (22, 24) sts. Dec 1 st at neck edge every row 5 times—13 (17, 19) sts. Work 4 rows even. Bind off all sts.

SLEEVE (MAKE 2)

Using smaller needles and B, cast on 36 sts. Knit 1 row (WS); fasten off B. Change to larger needles and work Stripe pat, beg with Row 3 and AT THE SAME TIME inc 1 st each edge every 5th row, then every 4th (3rd, 3rd) row 8 (10, 14) more times—54 (58, 66) sts. Cont even in Stripe pat until piece measures 6 (6½, 8)" from beg, ending with a WS row. Bind off all sts.

FINISHING

Sew Back to Front at right shoulder seam.

Neckband

With RS facing and using smaller needles and A, pick up and knit 64 (68, 68) sts evenly along neck edge. K1 row. Change to MC; k 1 row. Bind off with knit sts.

Place Back left shoulder button flap under Front left shoulder; sew shoulders tog at the armhole edge. Sew Sleeves to armholes. Sew side and sleeve seams. Sew buttons to button flap opposite buttonholes.

HAT

Using smaller needles and C, cast on 82 (90, 94) sts. K 5 rows, end on WS. Fasten off C. Change to larger needles and MC. Beg with a k row, work 10 rows in St st.

Next row (RS): Using MC, k1; *using A, k1; using MC, k3; rep from * to last st, using A, k1 .

Next row: Using MC, p2; *using A, p1, with MC, p3; rep from * across. Fasten off MC. Using A, work 10 rows in St st.

Next row (RS): *Using A, k1; using B, k1; rep from * across.

Next row: *Using A, p1; using B, p1; rep from * across. Fasten off A. Using B, work in St st until piece measures 4 (4½, 5)" from beg, dec 2 (4, 2) sts evenly spaced across last WS row—80 (86, 92) sts.

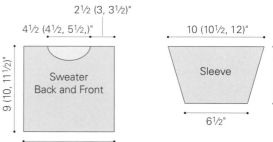

Shape top
Row 1 (RS): K1, *k4, k2tog; rep from * to last st, k1—67 (72, 77) sts.
Row 2 and all WS rows: Purl.
Row 3: K1, *k3, k2tog; rep from * to last st, k1—54 (58, 62) sts.
Row 5: K1, *k2, k2tog; rep from * to last st, k1—41 (44, 47) sts.
Row 7: K1, *k1, k2tog; rep from * to last st, k1—28 (30, 32) sts.
Row 9: K2 tog across—14 (15, 16) sts. Cut yarn, leaving a long end. Thread end through rem sts; pull and fasten securely. Sew Hat seam.

Tassel
Wind C around a 3½"-wide piece of cardboard 12 times. Cut yarn, leaving a long end. Thread end through needle and slip needle through all loops; tie. Remove cardboard and wind yarn tightly around loops ¾" below fold; fasten. Cut through loops; trim ends. Sew tassel to Hat.

BOOTIE (MAKE 2)
Using smaller needles and A, cast on 33 (37) sts. Knit 1 row (WS). Change to MC and work Garter st (knit every row) until piece measures 1½ (2)" from beg, ending with a WS row. Change to B and work Garter st for 4 rows.
Next row—Eyelet row (RS): *K2tog, yo; rep from * to last st, k1. Work Garter st for 3 rows.

Divide for instep
Next row (RS): K 22 (25). Turn.
Next row (WS): P11 (13).
Beg with a k row (RS) and working on 11 (13) sts, work 14 (16) rows in St st. Cut yarn.

Attach yarn to beg of RS row. With RS facing, k first 11 (12) sts at beg of row, pick up and k10 (13) sts up right-hand side of instep, knit across 11 (13) instep sts on needle, pick up and k10 (13) sts down left-hand side of instep, knit rem 11 (12) sts—53 (63) sts. Work 11 rows in Garter st.

Shape sole
Row 1 (RS): [K1, k2tog, k21 (26), k2tog] twice, k1—49 (59) sts.
Rows 2, 4, and 6: K1, k2tog, k to last 3 sts, k2 tog, k1—35 (45) sts at the end of Row 6.
Row 3: [K1, k2tog, k18 (23), k2tog] twice, k1—43 (53) sts.
Row 5: [K1, k2tog, k15 (20), k2tog] twice, k1—37 (47) sts. Bind off all sts.

Tie (MAKE 2)
Using smaller needles and C, cast on 66 sts. Bind off all sts.

FINISHING
Sew back and sole seams. Thread ties through eyelets.

christening
LACE BLANKET

Designed by **Joyce Nordstrom**   Photographed by **Greg Scheidemann**

■■■□ **Intermediate**

Sizes
Finished Measurements
40" square

Materials
Yarns
Light worsted weight,
2,200 yds. (1,980 m)
in white

Hooks & Extras
- Size G/6 (4 mm) crochet hook
  OR SIZE NEEDED TO OBTAIN GAUGE
- Blunt-end yarn needle
- Stitch marker

Notes
Gauge
4 blocks = 4" (10 cm); one 12-row
rep = 5.5" (14 cm). TAKE TIME TO
CHECK YOUR GAUGE.

Blanket is made on the diagonal,
beginning at one corner and increasing
in every row. Then stitches are
decreased on every row until opposite
corner is reached.

Crochet
PATTERN STITCHES
Puff: Working in the same st,
(yo and draw up a lp) 3 times, yo and draw
through all 7 lps on hook, ch 1 to close.

BLANKET
Row 1 (RS): Ch 6, dc in 4th ch from
hook and in next 2 ch—beg block made;
turn. Mark as RS.

Row 2: Ch 6, dc in 4th ch from hook and
next 2 ch—block made; sk 3 dc of beg
block, sl st around post of last dc; ch 3—
counts as dc, work 3 dc around same dc
post—2 blocks made; turn.
Row 3: Make beg block; (sk 3 dc of
block below, sl st around post of 4th
dc, ch 3, make 3 dc around same post)
twice—3 blocks made; turn.
Row 4: Work as for Row 3 up, having
1 more block in row—4 blocks.

Row 5: Ch 8, hdc in 6th ch from hook; *
ch 1, sk 3 dc of block below, sl st around
post of 4th dc, ch 4, hdc around same
post; rep from * across, ending with dc
over same post as last hdc—5 lps; turn.
Row 6: Work beg block; * sl st in lp,
ch 3—counts as dc; 3 dc in same lp; rep
from * across—6 blocks made; turn.

A blanket as pretty and delicate as this one easily rises to heirloom status. Crafted in a lacy field of puff, slip, and half-double crochet stitches, the design grows to 40 inches square when you add the eyelet-and-scalloped border.

Row 7: Ch 6, work Puff st in 5th ch from hook; * sk next 3 dc of previous block, sl st over next dc post, ch 4, make Puff st over same post; rep from * across row, ending with dc over same post as last Puff st—7 lps; turn.

Row 8: Rep Row 6—8 blocks.

Row 9: Rep Row 5—9 lps; turn.

Row 10: Rep Row 6—10 blocks.

Rows 11–16: Rep Row 3—16 blocks.

Rows 17–52: Rep Rows 5–16 three times—52 blocks after Row 52.

Rows 53 and 54: Rep Rows 5 and 6—54 blocks after Row 54.

Row 55 (last inc row): Rep Row 7—55 lps.

Decrease rows

Row 1: * Sl st in lp, ch 3—counts as dc; 3 dc in same lp; rep from * across 54 total times, sl st in last lp; turn.

Row 2: Sl st in first 3 dc, sl st around dc post, ch 4, hdc around same post; * ch 1, sk next 3 dc of previous block, sl st over last dc post, ch 4, hdc around same post; rep from * across, ending sl st over last dc post—53 lps; turn.

Row 3: Ch 1, * sl st in next lp, ch 3—counts as dc; 3 dc in same lp; rep from * across, ending sl st in last lp—52 blocks; turn.

Row 4: Sl st in first 3 dc, sl st over dc post; ch 3—counts as dc; 3 dc over same post; * sk next 3 dc of previous block, sl st over last dc post; ch 3—counts as dc; 3 dc over same post; rep from * across, ending sl st over last dc post—51 blocks; turn.

Rows 5–9: Rep Row 4—46 rem blocks after Row 9.

Row 10: Sl st in first 3 dc, sl st over next dc post; ch 4, hdc over same post; * ch 1, sk next 3 dc of previous block, sl st over next dc post, ch 4, hdc over post dc; rep from * across, ending sl st over last dc post—45 lps; turn.

Row 11: Rep Row 3—44 blocks.

Row 12: Sl st in first 3 dc; * sl st over next dc post, ch 4, Puff st), sk first 3 dc of next block; rep from * across, ending sl st over last dc post—43 lps; turn.

Rows 13–48: Rep Rows 1–12 three times—7 blocks after Row 48.

Cont as est until 1 block rem, sl st over last dc post. Fasten off.

BORDER

Rnd 1: With RS facing, join yarn with sl st in any corner, ch 1, 4 sc in same sp. Work 109 sc evenly along each edge with 4 sc in each corner around. At end, join with sl st in first sc.

Rnd 2: Ch 4—counts as dc and ch 1; * (dc in next sc, ch 1) 3 times; sk sc, (dc in next sc, ch 1) across side, ending sk sc; work dc and ch 1 in each corner sc; rep from * around, ending last rep with sk sc; join with sl st in 3rd ch of beg ch-4.

Rnd 3: * For Corner: (Sl st in ch-1 sp, ch 3, in same sp make 3 dc) 3 times. For Side: Sk 1 sp, (sl st in next sp; ch 3, in same sp make 3 dc) across, ending sk 1 sp. Rep from * around, ending last rep before first corner.

Rnd 4: Sk first ch-3, * sl st in sp before next dc, ch 4, in same sp work hdc, ch 1, sk next 3 dc; rep from * around.

Row 5: * Sl st in next ch-4 sp, ch 3, 3 dc in same sp; rep from * around. At end, join with sl st in 3rd ch of beg ch-3. Fasten off.

FINISHING

Pin to measurements on a flat, padded surface; cover with damp towels. Let dry.

SPLASHY
DUO

Babies go through towels and washcloths almost as fast as they do diapers. So for bathtime fun, only the softest accessories will do! This cotton chenille set, detailed with tiny border stripes and sweet picots, does the trick.

Designed by **Ann E. Smith**   Photographed by **Greg Scheidemann**

■■■□□ **Easy**

Sizes

Finished Measurements
Washcloth = 9×9"
Hooded Towel = 32×32"

Materials

Yarns
Worsted weight
100% cotton, 700 yds.
(640 m) in pink (MC)

Worsted weight 100% cotton,
100 yds. (91 m) in yellow (A)

Worsted weight 100% cotton,
200 yds. (182 m) in lilac (B)

Hooks & Extras

- Size G/6 (4 mm) crochet hook OR SIZE NEEDED TO OBTAIN GAUGE
- Blunt-end yarn needle

Notes

Gauge
12 sc and 12 rows = 4" (10 cm). TAKE TIME TO CHECK YOUR GAUGE.

This yarn relaxes after it has been crocheted, so the Hooded Towel may end up a bit larger than indicated.

Crochet
PATTERN STITCHES
Picot (p): In next sc, work sc, ch 2, and sl st.

WASHCLOTH
Using MC, ch 22.
Row 1: Sc in 2nd ch from hook and in each ch across—21 sts; turn.
Row 2: Ch 1, sc in each sc across; turn. Rep Row 2 for 19 more times—21 total rows. Fasten off.

Make border
Rnd 1: With RS facing, join A with sl st in top right sc, ch 1, 3 sc in same sc; (19 sc along edge, 3 sc in corner) 3 times, 19 sc along edge; join with sl st in first sc. Fasten off.
Rnd 2: With RS facing, join B with sl st in center sc of right corner, ch 1, 3 sc in same sc; (21 sc along edge, 3 sc in corner) 3 times, 21 sc along edge.

Rnd 3: Sc in next sc, 3 sc in next sc; (23 sc along edge, 3 sc in corner) 3 times, 22 sc along last edge; join. Fasten off.
Rnd 4: With RS facing, join MC with sl st in center sc of right corner, ch 1, in same sc work sc, ch 2, and sl st—p made.
  * Sc in next 5 sc, (p in next sc, sc in next 6 sc) twice, p in next sc, sc in next 5 sc **, p in corner sc; rep from * around, ending last rep at **; join with sl st in first sc. Fasten off.

TOWEL
Hood
Using MC, ch 4.
Row 1: Sc in 2nd ch from hook, 3 sc in next ch, sc in last ch—5 sc; turn.
Row 2: Ch 1, 2 sc in first sc, sc in each sc across, ending 2 sc in last sc—7 sc; turn.
Row 3: Ch 1, sc in first 3 sc, 3 sc in next sc, sc in last 3 sc—9 sc; turn.
Row 4: Rep Row 2—11 sc; turn.

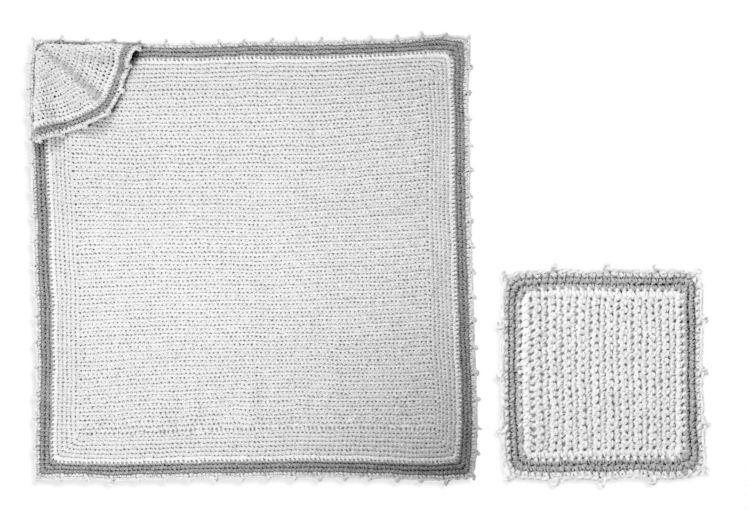

Row 5: Ch 1, sc in first 5 sc, 3 sc in next sc, sc in last 5 sc—13 sc; turn.

Row 6: Ch 1, sc in first 6 sc, 3 sc in next sc, sc in last 6 sc—15 sc. Cont in pat as est until there are 39 sts. Do not turn. Ch 1, work 18 sc evenly spaced along side to point, 3 sc in point, 18 sc evenly spaced along opposite edge. Fasten off. With RS facing, join A with sl st at lower edge, ch 1, work 41 sc evenly spaced across. Fasten off. Using B, work 2 sc rows.

Picot edge: With RS facing, join MC with sl st in first sc, ch 1, sc in same sc and next sc; * p in next sc, sc in next 5 sc; rep from * across, ending p in next sc, sc in last 2 sc. Fasten off.

Towel

Using MC, ch 86.

Row 1: Sc in 2nd ch from hook and in each ch across—85 sts; turn.

Row 2: Ch 1, sc in each sc across; turn. Rep Row 2 for 83 more times—total of 85 rows from Row 1.

Make border

Rnd 1: Using MC, ch 1, 3 sc in first sc, sc in next 83 sc, 3 sc in last sc. Work 83 sc along each edge with 3 sc in each corner, ending before first corner. Join with sl st in first sc.

Rnd 2: Ch 1, sc in same sc as joining, 3 sc in next sc; (make 85 sc along edge, 3 sc in corner) 3 times, 84 sc along last edge; join.

Rnd 3: Ch 1, sc in first 2 sc, 3 sc in next sc; (make 87 sc along edge, 3 sc in corner) 3 times, 85 sc along last edge; join.

Rnd 4: Ch 1, sc in first 3 sc, 3 sc in next sc; (make 89 sc along edge, 3 sc in corner) 3 times, 86 sc along last edge; join.

Rnd 5: Ch 1, sc in first 4 sc, 3 sc in next sc; (make 91 sc along edge; 3 sc in corner) 3 times, 87 sc along last edge; join. Fasten off.

Rnd 6: With RS facing, join B with sl st in center sc of corner, ch 1, 3 sc in same sc.

Work (93 sc along edge, 3 sc in corner) 3 times, 93 sc along last edge; join. Fasten off.

Rnd 7: With RS facing, join B with sl st in center sc of corner, ch 1, 3 sc in same sc. Work (95 sc along edge, 3 sc in corner) 3 times, 95 sc along last edge; join.

Rnd 8: Ch 1, sc in first sc; (3 sc in next sc, sc in next 97 sc) 3 times, 3 sc in next sc, sc in 96 sc; join.

Rnd 9 (joining Hood to Towel): Ch 1, sc in 2 sc, 3 sc in next sc, sc in next 76 sc.

Holding WS of Hood to RS of Towel and working through both layers, sc in next 23 sts, 3 sc in next st, sc through next 23 sts, then sc in next 76 sts along side. Work 3 sc in next sc, sc in next 99 sts, 3 sc in next sc, sc in rem 97 sts; join. Fasten off.

Rnd 10: With RS facing, join MC with sl st in center sc of corner, ch 1, in same sc make sc, ch 2, sl st in same sc—beg p made.

(Sc in next 5 sc, p in next sc) around, ending last rep with sc in 5 sc; join. Fasten off.

irresistible
DOTS INFANT SET

■■■□ Intermediate

Sizes

6 (12, 18) months
Instructions are written for the smallest size with changes for larger sizes given in parentheses. When only one number is given, it applies to all sizes.
Note: For ease in working, circle all numbers pertaining to the size you're knitting.

Finished Measurements
Cardigan: Chest = 21 (23, 24)"
Hat: Circumference = 12 (14, 16)"
Blanket: 19×24"

Materials

Yarns
Cardigan and Hat: Worsted weight, approx 600 yds. (540 m) in cream (MC)

Worsted weight, 200 yds. (180 m) *each* in gold (A), dark red (B), blue (C), and dark green (D)

Blanket: Worsted weight, approx 600 yds. (540 m) in cream (MC)

Worsted weight, 200 yds. (180 m) *each* in gold (A), dark red (B), blue (C), and dark green (D)

Needles & Extras
Cardigan and Hat:
- Size 5 (3.75 mm) needles OR SIZE NEEDED TO OBTAIN GAUGE
- Two stitch holders
- Four ¾"-diameter buttons
- Blunt-end yarn needle

Blanket:
- Size 5 (3.75 mm) needles OR SIZE NEEDED TO OBTAIN GAUGE
- Bobbins
- Stitch markers
- Blunt-end yarn needle

Notes

Gauge
20 sts and 28 rows = 4" (10 cm) in St st (knit all RS rows, purl all WS rows). TAKE TIME TO CHECK YOUR GAUGE.

In Seed st, always purl the knit sts and knit the purl sts as the work faces you.
  Stitches for hearts and letters A, B, and C are worked in St st. Use dark red (B) for hearts and letter B, use blue (C) for letter A, and use dark green (D) for letter C. Wrap colors A, B, C, and D onto bobbins. Each blanket square is 25 sts by 40 rows.

Knit
PATTERN STITCHES
Seed Stitch (over odd number of sts: multiple of 2 sts + 1; 1-row pat rep)
Pat row: K1, (p1, k1) across.
  Rep row for pat.

Seed Stitch (over even number of sts: multiple of 2 sts; 2-row pat rep)
Row 1: (P1, k1) across.
Row 2: (K1, p1) across.
  Rep Rows 1 and 2 for pat.

Dotted Pattern (multiple of 4 sts + 1; 24-row pat rep)
Row 1 (RS): Using MC, k2; using A, k1; *using MC, k3; using A, k1; rep from * to last 2 sts, using MC, k2.

This cream-colored set—including pom-pom hat, letters-and-hearts throw, and button-front cardigan—will steal the show at any baby shower. The throw is done in one piece with three columns of knitted-in designs.

Designed by **Jean Guirguis**
Photographed by **Tony Lattari**

Rows 2–6: Using MC, work in St st.
Row 7: Using MC, k4; using B, k1;
*using MC, k3; using B, k1; rep from *
to last 4 sts, using MC, k4.
Rows 8–12: Using MC, work in St st.
Row 13: Using MC, k2; using C, k1;
*using MC, k3; using C, k1; rep from *
to last 2 sts, using MC, k2.
Rows 14–18: Using MC, work in St st.
Row 19: Using MC, k4; using D, k1;
*using MC, k3; using D, k1; rep from *
to last 4 sts, using MC, k4.
Rows 20–24: Using MC, work in St st.
Rep Rows 1–24 for Dotted pat.

Notes: Instructions are written for baby
girl with buttons sewn to Left Front. For
baby boy, work Right Front first, omitting
buttonholes and marking position of
buttons along Seed st band. Then work
Left Front, creating buttonholes opposite
markers and following buttonhole
instructions for Right Front.

CARDIGAN
BACK

Using MC, cast on 53 (57, 61) sts. Work
in Seed st for 2". K 1 row; p 1 row.
Beg Dotted pat and work until piece
measures 10½ (11, 12)" from beg. Bind
off all sts.

LEFT FRONT

Using MC, cast on 31 (35, 39) sts. Work
in Seed st for 2".
Next row (RS): Knit to last 6 sts;
knit last 6 sts in Seed st as est to match
previous row.
Next row: Work 6 sts in Seed st as est;
p rem sts.
   Keeping last 6 sts in Seed st for front
band, work rem sts in Dotted pat until
piece measures 8½ (9, 10)" from beg
ending with a RS row.

Shape neck

Cont in Dotted pat, bind off at neck edge,
9 sts once, 3 sts once, 2 sts 3 (3, 4)
times—13 (17, 19) sts. Work until piece
measures same as Back; bind off all sts.
Mark position of 4 buttons evenly spaced
along Seed st band.

RIGHT FRONT
POCKET LINING

Using MC, cast on 13 sts. Work in St st
for 16 rows. Place sts on holder.

RIGHT FRONT

Work same as Left Front, working
6 Seed sts at beg of RS rows, creating
pocket when piece measures 3½" from
beg at end of a WS row, and AT THE
SAME TIME creating buttonholes
opposite markers, as foll:

Buttonholes (worked on Seed st band)

Working Seed st as est, work 2 sts, bind
off 2 sts, work 2 sts. On next row, cast on
2 sts over bound-off sts of previous row.

Pocket

RS row: Work 6 Seed sts and next
5 sts as established, sl next 13 sts onto
holder, k13 pocket lining sts from holder,
finish row. Cont knitting across lining sts
for remainder of Right Front, leaving
first sts on holder for front of pocket.
Cont working same as Left Front,
reversing neck shaping. Working on WS,
sew pocket lining in place.

SLEEVE (MAKE 2)

Using MC, cast on 29 (33, 37) sts. Work
in Seed st for 1", ending with a WS row.
Working in Dotted pat, inc 1 st at each
edge every 5 rows 8 (9, 9) times—
45 (51, 55) sts. Work even until Sleeve
measures 6½ (7, 7½)". Bind off all sts.

FINISHING

Sew shoulder seams.

Collar

With right side facing and using MC, pick
up and k61 (63, 65) sts evenly spaced
around neck edge (pick up and knit into
St sts only; do not pick up and knit into
Seed sts). Work in Seed st for 2".
Bind off in Seed st.

Pocket edging

With right side facing and using MC,
pick up and k13 sts from holder on
Right Front. Work in Seed st for 4 rows.
Bind off in Seed st. Sew ends of pocket
edging in place.

Sleeve placement

Mark center of top edge of Sleeve; pin marked center to shoulder seam, then pin entire top edge of Sleeve along Front and Back pieces. Sew Sleeves into place. Sew side and sleeve seams. Sew buttons opposite buttonholes.

HAT

Using MC, cast on 61 (71, 81) sts. Work in Seed st for 1½", ending with a RS row.
Next row: Purl.
Next row: Knit.
Next row: Purl.
Work Rows 1–19 of Dotted pat.
Row 20 (WS): Cont with MC only, p to last 2 sts, p2tog—60 (70, 80) sts.
Row 21: *K8, k2tog; rep from * across—54 (63, 72) sts.
Row 22 and all even-numbered rows: Purl.
Row 23: *K7, k2tog; rep from * across—48 (56, 64) sts.
Row 25: *K6, k2tog; rep from * across—42 (49, 56) sts.
Row 27: *K5, k2tog; rep from * across—36 (42, 48) sts.
Row 29: *K4, k2tog; rep from * across—30 (35, 40) sts.
Row 31: *K3, k2tog; rep from * across—24 (28, 32) sts.
Row 32: P2tog across—12 (14, 16) sts.

FINISHING

Cut yarn, leaving a long tail. Thread tail through rem sts, pull tightly, and fasten off. Use remainder of tail to sew seam. Make four 1½"-diameter pom-poms, one each using colors A, B, C, and D. Sew pom-poms to top of Hat.

BLANKET

Pattern row: K1, (pl, k1) across.
Rep row for Seed st.

Dot Stitch (worked over 25 sts and 40 rows using MC and color A, B, C, or D for CC—as directed in instructions)
Row 1 (RS): Using MC, k across.
Row 2: Using MC, p across.
Row 3: Carrying yarn in back of work, *using MC, k1; using CC, k1; rep from * to last st; using MC, k1.
Row 4: Using MC, p across.
Row 5: Using MC, k across.
Row 6: Carrying yarn in front of work, *using CC, p1; using MC, p1; rep from * to last st; using CC, p1.
Rows 7–36: Rep Rows 1–6 five times.
Rows 37–40: Rep Rows 1–4.

Make bottom border

Using MC, cast on 95 sts. Work in Seed st for 2".

Block Band 1

Row 1 (RS): Using MC, work 5 sts in Seed st, place marker (pm), work Row 1 of Letter C Chart, *page 139,* across 25 sts, pm, work 5 sts in Seed st, pm, work Row 1 of Dot st across next 25 sts, pm, work 5 sts in Seed st, pm, work Row 1 of Heart Chart, *page 139,* across 25 sts, pm, work 5 sts in Seed st.
Rows 2–40: Cont working Seed st sections and follow charts, *page 139,* working in St st and using A for Dot st.

Seed st Band

Rows 1–6: Using MC, work Seed st across 95 sts.

Block Band 2

Row 1 (RS): Using MC, work 5 sts in Seed st, work Row 1 of Dot st across 25 sts, work 5 sts in Seed st, work Row 1 of Letter B Chart, *page 139,* across 25 sts, work 5 sts in Seed st, work Row 1 of Dot st across 25 sts, work 5 sts in Seed st.
Rows 2–40: Cont working Seed st sections and follow charts (working in St st); use C for first Dot st block and use D for second Dot st block.

Seed st band

Rows 1–6: Using MC, work Seed st across 95 sts.

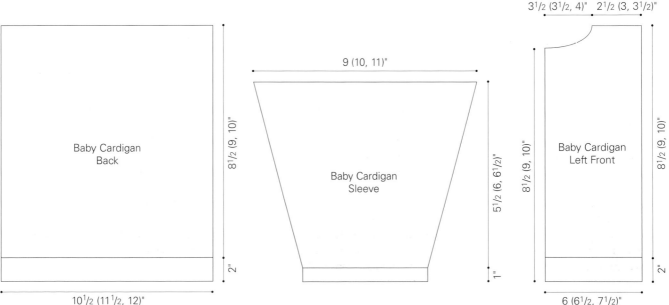

3½ (3½, 4)"   2½ (3, 3½)"

9 (10, 11)"

Baby Cardigan Back

8½ (9, 10)"

2"

10½ (11½, 12)"

Baby Cardigan Sleeve

5½ (6, 6½)"

1"

Baby Cardigan Left Front

8½ (9, 10)"

8½ (9, 10)"

2"

6 (6½, 7½)"

Block band 3

Row 1 (RS): Using MC, work 5 sts in Seed st, work Row 1 of Heart Chart across 25 sts, work 5 sts in Seed st, work Row 1 of Dot st across 25 sts, work 5 sts in Seed st, work Row 1 of Letter A Chart across 25 sts, work 5 sts in Seed st.

Rows 2–40: Cont working Seed st sections and follow charts; use A for Dot st.

Make top border

Using MC, work in Seed st for 2". Bind off all sts in pat.

FINISHING

Make one 1½"-diameter pom-pom in each of colors A, B, C, and D. Tie a pom-pom to each corner of the blanket.

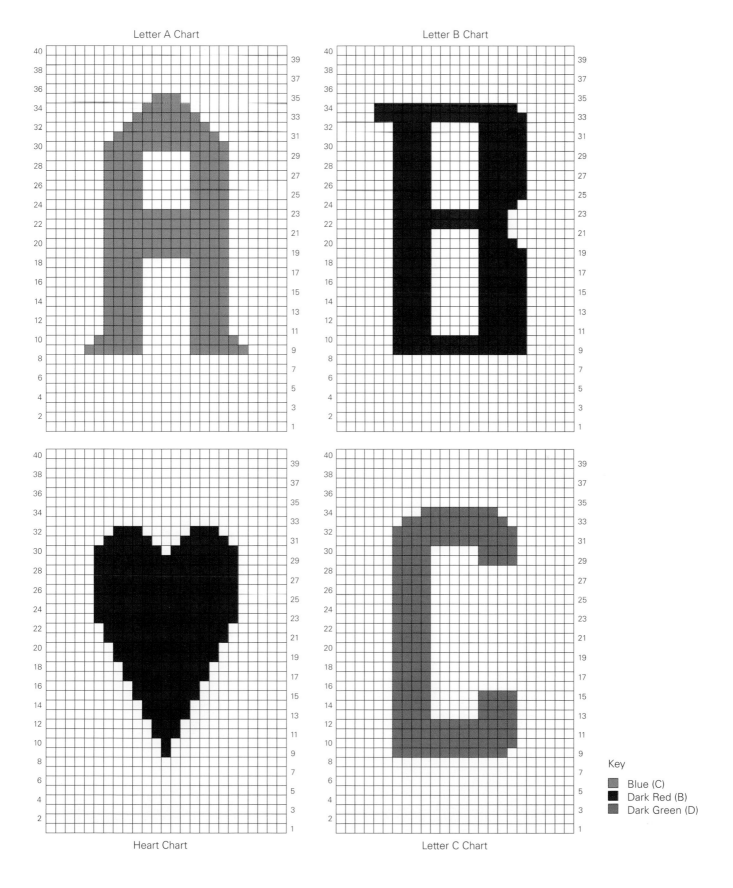

Letter A Chart

Letter B Chart

Heart Chart

Letter C Chart

Key

- Blue (C)
- Dark Red (B)
- Dark Green (D)

nursery
BUDDY

Single crochet stitches and doubled yarn make this toy especially durable. Plus, it's stitched all in one piece. You simply crochet a section, stuff it, and close it; then change color and move on to the next segment.

Designed by **Linda Cyr**
Photographed by **Greg Scheidemann**

Sizes

Finished Measurement

Length = 18"

Materials

Yarns

DK weight, 460 yds. (415 m) *each* in bright green (A), bright yellow (B), and soft purple (C)

Hooks & Extras

- Size I/9 (5.5 mm) crochet hook OR SIZE NEEDED TO OBTAIN GAUGE
- Stitch marker
- Polyester fiberfill
- Blunt-end yarn needle

Notes

Gauge

Using a double strand of yarn, 12 sc and 12 rnds = 4" (10 cm). TAKE TIME TO CHECK YOUR GAUGE.

Use a double strand of yarn throughout project.

Crochet

BODY

Beg with the tail, using A, ch 2.

Rnd 1: Work 8 sc in 2nd ch from hook, place marker to mark beg of rnd.

Rnd 2: (Sc in sc, 2 sc in next sc—inc made) around—12 sts.

Rnd 3: Rep Rnd 2—18 sts.

Rnd 4: (Sc in 2 sc, inc in next sc) around—24 sts.

Rnds 5–7: Sc in each sc around.

Rnd 8: (Sc in 2 sc, sc2tog) around—18 sts.

Rnd 9: (Sc in sc, sc2tog) around—12 sts. Stuff with polyester fiberfill and change to B.

* Rnd 1: (Sc in sc, inc in next sc) around—18 sts.

Rnd 2: (Sc in 2 sc, inc in next sc) around—24 sts.

Rnd 3: Rep Rnd 2—32 sts.

Rnds 4–8: Sc in each sc around.

Rnd 9: (Sc in 2 sc, sc2tog) around—24 sts.

Rnd 10: Rep Rnd 9—18 sts.

Rnd 11: (Sc in sc, sc2tog) around—12 sts **. Stuff with polyester fiberfill and change to C; rep from * to **. Stuff with polyester fiberfill and change to A, rep from * to **. Stuff with polyester fiberfill and change to B, rep from * to **. Stuff with polyester fiberfill and change to C.

Head

Beg at * and work Rnds 1–3—32 sts.

Rnd 4: (Sc in 3 sc, inc in next st) around—40 sts.

Rnds 5–11: Sc in each sc around.

Rnd 12: (Sc in 3 sc, sc2tog) around—32 sts.

Rnd 13: (Sc in 2 sc, sc2tog) around—24 sts.

Rnd 14: (Sc in 2 sc, sc2tog) around—18 sts.

Rnd 15: (Sc in sc, sc2tog) around—12 sts. Stuff with polyester fiberfill.

Rnd 16: (Sc in sc, sc2tog) around—8 sts.

Rnd 17: (Sc2tog) 4 times. Fasten off.

FINISHING

Nose

Using A, ch 2.

Rnd 1: Work 6 sc in 2nd ch from hook.

Rnd 2: Sc in each sc around.

Rnd 3: Sl st in each sc around. Fasten off. Stuff and sew to head, centered over Rnd 17.

Eye (make 2)

Using A, work as for nose through Rnd 1; change to B.

Rnd 2: Working in back lps only, sl st in each sc around, loosely. Fasten off. Sew to head ½" above nose and 1½" apart.

Antenna (make 2)

Place markers for 2 antennae 2½" above nose and 1" apart.

Cut two 24" strands of B; fold in half. Insert hook under 2 sts at 1 marker, hook center of folded strands and pull up onto hook. Ch 10. Fasten off.

Cut two 6" strands each of A and C. Pull strands through end of B ch, line up ends, and tie in an overhand knot; trim.

animal
INSTINCT
trio

Among this cache is a cuddly critter destined to charm a child you cherish. A winsome elephant, a proud lion, and a huggable hippo all await your crafty touches.

Designed by **Michele Wilcox**
Photographed by **Greg Scheidemann**

Elegant Elephant ■■■□□ Easy

Sizes

Finished Measurements
10×7½" (viewed from the side, excluding trunk)

Note: All pieces are worked in rnds, but do not join rnds. Mark beg of each rnd with a colored thread.

Materials

Yarns
Worsted weight, 300 yds. (274 m) in gray (MC)

4 MEDIUM

Worsted weight, scraps of light pink (A) and white (B)

Hooks & Extras
• Size F/5 (3.75 mm) crochet hook OR SIZE NEEDED TO OBTAIN GAUGE
• Polyester fiberfill
• 1 yd. of black perle cotton for embroidery
• ½ yd. of ⅜"-wide satin ribbon
• Blunt-end yarn needle

Notes

Gauge
Worked in rnds, 12 sc and 16 rows = 4" (10 cm). TAKE TIME TO CHECK YOUR GAUGE.

Special Abbreviations
sc2tog = [Insert hook in next stitch and draw up a loop (lp)] twice, yarn over and draw through all 3 loops on hook.

Crochet

BODY

Beg at back and using MC, ch 2.

Rnd 1: 6 sc in 2nd ch from hook.

Rnd 2: 2 sc in each sc around—12 sc.

Rnd 3: (Sc in next sc, 2 sc in next sc) 6 times—18 sc.

Rnd 4: (Sc in each of next 2 sc, 2 sc in next sc) 6 times—24 sc.

Rnd 5: (Sc in each of next 3 sc, 2 sc in next sc) 6 times—30 sc.

Rnd 6: (Sc in each of next 4 sc, 2 sc in next sc) 6 times—36 sc.

Rnd 7: (Sc in each of next 5 sc, 2 sc in next sc) 6 times—42 sc.

Rnd 8: Sc in each sc around.

Rnd 9: (Sc in each of next 6 sc, 2 sc in next sc) 6 times—48 sc.

Rnds 10–17: Sc in each sc around.

Rnd 18: (Sc in each of next 6 sc, sc2tog over next 2 sc) 6 times—42 sc.

Rnds 19–26: Sc in each sc around.

Rnd 27: (Sc in each of next 5 sc, sc2tog over next 2 sc) 6 times—36 sc.

Rnd 28: Sc in each sc around.

Rnd 29: (Sc in each of next 4 sc, sc2tog over next 2 sc) 6 times—30 sc.

Rnd 30: (Sc in each of next 3 sc, sc2tog over next 2 sc) 6 times—24 sc. Stuff Body firmly.

Rnd 31: (Sc in each of next 2 sc, sc2tog over next 2 sc) 6 times—18 sc.

Rnd 32: (Sc in next sc, sc2tog over next 2 sc) 6 times—12 sc. Finish stuffing and fasten off. Draw rem sts tog tightly.

HEAD

Beg at tip of trunk and using MC, ch 2.

Rnd 1: 6 sc in 2nd ch from hook.

Rnd 2: Working in back lp only of each st, sc in each sc around.

Rnds 3–10: Sc in each sc around, stuffing as you go.

Rnd 11: (Sc in each of next 2 sc, 2 sc in next sc) twice—8 sc.

Rnd 12: (Sc in next sc, 2 sc in next sc) 4 times—12 sc.

Rnd 13: Sc in each sc around.

Rnds 14–17: Rep Rnds 3–6 of Body—36 sc.

Rnds 18–25: Sc in each sc around.

Rnds 26–29: Rep Rnds 29–32 of Body—12 sc; fasten off.

Sew Head securely in place on front of Body. Embroider satin sts with perle cotton for eyes.

CHIN

Using MC, ch 2.

Rnd 1: 6 sc in 2nd ch from hook.

Rnd 2: (Sc in next sc, 2 sc in next sc) 3 times—9 sc.

Rnds 3–4: Sc in each sc around; fasten off. Stuff lightly and sew in position under trunk.

TUSK (MAKE 2)

Using B, ch 2.

Rnd 1: 6 sc in 2nd ch from hook.

Rnds 2–5: Sc in each sc around; fasten off.

Do not stuff. Sew in position along side of trunk.

OUTER EAR (MAKE 2)

Note: Ears are worked in rows. Turn at end of each row.

Using MC, ch 2.

Row 1: 6 sc in 2nd ch from hook; turn.

Row 2: Ch 1, sc in next sc, 2 sc in each of next 4 sc, sc in last sc; turn—10 sc.

Row 3: Ch 1, sc in each of next 3 sc, 2 sc in each of next 4 sc, sc in each of last 3 sc; turn—14 sc.

Row 4: Ch 1, sc in each of next 5 sc, 2 sc in each of next 4 sc, sc in each of last 5 sc; turn—18 sc.

Row 5: Ch 1, sc in each sc across; fasten off.

INNER EAR (MAKE 2)

Using A, work as for Outer Ear until Row 4 is complete. Work Row 5 with MC.

Join Outer Ear to Inner Ear with MC, working 1 row of sc through both thicknesses in back lps only of the 18 sc. Sew Ears in position.

LEG (MAKE 4)

Using MC, ch 2.

Rnds 1–4: Work same as Rnds 1–4 of Body—24 sc.

Rnd 5: Working in back lp only of each st, sc in each sc around.

Rnds 6–17: Sc in each sc around.

Fasten off at end of Rnd 17. Stuff firmly.

FOUR TOES PIECE (MAKE 4)

Using A, ch 12.

Row 1: 3 hdc in 2nd ch from hook, (sl st in each of next 2 ch, ch 1, 3 hdc in next ch) 3 times, sl st in last ch; fasten off. Sew Four Toes Piece to front of foot along edge of Rnd 5 of each leg. Sew legs in position.

TAIL

Using MC, ch 10, sl st in 2nd ch from hook and each rem ch across; fasten off. Sew in position. Cut four 3" strands of MC. Tie them tightly in the center and fasten to end of Tail; trim.

Little Lion

■■■□□ Easy

Sizes

Finished Measurements

9×7" (viewed from the side

Note: All pieces are worked in rnds, but do not join rnds. Mark beg of each rnd with a colored thread.

Materials

Yarns

Worsted weight, 223 yds. (205 m) in gold (MC)

Worsted weight, scraps in rust (CC)

Hooks & Extras

• Size F/5 (3.75 mm) crochet hook OR SIZE NEEDED TO OBTAIN GAUGE
• Polyester fiberfill
• 3 yds. of black pearl cotton for embroidery
• Blunt-end yarn needle

Notes

Gauge

Worked in rnds, 16 sc and 18 rows = 4" (10 cm). TAKE TIME TO CHECK YOUR GAUGE.

Special Abbreviations

sc2tog = [Insert hook in next st and draw up a loop (lp)] twice, yarn over and draw through all 3 lps on hook.

Crochet

FRONT OF HEAD

Using MC, ch 2.

Rnd 1: 6 sc in 2nd ch from hook.

Rnd 2: 2 sc in each sc around—12 sc.

Rnd 3: (Sc in next sc, 2 sc in next sc) 6 times—18 sc.

Rnd 4: (Sc in each of next 2 sc, 2 sc in next sc) 6 times—24 sc.

Rnd 5: (Sc in each of next 3 sc, 2 sc in next sc) 6 times—30 sc.

Rnd 6: Sc in each sc around.

Rnd 7: (Sc in each of next 4 sc, 2 sc in next sc) 6 times—36 sc.

Rnd 8: (Sc in each of next 5 sc, 2 sc in next sc) 6 times—42 sc.

Rnds 9–10: Sc in each sc across; fasten off at end of Rnd 10.

BACK OF HEAD

Work as for Front of Head. Sew Back and Front of Head tog through back lps of Rnd 10, stuffing before closing.

MANE

Wrap CC around a 3" piece of cardboard 80 times. Cut one end (you will have eighty 6" lengths of yarn). Make one fringe using 2 strands of yarn in each unworked (front) lp from Rnd 10 of both Front and Back of Head. Cut more strands as needed. Trim fringes. Brush Mane lightly with a hairbrush to fluff.

NOSE

Using MC, ch 5.

Rnd 1: Sc in 2nd ch from hook and in each of next 2 ch, 3 sc in last ch, on opposite side of ch, work sc in each of next 2 ch, 2 sc in last ch.

Rnd 2: 2 sc in first sc, sc in each of next 2 sc, 2 hdc in each of next 3 sc, sc in each of next 2 sc, 2 sc in each of last 2 sc.

Rnd 3: Sc in each st around; fasten off. Sew lengthwise to center front of face, stuffing lightly. Using pearl cotton, satin-stitch the nose detail and eyes and straight-stitch the mouth.

EAR (MAKE 2)

Using MC, ch 2.

Rnd 1: 6 sc in 2nd ch from hook.

Rnd 2: (Sc in next sc, 2 sc in next sc) 3 times—9 sc.

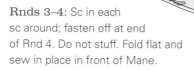

Rnds 3–4: Sc in each sc around; fasten off at end of Rnd 4. Do not stuff. Fold flat and sew in place in front of Mane.

BODY

Beg at back end, using MC, ch 2.

Rnds 1–5: Rep Rnds 1–5 of Front of Head—30 sc.

Rnd 6: (Sc in each of next 4 sc, 2 sc in next sc) 6 times—36 sc.

Rnd 7: (Sc in each of next 5 sc, 2 sc in next sc) 6 times—42 sc.

Rnd 8: Sc in each sc around.

Rnd 9: (Sc in each of next 6 sc, 2 sc in next sc) 6 times—48 sc.

Rnds 10–22: Sc in each sc around.

Rnd 23: (Sc in each of next 6 sc, sc2tog over next 2 sc) 6 times—42 sc.

Rnds 24–30: Sc in each sc around.

Rnd 31: (Sc in each of next 5 sc, sc2tog over next 2 sc) 6 times—36 sc.

Rnd 32: (Sc in each of next 4 sc, sc2tog over next 2 sc) 6 times—30 sc.

Rnd 33: (Sc in each of next 3 sc, sc2tog over next 2 sc) 6 times—24 sc.

Rnd 34: (Sc in each of next 2 sc, sc2tog over next 2 sc) 6 times—18 sc. Stuff Body firmly.

Rnd 35: (Sc in next sc, sc2tog over next 2 sc) 6 times; fasten off. Draw rem sts tog tightly. Sew Head firmly to Body with face looking sideways.

LEG (MAKE 4)

Using MC, ch 2 (bottom of foot).

Rnds 1–3: Rep Rnds 1–3 of Front of Head—18 sc.

Rnd 4: 2 sc in each of first 6 sc, sc in each of rem 12 sc—24 sc.

Rnd 5: Sc in each sc around.

Rnd 6: (Sc2tog over next 2 sc) 6 times, sc in each of next 12 sc—18 sc.

Rnds 7–17: Sc in each sc around; fasten off. Stuff.

Shape paws

Thread MC onto blunt-end yarn needle. Sewing through all thicknesses, form paws by drawing thread through and around Rnd 3 and Rnd 8; tug to shape and fasten in place. Rep 2 more times. Sew Legs to Body.

TAIL

Using MC, ch 2.

Rnd 1: 6 sc in 2nd ch from hook.

Rnds 2–8: Sc in each sc around; fasten off at end of Rnd 8.

Cut eight 8" lengths of CC. Attach as fringe to end of Tail. Sew Tail in position. Brush Tail lightly with a hairbrush to fluff.

Happy Hippo

■ ■ □ □ Easy

Sizes

**Finished
Measurements**

9×7" (viewed from side)

Note: All pieces are worked in rnds, but do not join rnds. Mark beg of each rnd with a colored thread.

Materials

Yarns
Worsted weight, 380 yds. (348 m) in gray (MC)

Worsted weight, scraps of light pink (A) and white (B)

Hooks & Extras
• Size F/5 (3.75 mm) crochet hook OR SIZE NEEDED TO OBTAIN GAUGE
• Polyester fiberfill
• 1 yd. of black perle cotton for embroidery
• ½ yd. of ⅜"-wide satin ribbon

Notes

Gauge
Worked in rnds, 15 sc and 16 rows = 4" (10 cm). TAKE TIME TO CHECK YOUR GAUGE.

Special Abbreviations
sc2tog = [Insert hook in next st and draw up a loop (lp)] twice, yarn over and draw through all 3 lps on hook.

Crochet

HEAD

Using MC, ch 2.
Rnd 1: 6 sc in 2nd ch from hook.
Rnd 2: 2 sc in each sc around—12 sc.
Rnd 3: (Sc in next sc, 2 sc in next sc) 6 times—18 sc.
Rnd 4: (Sc in each of next 2 sc, 2 sc in next sc) 6 times—24 sc.

Rnd 5: (Sc in each of next 3 sc, 2 sc in next sc) 6 times—30 sc.
Rnd 6: Sc in each sc around.
Rnd 7: (Sc in each of next 4 sc, 2 sc in next sc) 6 times—36 sc.
Rnds 8–14: Sc in each sc around.
Rnd 15: *Sc in each of next 4 sc, sc2tog over next 2 sc; rep from * around—30 sc.

Rnd 16: Sc in each sc around.
Rnd 17: (Sc in each of next 4 sc, 2 sc in next sc) 3 times, ch 6, sk last 15 sc.
Rnd 18 (begin upper jaw): Sc in each of next 18 sc, sc in each of next 6 ch—24 sc.
Rnds 19–20: Sc in each sc around.

Rnd 21: *Sc in each of next 2 sc, sc2tog over next 2 sc; rep from * around—18 sc.

Rnds 22–24: Sc in each sc around.

Rnd 25: (Sc2tog over next 2 sc) 9 times—9 sc.

Rnd 26: (Sc2tog over next 2 sc) 4 times, sc in last sc—5 sc; fasten off. Stuff back of Head and top of jaw.

BOTTOM JAW

Join MC with sc in first unworked st of Rnd 17, sc in each of next 14 unworked sc, sc in opposite side of 6 ch—21 sc.

Rnds 18–22: Sc in each sc around— 21 sc.

Rnd 23: (Sc2tog over next 2 sc) 10 times, sc in last sc—11 sc; stuff.

Rnd 24: (Sc2tog over next 2 sc) 5 times, sc in last sc; fasten off. Draw rem sts tog tightly.

INSIDE OF MOUTH

Using A, ch 6.

Rnd 1: Sc in 2nd ch from hook and in each of next 3 ch, 3 sc in last ch, working on opposite side of ch, sc in each of next 3 ch, 2 sc in last ch—12 sc.

Rnd 2: 2 sc in next sc, sc in each of next 3 sc, 2 sc in each of next 3 sc, sc in each of next 3 sc, 2 sc in each of next 2 sc—18 sc.

Rnd 3: *Sc in each of next 7 sc, 2 sc in each of next 2 sc; rep from * around— 22 sc. Fasten off. Sew in position.

TOOTH (MAKE 4)

Using B, ch 2.

Rnd 1: 4 sc in 2nd ch from hook.

Rnd 2: Working in back lps only, sc in each sc around; fasten off. Sew in position.

NOSTRIL (MAKE 2)

Using MC, ch 2.

Rnd 1: 6 sc in 2nd ch from hook; fasten off. Draw sts tog tightly; sew to top of upper jaw as shown.

EAR (MAKE 2 EACH IN MC AND 2 EACH IN A [A NOT VISIBLE IN PHOTO])

Using MC, ch 3.

Rnd 1: Sc in 2nd ch from hook, 3 sc in next ch; on opposite side of ch, work 1 sc in next ch. Fasten off.

With MC, work 1 row of sc around 1 MC Ear and 1 A Ear to join. Sew in position.

BODY

Beg at back end and using MC, ch 2.

Rnds 1–5: Work same as Rnds 1–5 of Head—30 sc.

Rnd 6: (Sc in each of next 4 sc, 2 sc in next sc) 6 times—36 sc.

Rnd 7: (Sc in each of next 5 sc, 2 sc in next sc) 6 times—42 sc.

Rnd 8: (Sc in each of next 6 sc, 2 sc in next sc) 6 times—48 sc.

Rnd 9: Sc in each sc around.

Rnd 10: (Sc in each of next 7 sc, 2 sc in next sc) 6 times—54 sc.

Rnd 11–20: Sc in each sc around.

Rnd 21: (Sc in each of next 7 sc, sc2tog over next 2 sc) 6 times—48 sc.

Rnd 22: Sc in each sc around.

Rnd 23: (Sc in each of next 6 sc, sc2tog over next 2 sc) 6 times—42 sc.

Rnds 24–34: Sc in each sc around.

Rnd 35: (Sc in each of next 5 sc, sc2tog over next 2 sc) 6 times—36 sc.

Rnd 36: Sc in each sc around.

Rnd 37: (Sc in each of next 4 sc, sc2tog over next 2 sc) 6 times—30 sc.

Rnd 38: (Sc in each of next 3 sc, sc2tog over next 2 sc) 6 times—24 sc.

Rnd 39: (Sc in each of next 2 sc, sc2tog over next 2 sc) 6 times—18 sc. Fasten off. Stuff Body firmly. Sew back of Head securely to opening at front of Body.

TAIL

Using MC, ch 2.

Rnd 1: 6 sc in 2nd ch from hook

Rnds 2–10: Sc in each sc around, do not fasten off; flatten work and work 3 sc across through both thicknesses, leaving end of yarn for sewing. Sew tail to back of Body. Cut twelve 5" strands of MC. Tie center of strands to end of Tail.

LEG (MAKE 4)

Using MC, ch 2.

Rnds 1–3: Work same as Rnds 1–3 of Head—18 sc.

Rnd 4: Working in back lp only of each st, sc in each sc around.

Rnds 5–12: Sc in each sc around; fasten off at end of Rnd 12. Stuff firmly. Sew in position.

FINISHING

Embroider eyes with black perle cotton and satin st. Tie satin ribbon into a bow around neck.

This matching sweater and pants duet for a toddler is adorable and practical. Bursts of Garter stitch and French knots punctuate the sweater front and sleeves. An I-cord drawstring at the waist makes the pants easy to slip on and off.

baby
kimono set

Designed by **Ann E. Smith**   Photographed by **Greg Scheidemann**

Sizes

12 (18, 24) months

Instructions are written for the smallest size with changes for larger sizes given in parentheses. When only one number is given, it applies to all sizes.

Note: For ease in working, circle all numbers pertaining to the size you're knitting.

Finished Measurements

Kimono

Chest (buttoned) = 25 (27, 29)"
Length = 12½ (13½, 14½)"

Pants

Waist = 20 (21½, 22)"
Length (total) = 17 (19, 21)"

Materials

Yarns

Sport weight, 920 (920, 1,380) yds. [825, (825, 1,240) m] in cream (MC)

Sport weight, 460 yds. (415 m)—all sizes—in pink (CC)

Needles & Extras

- Size 6 (4 mm) knitting needles OR SIZE NEEDED TO OBTAIN GAUGE
- Size 4 (3.5 mm) knitting needles
- Size 4 (3.5 mm) 16" circular needle
- Two sets of snap fasteners for Kimono
- Size F/5 (3.75 mm) crochet hook for Pants drawstring
- Blunt-end yarn needle

Notes

Gauge

22 sts and 29 rows = 4" (10 cm) in Body pat with larger needles. 22 sts and 28 rows = 4" (10 cm) in St st (k all RS rows, p all WS rows) with larger needles. TAKE TIME TO CHECK YOUR GAUGE.

Special Abbreviations

ssk (slip, slip, knit) = Slip next 2 sts to right-hand needle singly and knitwise; insert tip of left-hand needle through the front loop of both stitches and knit them together.

Knit
KIMONO
BACK

Using larger needles and MC, cast on 68 (72, 80) sts.

Work Body pat as follows:

Row 1: Purl.
Row 2: K4 (1, 0); *k4, p6, rep from * across; end with k4 (1, 0).
Row 3: Purl.
Row 4: Knit.
Row 5: Purl.
Row 6: K3 (1, 0), p6 (5, 5); *k4, p6, rep from * across; end with k9 (6, 5).
Row 7: Purl.
Row 8: Knit.

Rows 1–8 for Body pat until piece measures 6½ (7, 7½)" from beg, ending with a WS row.

Shape armholes

Bind off 6 sts at beg of next 2 rows. Work even on 56 (60, 68) sts until piece measures 12 (13, 14)" from beg, ending with a WS row. Bind off.

RIGHT FRONT

Using larger needles and MC, cast on 37 (41, 45) sts.

Work Body pat as follows:

Rows 1, 3, 5, 7: Purl.

Row 2: K7 (5, 4); *p6, k4, rep from * across; end with p0 (6, 6), k0 (0, 5).

Rows 4 and 8: Knit.

Row 6: P0 (0, 5), k2 (0, 4); *p6, k4, rep from * across; end last rep with p5 (6, 6), k0 (5, 0).

Rep Rows 1–8 for Body pat until piece measures 6½ (7, 7½)" from beg, ending with a WS row.

Shape neck and armhole

Next row: K1, ssk (for first neck dec), work pat to end.

Next row: Bind off 6 sts for armhole. Dec 1 st at neck edge NOW and every other row 8 (12, 16) times more, then every 4th row 4 (3, 2) times. Work even on rem 17 (18, 19) sts to same length as Back, ending with a WS row. Bind off.

LEFT FRONT

Using larger needles and MC, cast on 37 (41, 45) sts.

Work Body pat as foll:

Rows 1, 3, 5, 7: Purl.

Row 2: K5 (0, 5); *p6, k4, rep from * across; end last rep with p5 (0, 0), k0 (1, 0).

Rows 4 and 8: Knit.

Row 6: P3 (0, 6), k4 (5, 4); *p6, k4, rep from * across; end last rep with p0 (6, 5).

Rep Rows 1–8 for Body pat until piece measures 6½ (7, 7½)" from beg, ending with a WS row.

Shape neck and armhole

Next row: Bind off 6 sts, work pat across to last 3 sts, k2tog, k1.

Work 1 row even.

Dec row: Work pat across, ending with k2tog, k1. Rep Dec row every other row 8 (12, 16) times more, then every 4th row 4 (3, 2) times—17 (18, 19) sts. Complete as for Right Front.

SLEEVE (MAKE 2)

Using smaller needles and CC, cast on 44 sts. (P 1 row, k 1 row) twice. Change to MC and knit across. Change to larger needles and work Body pat as follows:

Rows 1, 3, 5, 7: Purl.

Row 2: K2; (k4, p6) across, ending with k2.

Rows 4 and 8: Knit.

Row 6: K1; (p6, k4) across, ending with p3.

Rep Rows 1–8 for Body pat. AT THE SAME TIME, after working first 7 pat rows, inc 1 st each edge NOW and every 8th (6th, 4th) row 4 (7, 10) more times. Including new sts in pattern as they accumulate, work even on the total 54 (60, 66) sts until piece measures 6½ (7½, 8½)" from first pat row, ending with a WS row. Bind off.

FINISHING

Join shoulder seams. Set in Sleeves, joining bound-off sts to Sleeve sides for square armholes. Join underarm and side seams.

With RS facing and using circular needle and CC, beg at center of back neck. Pick up and k11 (12, 14) sts to shoulder, 31 (34, 36) sts to first neck shaping row, 36 (38, 41) sts to lower edge. Pick up and k1 st in each cast-on st along lower edge, 36 (38, 41) sts to first neck shaping row, 31 (34, 36) sts to shoulder, and 11 (12, 14) sts to center of back neck. Turn. (K 1 row, p 1 row) twice. Bind off kwise. Sew Back neck seam.

For snaps

Sew one snap on WS of Right Front near border and at first neck dec row. Sew second snap 1" from first, in a horizontal line. Sew second half of snaps to correspond on RS of Left Front.

Thread a double strand of CC into yarn needle; make French knots on fronts only by referring to photo, *opposite*, for placement.

PANTS
RIGHT LEG

Beg at the top and beneath the waistband and using larger needles and MC, cast on 55 (59, 61) sts. P 1 row.

Wrapping

On a knit side, k to the last stitch indicated. With yarn in back, sl the next st to the right-hand needle as if to knit. Turn work so that the yarn is in front. Bring yarn around the slipped st to the back. Sl the slipped stitch again as if to knit. Bring yarn to the front between the slipped st and the next st. P back across the row.

Shape back

Row 1: K10, wrap next st and purl back.

Row 2: K15, wrap next st and purl back.

Cont as est, working 5 more sts every RS row until 30 sts have been worked; turn, p to end, working each wrap with the st it wraps. Work St st across all sts until piece measures 6½ (7, 8)" from beg on shaped side, ending with a WS row.

Shape crotch

Inc 1 st each edge on next row and every RS row 3 times more—63 (67, 69) sts. P 1 row. Cast on 4 sts at beg of next 2 rows—71 (75, 77) sts. Work 8 rows even. Dec 1 st each edge on next row. Rep last 9 rows 4 (5, 4) times more—61 (63, 67) sts. Work even until piece measures 7¾ (9¼, 10¼)" from cast-on sts at crotch; ending with a RS row.

Border

With smaller needles and CC, p 2 rows, k 1 row, p 1 row. Bind off kwise.

LEFT LEG

Cast on and p 1 row as for Right Leg. K 1 row.

Wrapping

On a purl side, p to the last st indicated. With yarn in front, sl the next st to the

right-hand needle as if to purl. Turn work so yarn is now in back. Bring yarn forward around the slipped st. Sl the slipped st again as if to purl. Bring the yarn to the back between the slipped st and the next st. Knit back across the row.

Shape back

Row 1: P10, wrap next st and knit back.
Row 2: P15, wrap next st and knit back.
Cont as est, working 5 more sts every WS row until 30 sts have been worked;

turn, k to end, working each wrap with the st it wraps.
Reversing all shapings, complete as for Right Leg.

FINISHING

Join crotch and leg seams.
With RS facing and using circular needle and CC, pick up and k108 (116, 120) sts evenly spaced around waist. Place marker to indicate beg of rnd. Join.
Rnds 1–4: Work k2, p2 rib around.

Eyelets

Rnd 5: (K2, p2tog, yo) around.
Rnds 6–9: (K2, p2) around. Bind off kwise.

Drawstring

With crochet hook and a double strand of CC, ch 125 (135, 145). Sl st in second ch from hook and in each ch across. Fasten off. Thread drawstring through eyelets so that it begins and ends at center front. Tie each end in an overhand knot.

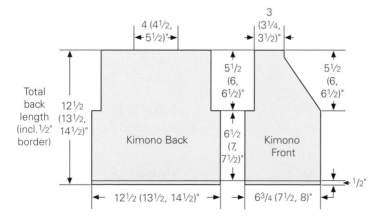

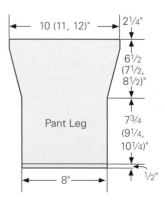

Pastel tones in nubby yarn give this baby afghan a quilted look. Knit the blanket square by square, forming the mitered corners as you go.

rainbow BLANKET

Designed by **Wendy Rogers**   Photographed by **Greg Scheidemann**

■■■□□ Easy

Sizes

Finished Measurement

33" square

Materials

Yarns

Bulky weight, 370 yds. (334 m) *each* in blue (A), yellow (B), lavender (C), light green (D), and pink (E)

Note: To achieve the effect shown here, use a nubby yarn.

Needles & Extras

•Size 10 (6mm) 36" circular needle OR SIZE NEEDED TO OBTAIN GAUGE
• Blunt-end yarn needle

Notes

Gauge

14 sts and 20 rows = 4" (10cm) over St st (knit all RS rows, purl all WS rows). TAKE TIME TO CHECK YOUR GAUGE.

Blanket is worked square by square, starting in the bottom left corner. See diagram, *below,* for colors and the order in which the squares are made and assembled.

Special Abbreviations

sk2p = Double decrease worked by slipping 1 stitch knitwise, knitting 2 together, passing slipped stitch over.

Knit

BASIC SQUARE

Note: MC indicates larger area of color in each square; CC indicates smaller area of color at top right corner of square.

Using MC, cast on 25 sts.

Row 1 (and all WS rows): Using MC, knit.

Row 2: K11, sk2p, k11.

Row 4: K10, sk2p, k10.

Row 6: K9, sk2p, k9.

Row 8: K8, sk2p, k8.

Row 10: K7, sk2p, k7.

Row 12: Change to CC, k6, sk2p, k6.

Row 14: K5, sk2p, k5.

Row 16: K4, sk2p, k4.

Row 18: K3, sk2p, k3.

Row 20: K2, sk2p, k2.

Row 22: K1, sk2p, k1.

Row 24: Sk2p.

Cut yarn and pull through rem st to secure.

SQUARE 1

With MC, cast on 25 sts and follow directions for Basic Square.

SQUARES 2–7

Using new MC (see color diagram, *below*), pick up 12 sts along top of square just worked, cast on 13 sts. Follow directions for Basic Square (see color diagram for new CC).

SQUARE 8

Using new MC (see color diagram), cast on 13 sts, pick up 12 sts along right side of Square 1. Follow directions for Basic Square (see color diagram for new CC).

SQUARE 9

Using new MC (see color diagram), pick up 12 sts along top of square just worked, pick up 1 st at corner of Square 1, and pick up 12 sts along right side of Square 2. Follow directions for Basic Square.

SQUARES 10–14

Follow directions for Square 9.

Following the color diagram, continue making remaining squares (15-43) using appropriate cast-on and pick-up techniques.

BORDER

With RS facing and using B, pick up and k84 sts along one edge.

Row 1 (WS): Knit.

Row 2 (RS): Inc 1 by knitting into front and back of st, k to last st, inc 1.

Row 3: Knit.

Rep Rows 2 and 3 three more times. Change to D and rep Row 2. Bind off.

Rep Border on 3 rem edges.

FINISHING

Sew border seams. Weave in ends.

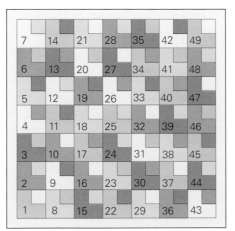

Color Diagram

On a roll

Here's a toy perfect for baby's play! Filled with cushy fiberfill, the 8-inch-diameter ball is made from six individual wedges. The shapes are joined with rows of white single-crochet stitches and then capped at the top and bottom in small circles of crochet.

Designed by **Linda Cyr**
Photographed by **Greg Scheidemann**

■■■□□ Easy

Sizes

Finished Measurements

Circumference (stuffed) = 23"

Materials

Yarns

Medium sport weight,
200 yds. (182 m) *each*
in light green (A),
light yellow (B),
lavender (C), and white (D)

Hooks & Extras

- Size I/9 (5.5 mm) crochet hook
  OR SIZE NEEDED TO OBTAIN
  GAUGE
- Polyester fiberfill stuffing
- Blunt-end yarn needle

Notes

Gauge

Using a double strand of yarn,
12 sc and 16 rows = 4" (10 cm).
TAKE TIME TO CHECK YOUR
GAUGE.

Use a double strand of yarn
throughout project.

Crochet

SIDE PANEL (MAKE 2 EACH USING A, B, AND C FOR A TOTAL OF 6)

Using A, ch 4.

Row 1: Sc in 2nd ch from hook and in each ch across—3 sts; turn.

Row 2: Ch 1, sc in each sc across; turn.

Row 3: Ch 1, sc in each sc across, ending 2 sc in last sc—4 sts; turn.

Rows 4–6: Rep Row 3—7 sts.

Row 7: Rep Row 2.

Rows 8 and 9: Rep Row 3—9 sts.

Rows 10 and 11: Rep Row 2.

Rows 12 and 13: Rep Row 3—11 sts.

Rows 14–19: Rep Row 2.

Row 20: Ch 1, sk sc, sc across—10 sts; turn.

Row 21: Rep Row 20—9 sts.

Rows 22 and 23: Rep Row 2.

Rows 24 and 25: Rep Row 20—7 sts.

Row 26: Rep Row 2.

Rows 27–30: Rep Row 20—3 sts.

Row 31: Rep Row 2. Fasten off.

END (MAKE 2)

Using D, ch 2.

Rnd 1: Work 6 sc in 2nd ch from hook.

Rnd 2: Work 2 sc in each sc around—12 sts.

Rnd 3: (Sc in sc, 2 sc in next sc) around—18 sts.

Rnd 4: (Sc in 2 sc, 2 sc in next sc) around—24 sts. Fasten off.

FINISHING

Alternating color panels, hold 2 panels tog and using D, sc across to join; turn.

Sl st in each sc across. Fasten off. Rep until all panels are joined. Stuff ball with fiberfill.

Sew ends to ball, covering edges of panels.

Topped with a tasseled hood, this little sweater buttons up the front for easy-on/easy-off styling. Stitch the double-crochet pattern in pastels, using soft contrasting bands for newborns. Spice it up for toddlers in bold colors with rainbow hues for banding.

snuggle-up hoodie

Designed by **Michelle Thompson**   Photographed by **Greg Scheidemann**

■■■□□ Easy

Sizes

6 (12, 24, 36, 48) months
Instructions are given for the smallest size with changes for larger sizes in parentheses. When only one number is given, it applies to all sizes.
Note: For ease in working, circle all numbers pertaining to the size you're crocheting.

Finished Measurements
Chest = 25 (27, 29, 31, 33)"
Length (Back) = 12 (13, 14, 15, 16)"

Materials
Yarns
DK, 460 yds. (413 m)—
all sizes—*each* in light blue (A) and lavender (B)

5 BULKY

Bulky weight 100% polyester, 220 (220, 275, 275, 330) yds. [200 (200, 250, 250, 300) m] in light blue (C)

5 BULKY

Hooks & Extras
- Size K/10½ (6.5 mm) crochet hook OR SIZE NEEDED TO OBTAIN GAUGE
- Stitch markers
- Five ¾"-diameter buttons
- Blunt-end yarn needle

Notes
Gauge
With C, 8 dc = 4" (10 cm); 6 rows = 5" (12.7 cm). TAKE TIME TO CHECK YOUR GAUGE.

Crochet
BACK
Starting at bottom edge using C, ch 24 (26, 28, 30, 32).
Row 1 (RS): Dc in 4th ch from hook and in each ch across—22 (24, 26, 28, 30) sts; turn.
Row 2: Ch 3—counts as dc; dc in each dc across; turn.
   Rep Row 2 until piece measures 11 (12, 13, 14, 15)" from beg. Fasten off.

BACK TRIM
Rnd 1: With RS facing, join 1 strand each of A and B held tog in top right corner st. Ch 1, working loosely, sc evenly spaced around, working 3 sc in each corner st; join with sl st in first sc; turn.
Rnd 2: Ch 1, sc in each sc around, working 3 sc in each corner st; join with sl st in first sc. Fasten off.

FRONT (MAKE 2)
Starting at bottom edge using C, ch 12 (13, 14, 15, 16).

Row 1 (RS): Dc in 4th ch from hook and in each ch across—10 (11, 12, 13, 14) sts; turn.
Row 2: Ch 3—counts as dc; dc in each dc across; turn.
   Rep Row 2 until piece is 2 rows shorter than finished Back.

Shape neck
Sl st in first 4 sts, ch 3—counts as dc; dc in each rem st to end. Work 1 row even on rem 7 (8, 9, 10, 11) dc. Fasten off.

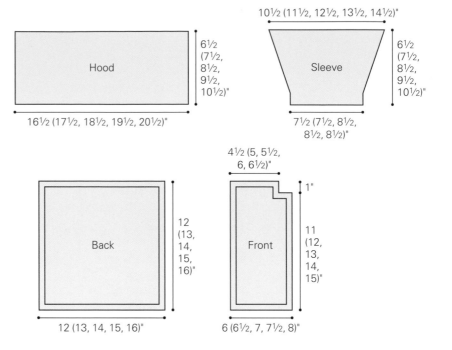

FRONT TRIM

Work as for Back Trim.

SLEEVE (MAKE 2)

Starting at lower edge with C, ch 17 (17, 19, 19, 19).

Row 1 (RS): Dc in 4th ch from hook and in each ch across—15 (15, 17, 17, 17) sts; turn. Work in dc, inc 1 dc each edge every row 3 (4, 4, 5, 6) times—21 (23, 25, 27, 29) sts. Work even until piece measures approx 6½ (7½, 8½, 9½, 10½)" from beg. Fasten off.

CUFF

With RS facing and working across opposite side of foundation ch on cuff edge, join 1 strand each of A and B in first ch. Ch 1, working loosely, sc in each ch across—15 (15, 17, 17, 17) sc; join with sl st in first sc. Ch 1, sc in each sc around; join and fasten off.

HOOD

Using C, ch 35 (37, 39, 41, 43).

Row 1 (RS): Dc in 4th ch from hook and in each ch across—33 (35, 37, 39, 41) sts; turn. Work even until piece measures 6½ (7½, 8½, 9½, 10½)" from beg. Fasten off C.

HOOD EDGING

Join 1 strand each of A and B held tog and work 2 sc rows loosely on last edge only. Fasten off.

FINISHING

Sew Fronts to Back at shoulders.

Place markers 5½ (6, 6½, 7, 7½)" down from shoulder seams on each side of Fronts and Back. Set in Sleeves bet markers.

Join underarm and side seams.

Button band

Row 1: On Left Front for girls/Right Front for boys, with RS facing, and 1 strand each of A and B, join yarn at top/bottom of front edge.

Ch 1, sc evenly spaced across front edge; turn.

Work even in sc for 2 more rows. Fasten off.

Buttonhole band

Mark positions for 5 evenly spaced buttonholes on opposite front edge.

Row 1: With RS facing and 1 strand each of A and B, join yarn at bottom/top of front edge. Ch 1, sc evenly spaced across, working (ch 1, sk 1 sc) at each marker; turn.

Row 2: Ch 1, sc in each sc and each ch 1-sp across; turn. Work 1 row even in sc. Fasten off.

Sew buttons to button band opposite the buttonholes.

Fold Hood in half, matching sts on bottom edge; with matching yarn, sew back seam.

With hood edging in front, sew bottom edge of Hood along neck edge bet buttonhole band and button band, easing in fullness. Weave in loose ends.

Tassel

Wrap A and B tog 25 times around a 3" piece of cardboard. Tie 1 strand each of A and B through 1 end of bundle. Cut opposite end of bundle. Wrap a separate strand of A and B several times around bundle, 1" below folded end; fasten off and secure. Attach Tassel to back tip of Hood.

stuffed bunny

It won't take long for this cheerful floppy-eared bunny to become a child's constant companion. Knitting it in simple stockinette stitch is a breeze.

Designed by **Charlotte Parry**   Photographed by **Greg Scheidemann**

▮▮ ▮▮ ▭ ▭ **Easy**

Sizes

Finished Measurement

Height (without extending ears) = 14"

Materials

Yarns

Worsted weight 100% cotton, 170 yds. (156 m) *each* in white (A), blue (B), green (C), and pink (D)

Needles & Extras

• Size 6 (4 mm) needles OR SIZE NEEDED TO OBTAIN GAUGE
• Blunt-end yarn needle
• Stitch marker
• Polyester fiberfill

Notes

Gauge

20 sts and 28 rows = 4" (10 cm) in St st (knit all RS rows, purl all WS rows). TAKE TIME TO CHECK YOUR GAUGE.

Special Abbreviations

sk2p = Slip 1, knit 2 sts together, pass slipped st over the 2 sts knit tog

Knit

HEAD

Center gusset

Using A, cast on 10 sts for neck edge at back of Head. K 2 rows. Beg with a p row, work St st (k RS rows, p WS rows) until piece measures 4" from cast-on edge, ending with a WS row.

Next row (RS): K1, ssk, k to last 3 sts, k2tog, k1—8 sts.

Work St st for 5 rows. Rep these 6 rows twice—4 sts.

Next row (RS): K1, k2tog, k1—3 sts.

Purl 1 row. Bind off all sts.

RIGHT SIDE

Using A, cast on 13 sts for neck edge at side of Head. K 2 rows; p 1 row.

Next row (RS): K1, make 1 (M1), k to end—14 sts.

Work St st for 3 rows. Rep these 4 rows twice—16 sts. Mark end of row.

Next row (RS): Bind off 3 sts, k to end—13 sts. P 1 row.

Next row (RS): Bind off 2 sts, k to last 3 sts, k2tog, k1—10 sts. P 1 row. Rep last 2 rows twice—4 sts.

Next row (RS): Bind off 2 sts, k1—2 sts. P 1 row. Bind off rem 2 sts.

LEFT SIDE

Using A, cast on 13 sts for neck edge at side of Head. K 2 rows; p 1 row.

Next row (RS): K to last st, M1, k1—14 sts.

Work St st for 3 rows. Rep these 4 rows once—15 sts.

Next row (RS): K14, M1, k1—16 sts.

Work St st 2 rows. Mark end of row.

Next row (WS): Bind off 3 sts, p to end—13 sts. K 1 row.

Next row (WS): Bind off 2 sts, p to last 3 sts, p2tog, p1—10 sts. K 1 row. Rep these last 2 rows twice—4 sts.

Next row (WS): Bind off 2 sts, p1—2 sts. K1 row. Bind off rem 2 sts.

FINISHING

Sew side edges of center gusset to edge of Right Side and Left Side, ending at markers. Sew Left and Right Side pieces together along remaining edges. Stuff Head with fiberfill. Using straight stitches, embroider eyes using B and mouth and nose using D, referring to photo, *opposite*, as a guide.

EARS (MAKE 1 USING B, 1 USING D)

Cast on 10 sts.

Row 1 (RS): Knit.

Row 2: K2, p6, k2. Rep these 2 rows until piece measures 3", ending with a WS row.

Next row (RS): K2, ssk, k to last 4 sts, k2tog, k2—8 sts.

Next row (WS): K2, p4, k2.

Next row (RS): Knit.

Next row (WS): K2, p4, k2. Rep these last 4 rows once—6 sts.

Next row (RS): K2, k2tog, k2—5 sts.

Work 1 row even as est.

Next row (RS): K1, sk2p, k1—3 sts.

Work 2 rows even as est. Bind off all sts. Sew cast-on edge of Ear to center/side seam at top of Head (see photo, *right*, for placement).

RIGHT SIDE BODY

Leg

Using B, cast on 11 sts. K 1 row, p 1 row.

Next row (RS): Inc 1 in each st across—22 sts.

Work in St st until piece measures 6", ending with a WS row. (Cont working on same piece for chest.)

Shape chest

Bind off 1 st at beg of next 2 rows—20 sts.

Next row (RS): K1, ssk, k to last 3 sts, k2tog, k1—18 sts. P 1 row.

Next row (RS): K1, M1, k to end—19 sts. P 1 row. Rep these 2 rows twice more—21 sts.

Work in St st until piece measures 10" from beg, ending with a WS row.

Next row (RS): K2, ssk, k to end—20 sts. P 1 row. Rep these 2 rows twice more—18 sts.

Next row (RS): K1, (ssk, k2) twice, (k2, k2tog) twice, k1—14 sts. P 1 row. Bind off.

LEFT SIDE BODY

Leg

With D, cast on 11 sts. K 1 row, p 1 row.

Next row (RS): Inc 1 in each st across—22 sts.

Work in St st until piece measures 6", ending with a WS row. (Cont working on same piece for chest.)

Shape chest

Bind off 1 st at beg of next 2 rows—20 sts.

Next row (RS): K1, ssk, k to last 3 sts, k2tog, k1—18 sts. P 1 row.

Next row (RS): K to last st, M1, k1—19 sts. P 1 row. Rep these 2 rows twice more—21 sts.

Work in St st until piece measures 10" from beg, ending with a WS row.

Next row (RS): K to last 3 sts, k2tog, k1—20 sts. P 1 row. Rep these 2 rows twice more—18 sts.

Next row (RS): K1, (k2tog, k2) twice, (k2, ssk) twice, k1—14 sts. P 1 row. Bind off.

FINISHING

Fold leg sections in half and sew seams. Sew Right Side Body to Left Side Body along front and back seams. Stuff with fiberfill. Sew Head to Body.

ARM (MAKE 2)

Using C, cast on 10 sts. Work in St st, inc 1 st each edge every other row 5 times—20 sts. Work even until piece measures 5" from beg, ending with a WS row.

Next row (RS): Dec 1 st at each edge—18 sts. P 1 row. Rep these 2 rows 4 times—10 sts.

Bind off. Fold Arm in half and sew seam, beginning at cast-on edge and ending ½" from bound-off edge. Stuff Arm with fiberfill and sew to side of Body.

super-soft
blanket & pullover

Super-Soft Blanket

■ ■ □ □ □ Easy

Sizes
Finished Measurements
28×32"

Materials
Yarns
Light worsted,
1,380 yds. (1, 240 m)
in light green (MC)

Bulky weight 100% polyester,
55 yds. (50 m) in
light pink (CC)

Needles & Extras
- Size 11 (8 mm) 29" circular
  needle OR SIZE NEEDED TO
  OBTAIN GAUGE
- Size K/10½ (6.5 mm) crochet
  hook
- Blunt-end yarn needle
- Sewing needle and thread
  to match CC

Notes
Gauge
15 sts and 24 rows = 4" (10 cm)
in pattern with a double strand
of MC. TAKE TIME TO CHECK
YOUR GAUGE.

Knit this blanket using a double
strand of MC; then crochet
flowers with CC to add later. To
accommodate the large number
of stitches, work back and forth
on a circular needle.

Stitch this unbelievably soft set
with chenille yarn and add
contrasting crocheted flowers for a
look that's perfect for a little girl.

Designed by **Jodi Lewanda** (blanket) and **Aliza Gebiner** (pullover)
Photographed by **Greg Scheidemann**

Knit

Using a double strand of MC, cast on 106 sts. K 6 rows for Garter st border.

BLANKET PATTERN

Row 1 (WS): K4; (p14, k14) 3 times, p14, k4.

Row 2: Knit.

Rows 3–20: Rep Rows 1 and 2.

Row 21 (WS): K4; (k14, p14) 3 times, k18.

Row 22: Knit.

Rows 23–40: Rep Rows 21 and 22.

Rep Rows 1–40 three more times—160 rows. Rep Rows 1–20 again. K 5 rows for Garter st border. Bind off kwise.

FLOWER (MAKE 10)

Using crochet hook and CC, ch 6; sl st in first ch to form ring. Ch 1, sc in ring; (ch 5, sc in ring) 5 times, ch 5; join with sl st in first sc. Fasten off.

FINISHING
Overcast edging

Thread CC into the yarn needle. With RS facing, bring the needle from WS to RS about 1" from any edge of the Blanket and pull the yarn through. *Take the needle and yarn over the edge, then insert the needle from WS to RS about 1" from the last stitch and pull the yarn through; rep from * around entire Blanket, keeping the loops snug but not so tight as to distort the edge. At the end, make a tiny stitch on WS to secure. Cut the yarn. Weave in all loose ends along WS.

Arrange Flowers onto RS of stockinette squares as shown in photo, *below.* Sew them securely in place with the sewing needle and matching thread.

Pretty-in-Pink Pullover

■■■□□□ Easy

Sizes

6 (12, 18) months

Instructions are given for the smallest size with changes for larger sizes given in parentheses. When only one number is given, it applies to all sizes.

Note: For ease in working, circle all numbers pertaining to the size you're knitting.

Finished Measurements

Chest = 24 (26, 28)"
Length = 11 (11½, 12)"

Materials

Yarns

Bulky weight 100% polyester, approx 165 (220, 220) yds. [150 (200, 200) m] in light pink (MC)

Medium sport weight, 50 yds. (45 m)—all sizes—in light green (CC)

Needles & Extras

• Size 10½ (6.5 mm) knitting needles OR SIZE NEEDED TO OBTAIN GAUGE
• Size 7 (4.5 mm) crochet hook
• Stitch holder
• Stitch markers
• Blunt-end yarn needle

Notes
Gauge

8 sts and 16 rows = 4" (10 cm) in St st (k all RS rows, p all WS rows). TAKE TIME TO CHECK YOUR GAUGE.

Knit

BACK

Using MC, cast on 24 (26, 28) sts. Knit 4 rows for Garter st border, noting that first row is RS. Then work St st (k 1 row, p 1 row) until piece measures 8 (8½, 9)" from beg. Then work Garter st (k every row) until piece measures 11 (11½, 12)" from beg, ending with a WS row. Bind off loosely.

FRONT

Work as for Back to 8 (8½, 9)" from beg.

Shape neck

First side: K12 (13, 14) sts; turn. Place rem sts onto holder. K every row until piece measures same as Back, ending with a WS row. Bind off loosely.
Second side: Join yarn at neck edge and k12 (13, 14) sts; turn. Finish as for first side.

Join 7 (8, 9) shoulder sts at each edge, leaving center 10 back sts free for Back neck and 5 sts free at each Front neck edge for turn-back collar.

SLEEVE (MAKE 2)

Work 3" in Garter st, then 3" in St st; work Garter st to specified length.

Place markers 4½ (5, 5½)" from shoulder seam and along each side edge.

With RS facing and using MC, pick up and k18 (20, 22) sts between markers.

Knit 3 rows. Dec 1 st each edge NOW and every 6th row until 10 (12, 12) sts rem. Work even to 6" from beg. Work 1 (1½, 2)" in Garter st; bind off kwise on RS.

FINISHING

Join underarm and side seams. Sew sleeves in place. Turn back edges of Front neck opening and sew in place.

Edging

Thread a double strand of CC into yarn needle. With RS facing, bring needle from WS to RS near a side seam and just above last Garter st row at lower edge; take to WS just below first Garter st row and one st to right or left of first st. Making sts ½" apart, cont around entire lower edge. Secure in place on WS of fabric.

FLOWER (MAKE 3 OR 5)

Using a crochet hook and a double strand of CC, ch 6; sl st in first ch to form ring. Ch 1, sc in ring; (ch 5, sc in ring) 5 times, ch 5; join with sl st in first sc. Fasten off.

Arrange 3 Flowers on left Front of Pullover as shown in photo, *above*, and sew in place. If you like, add 2 Flowers to left back yoke.

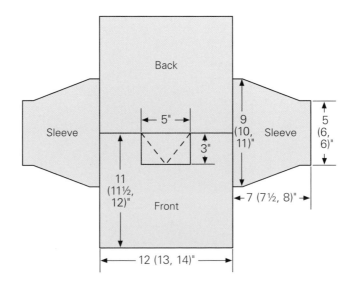

Bundle up your little one in this pair of sweet little mittens and a perky cap. Simple stockinette stitching is set off by a delightful fringe trim, made by just tying together the yarn tails from each color change.

candy-cane
hat & • mittens

Designed by **Ann E. Smith**
Photographed by **King Au**

Sizes

Finished Measurements

Mitten = 2½×4"

Hat = 18" in circumference
(including 11"-high rolled brim)

Materials

Yarns

Sport weight, 435 yds.
(398 m) in cream (MC)

Sport weight,
approx 200 yds. (180 m)
in dark red (CC)

Needles & Extras

• Size 4 (3.5 mm) knitting needles OR
SIZE NEEDED TO OBTAIN GAUGE
• Blunt-end yarn needle
• 24" length of narrow off-white ribbon

Notes

Gauge

6 sts and 8 rows = 1" (2.5 cm) in St st
(knit all RS rows, purl all WS rows). TAKE
TIME TO CHECK YOUR GAUGE.

Special Abbreviations

ssk (slip, slip, knit) = Slip next 2 sts
to right-hand needle singly and knitwise;
insert tip of left-hand needle through
front loops of both stitches and knit
them together.

Knit

MITTEN (MAKE 2)

Using MC, cast on 30 sts.

 *Leave 8" tails when joining colors.
Using MC, p 1 row, k 1 row, p 1 row.
Using CC, k 1 row. For Body pat, rep from
* for total of 6 times. Purl 1 row using MC.

Shape top

Row 1: Maintaining Stripe pat, (ssk, k11,
k2tog) twice.

Row 2: P26.

Row 3: (Ssk, k9, k2tog) twice.

Row 4: P22.

Row 5: K2tog across.

Row 6: P11. Leaving a 12" tail, cut yarn.

 Thread tail into yarn needle and back
through rem sts twice.

FINISHING

Take all tails to outside (RS). Matching
stripes, tie each of the 4 tails together
in an overhand knot all along side edge.
Trim to ½". With tail from top, sew
seam of side edge. Let lower edge roll
naturally.

HAT

Leaving an 8" tail and using MC, cast on
120 sts.

Row 1 and each following WS row:
P across.

Row 2: K28, k2tog, ssk, k56, k2tog, ssk,
k28—116 sts.

Row 4: K27, k2tog, ssk, k54, k2tog, ssk,
k27—112 sts.

Rows 6–7: Using MC, work even in St
st on 112 sts.

Row 8: *K1, yo, k2tog, rep from *
across—37 eyelets made.

Row 9: Purl.

Rows 10–19: Work even in St st on
112 sts.

Row 20: Using MC, k11, (k2tog, k20) 4
times, k2tog, k11—107 sts.

Note: When joining new color, leave 8"
tails at side edges.

Row 21: Using MC, purl.

Row 22: Using CC, knit.

Row 23: Using MC, purl.

Row 24: Using MC, knit.

Row 25: Using MC, purl.

Row 26: Using CC, knit.

Row 27: Using MC, purl.

Row 28: Using MC, (k19, k2tog) five
times, k2.

Row 29: Using MC, p102.

Rows 30 and 31: Rep Rows 22 and 23.

Row 32: Using MC, (k18, k2tog) times, k2.

Row 33: Using MC, p97.

Rows 34 and 35: Rep Rows 22 and 23.

Row 36: Using MC, (k17, k2tog) five
times, k2.

Row 37: Using MC, p92.

 Cont in 4-row Stripe pat, dec 5 sts
evenly spaced on each MC knit row until
12 sts rem.

Next row: K2tog across. P6. Cut yarn,
leaving an 8" tail. Thread tail into yarn
needle and back through sts. Draw up to
close opening. Sew to first stripe row.

FINISHING

The hat is not sewn together along the
opening where the tails are tied together.
Take all tails to outside (RS). Matching
stripes and working along side edge, tie
the 4 tails tog in an overhand knot. With
beg tail at lower edge, join MC rows
up to first stripe. Let this portion form
a natural roll. Weave ribbon in eyelets
made in Row 8. Tie ends together.

Pom-pom

Wind CC around a plastic card 25 times;
tie a separate strand tightly around
center. Carefully remove card. Cut ends
of pom-pom. Trim and sew to tip of Hat.

kids

Brighten a child's wardrobe with playful sweaters
and accessories that are comfy and fun to wear.

MULTICOLOR
PONCHO & LEG WARMERS

This poncho and leg warmer set needs no color changes while you knit (the fringe is an add-on). The secret to the stripes is in the variegated yarn—the design forms automatically as you work the pattern. Designed by **Lorna Miser**   Photographed by **Jay Wilde**

■■ ■■ □ **Intermediate**

Sizes

4–6 (7–9, 10–12) years

Finished Measurements
Poncho length at center front (excluding fringe and neck edging) = 12 (14, 16)"
Leg Warmer (excluding top edging) = 6 (8, 10)"

Materials

Yarns
Sport weight, 660 (990, 1,320) yds. [600 (900, 1,200) m] in multicolor stripe (MC)

Sport weight, 435 (435, 870) yds. [400 (400, 800) m] in cream (CC; for fringe)

Needles & Extras
- Size 5 (3.75 mm) needles, and 16" (40 cm) circular needle same size OR SIZE NEEDED TO OBTAIN GAUGE
- Size F/5 (3.75 mm) crochet hook
- Blunt-end yarn needle
- Long sewing pins with colored heads

Notes

Gauge
22 sts and 30 rows = 4" (10 cm) in St st (knit all RS rows, purl all WS rows).
TAKE TIME TO CHECK YOUR GAUGE.

Knit
PATTERN STITCHES
Ribbed Stitch
RS: K12, p2 ribbing
WS: K2, p12.
  Incorporate new sts into Ribbed st pat when there are enough sts.
Note: Poncho is knit from the neck down in 4 sections. After the sections are sewn together, pick up the neck edge and work in the round.

PONCHO
Work 4 sections the same.
  Using MC, cast on 28 (32, 36) sts.

Size 4–6 yrs. only
Row 1 (WS): P1, (k2, p10) twice, k2, p1.
First Inc row (RS): K1, yo, (p2, make 1 [M1], k10) twice, p2, yo, k1—32 sts.
Row 3: P2, (k2, p11) twice, k2, p2.
Second Inc row: K2, yo, (p2, M1, k11) twice, p2, yo, k2—36 sts.
Row 5: P3 (k2, p12) twice, k2, p3.

Sizes 7–9, 10–12 yrs. only
Row 1 (WS): P (1, 3) sts, (k2, p12) twice, k (2, 2) sts, p (1, 3) sts.
First Inc row (RS): K (1, 3) sts, yo, (p2, k12) twice, p (2, 2) sts, yo, k (1, 3) sts—(34, 38) sts
All WS rows: Work in pat as est, k the k sts, p the p sts and work the yo's in pat.
All RS rows: K1, yo, *k the k sts, p the p sts to last st, yo, k1.
  Rep the last rows until (10, 14) more inc have been made—(44, 52) sts.

Continue all sizes as follows

Continue 2 of the sections using the following shaping:

Note: Work new sts in St st until there are enough sts to incorporate them into the Ribbed st pat.

RS rows: K2tog, yo, work in Ribbed st pat to last st, yo, k1. When the row ends with 12 knit sts, work in pat to last st, yo, p1. Rep this once more on the next RS row to maintain est pat of k12, p2, then resume same as earlier rows.

WS rows: Work in pat as est, k the k sts, p the p sts, and work the yo's in pat. Rep these 2 rows until piece measures 12 (14, 16)" from cast-on edge, measuring straight up the center, ending with RS row. Knit 2 rows. Bind off loosely.

Continue remaining 2 sections as follows

Note: Work new sts in St st (k on RS rows, p on WS rows) until there are enough sts to incorporate them into the Ribbed st pat.

RS rows: K1, yo, work in Ribbed st pat to last 2 sts, yo, k2tog.

WS rows: K the k sts, p the p sts, and work the yo's in pat.

Rep these 2 rows until piece measures 12 (14, 16)" from cast-on edge, measuring straight up the center, ending with RS row. K 2 rows. Bind off loosely.

With WS tog, carefully match shoulders (edges with shaping only) and front and back pieces (edges with inc made every other row). Pin edges in place. Using CC, whipstitch seams together decoratively on the RS.

NECK EDGING

With RS facing and using circular needle and MC, pick up and knit 2 of every 3 sts around cast-on edge—about 74 (84, 96) sts. Knit every rnd for 1½". Bind off loosely. The edging will roll forward exposing the purl sts. Weave in loose ends.

FRINGE

Using CC, cut 2 strands each 8" long for each Fringe. Fold both strands in half, and using the crochet hook, pull strands halfway through one stitch in the k row above the bind-off edge. Insert Fringe ends through the fold, then pull ends to tighten and secure. Rep Fringe in every other stitch around the lower edge.

LEG WARMER (MAKE 2)

Using MC, cast on 49 (57, 65) sts.
Row 1 (WS): P1, (k2, p2) across row.
Row 2 (RS): (K2, p2) across row to last st, k1.

Rep these 2 rows until Leg Warmer measures 6 (8, 10)" from cast-on. Change to St st for 1½". Bind off. Sew side edges together. Weave in loose ends.

BAND OF BLOOMS

Small grannylike squares blossom across this sweet headband. Made using cotton crochet thread, the squares are sewn together in a strip and finished with end triangles and long chain-stitch ties.

Adapted from a block-motif design by **Jan Eaton**
Photographed by **Greg Scheidemann**

Sizes

One size fits most children.

Finished Measurements
8½" wide, not including ties

Materials

Yarns
Sport weight cotton or cotton blend, 150 yds. (137 m) *each* in light green (MC), pink (A), and blue (B)

2 FINE

Hooks & Extras
- Size F/5 (3.75 mm) crochet hook OR SIZE NEEDED TO OBTAIN GAUGE
- Blunt-end yarn needle
- Sewing thread to match yarn B
- Embroidery needle

Notes

Gauge
1 motif = 2" square (5 cm).
TAKE TIME TO CHECK YOUR GAUGE.

Crochet

GRANNY SQUARE FLOWER PATTERN

Foundation Ring: Using A (B), ch 6, join with sl st to form a ring.

Rnd 1 (RS): Ch 5—counts as dc, and ch 2; (dc in ring, ch 2) 7 times, join with sl st in 3rd ch of ch-5. Fasten off—8 dc and 8 ch-2 lps.

Rnd 2: With RS facing, join B (A) with sl st in next ch-2 sp, ch 1, in same sp work sc, hdc, 2 dc, hdc, sc—1 petal made; in each ch-2 sp around work sc, hdc, 2 dc, hdc, and sc; join with sl st in first sc. Fasten off.

Rnd 3: With RS facing, join MC in back lp of same sc as last sl st, ch 5; working in back lps, (sl st in first sc of next petal, ch 5) 7 times; join with sl st in first ch of ch-5.

Rnd 4: Sl st into next ch-5 sp, ch 1, 6 sc into same sp; * work 3 dc, ch 2, and 3 dc in next ch-5 sp **, 6 sc in next ch-5 sp; rep from * twice and from * to ** once again; join with sl st into first sc. Fasten off.

HEADBAND

Make 3 Granny Square Flower pats, crocheting 2 with B centers and 1 with an A center. Alternating colors, join squares in a strip.

END TRIANGLE (MAKE 2)

With RS facing, join MC with a sl st in a ch-2 corner at 1 end of strip.

Row 1: Ch 2—counts as hdc; (yo and draw up a lp in next dc) 2 times; yo and draw through all 5 lps on hook—hdc dec made; hdc in next 8 sts, hdc dec over next 2 dc; (sk ch-2 sp)—11 sts; turn.

Row 2: Ch 2—counts as hdc; sk next st, hdc dec, hdc in next 5 sts, hdc dec over next 2 sts—8 sts; turn.

Row 3: Ch 2—counts as hdc; sk next st, hdc dec over next 2 sts, hdc in next 2 st, hdc dec over next 2 sts—5 sts; turn.

Row 4: Ch 2—counts as hdc; sk next st, hdc in next 2 hdc, sk last st—3 sts; turn.

Row 5: Ch 2, sk next st, hdc in next hdc—2 sts. Do not fasten off thread.

CHAIN TIES

Using MC, ch 100, sc in 2nd ch from hook and in each ch across; end with sl st in corresponding hdc of Row 5. Fasten off.

on-the-go
BOY'S PULLOVER

Trimmed with rolled cuffs and hem and accented with button wheels, this sweater with a colorful car motif knits up quickly in stockinette stitch using chunky-weight yarn.

Designed by **Ann E. Smith**   Photographed by **Greg Scheidemann**

▬▬ ▬▬ ▬▬ ▭ **Intermediate**

Sizes

2 (4, 6, 8) years

Instructions are written for the smallest size with changes for larger sizes given in parentheses. When only one number is given, it applies to all sizes.

Note: For ease in working, circle all numbers pertaining to the size you're knitting.

Finished Measurements

Chest = 26 (28, 30, 32)"
Length (Back) = 15 (16½, 18, 19½)"

Materials

Yarns

Bulky weight, 305 (460, 460, 615 yds. [280 (420, 420, 560) m] in denim (MC)

Bulky weight, 155 yds. (140 m) in orange (CC)

Needles & Extras

- Size 10½ (6.5 mm) knitting needles OR SIZE NEEDED TO OBTAIN GAUGE
- Size 10 (6 mm) knitting needles
- Size 10 (6 mm) 16" circular needle
- Two 1"-diameter black buttons with four holes for wheels
- Two ring-type stitch markers
- Blunt-end yarn needle

Notes

Gauge

17 sts and 20 rows = 5" (12.5 cm) with larger needles in St st (knit all RS rows, purl all WS rows). TAKE TIME TO CHECK YOUR GAUGE.

An Intarsia car is added to the front only. While working the chart for St st car, use separate strands of yarn for each color section, bringing the new color from under the previous color for a "twist" to prevent holes. Read the chart from right to left for knit (RS) rows and from left to right for purl (WS) rows. See schematics and chart, *opposite*.

Knit

BACK

Using smaller needles and CC, cast on 43 (47, 51, 55) sts. Beg with a knit row, work 10 rows in St st. Change to larger needles.

Border

Row 1 (RS): (K1 in CC, k1 in MC) across, ending with k1 in CC.
Row 2: (P1 in CC, p1 in MC) across, ending with p1 in CC.

Using MC, work even in St st, beg with a knit row, until piece measures approx 9 (9½, 10, 10½)" from beg, ending with a WS row.

Shape armholes

Bind off 4 sts at beg of next 2 rows—35 (39, 43, 47) sts. Work even until piece measures 14 (15, 16, 17)" from beg, ending with a WS row. Bind off loosely.

FRONT

Work as for Back until piece measures approx 8 (8½, 9, 9½)" from beg, ending with a WS row and placing markers before and after 19 center sts for chart placement. Work Car Motif Chart, *opposite*, through Row 10, noting armhole shaping will be worked as for Back when piece measures approx 9 (9½, 10, 10½)" from beg.

Cont in St st using MC until piece measures approx 12 (13, 14, 15)" from beg, ending with a WS row.

Shape neck

Next row: K15 (16, 17, 18) sts, join a new ball of MC, and bind off center 5 (7, 9, 11) sts; k to end. Working sides separately and AT THE SAME TIME, bind off 2 sts at each neck edge twice and then 1 st at each neck edge twice. Work even on rem 9 (10, 11, 12) sts for each shoulder to same length as Back, ending with a WS row. Bind off loosely.

SLEEVE (MAKE 2)

Using smaller needles and CC, cast on 17 (21, 25, 29) sts. Beg with a knit row, work 10 rows in St st. Change to larger needles. Work 2 rows of border as for Back. Using MC, work in St st, inc 1 st each edge NOW and every 4th row 8 times more. Work even on 35 (39, 43, 47) sts until piece measures approx 11 (12, 13, 14)" from beg, ending with a WS row. Bind off loosely.

FINISHING
Neckband

Join shoulder seams. With RS facing and using circular needle and MC, pick up and k17 (19, 21, 23) sts evenly spaced along Back neck and 27 (29, 31, 33) sts evenly spaced along Front neck— 44 (48, 52, 56) sts. Place a marker for beg of rnd. Join.

Next 4 rnds: Work rib of k1, p1 around. Change to CC and k 1 rnd.

Next 4 rnds: With CC, work rib of k1, p1 around. Bind off k-wise. Turn neckband to inside and sew in place along pick-up rnd.

Set in Sleeves

Sew bound-off edges of Sleeves to armhole sections of Front and Back; sew upper side edges of Sleeve to 4 bound-off armhole sts. Join sleeve and side seams using matching color yarns.

Using CC, sew the buttons in place as wheels using a cross-stitch on each.

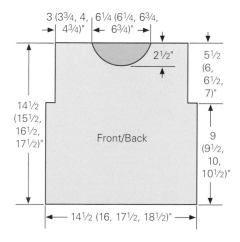

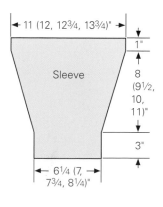

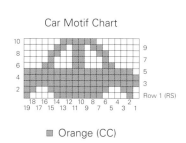

Car Motif Chart

■ Orange (CC)

GIRL'S
raglan cardigan
WITH CAPELET

Treat your little girl to this adorable cardigan-and-cape combo with Fair Isle flair. The pieces can be worn together or individually. The sweater has raglan shaping at the armholes but is worked in five separate segments.

Designed by **Deborah Newton**
Photographed by **Greg Scheidemann**

Sizes

4 (6, 8, 10) years

Instructions are written for the smallest size with changes for larger sizes given in parentheses. When only one number is given, it applies to all sizes.

Note: For ease in working, circle all numbers pertaining to the size you're knitting.

Finished Measurements

Cardigan

Chest = 26 (28, 30, 32)"

Length (Back) = 14 (16, 18, 20)"

Capelet

Length = 7 (8, 9, 10)"

Width (at lower edge including bands) = 46 (48, 50, 52)"

Materials

Yarns

Worsted weight, 715 yds. (650 m)—all sizes— in green (MC)

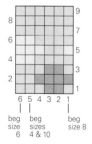

Worsted weight, approx 175 yds. (160 m)—all sizes—*each* in medium pink (A), light pink (B), and yellow (C)

Needles & Extras

- Size 7 (4.5 mm) 24" circular needle
  OR SIZE NEEDED TO OBTAIN GAUGE
- Size 6 (4 mm) 24" circular needle
- Size 8 (5 mm) 24" circular needle
- Blunt-end yarn needle
- 7 (7, 9, 9) ⅞"-diameter buttons: 4 (4, 5, 5) for Cardigan; 3 (3, 4, 4) for Capelet

Notes

Gauge

20 sts and 24 rows = 4" (10 cm) in St st with medium-size needles

20 sts and 24 rows = 4" (10 cm) over Color Border with largest needles.

TAKE TIME TO CHECK YOUR GAUGE.

Knit

PATTERN STITCHES

1×1 Rib Pattern (worked over an odd number of sts)

Row 1 (WS): P1, *kl, p1; rep from * across.

Row 2: K1, *p1, k1; rep from * across.
Rep Rows 1–2 for 1×1 Rib pat.

Chart Explanation

Chart 1 is for Cardigan Color Border; Chart 2 is for Capelet Color Border. Odd-numbered rows are RS rows (knitted) and are read from right to left. Even-numbered rows are WS rows (purled) and are read from left to right. When beginning Row 1 at any st other than st #1, knit from designated st to st #6, then knit sts #1–6 repeatedly across row. If fewer than 6 sts rem at end of row, knit st #1, st #2, etc. to end of row. Begin Row 2 where you finished Row 1. For example, if after knitting sts #1–6 across Row 1, you have 3 sts remaining and you knitted sts #1–3, then beg Row 2 (remember to follow Row 2 from left to right) by purling sts #3, #2 and #1, then purling sts 6–1 repeatedly across row.

CARDIGAN BACK

Using smallest needles and A, cast on 71 (77, 81, 87) sts. Change to MC and work 1×1 Rib pat for 2", ending with a RS row.

Next row (WS): Dec 5 (7, 5, 7) sts evenly spaced across row—66 (70, 76, 80) sts. Changing to largest needle if necessary to keep gauge, work Chart 1 for Color Border for 18 rows.

Using smallest needle and MC, work in St st (knit RS rows, purl WS rows) until piece measures 8 (9, 10, 11)" from beg, ending with a WS row.

Shape armholes

Bind off 2 sts at beg of next 2 rows—62 (66, 72, 76) sts.

Next row (RS): K1, ssk, k to last 3 sts, k2tog, k1—60 (64, 70, 74) sts.

Next row: Purl.

Rep last 2 rows 19 (20, 22, 23) times—22 (24, 26, 28) sts. Bind off.

LEFT FRONT

Using smallest needle and A, cast on 33 (35, 37, 39) sts. Change to MC and work 1×1 Rib pat for 2", ending with a RS row.

Next row (WS): Dec 3 (3, 1, 1) sts evenly spaced across row—30 (32, 36, 38) sts.

Changing to largest needle if necessary to keep gauge, work Chart 1 for Color Border for 18 rows.

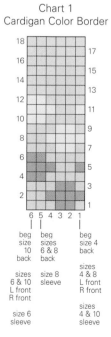

Chart 1
Cardigan Color Border

Chart 2
Capelet Color Border

Key

☐ Green (MC)
■ Medium Pink (A)
☐ Light Pink (B)
☐ Yellow (C)

Using MC, work in St st until piece measures 8 (9, 10, 11)" from beg, ending with a WS row.

Shape armhole

Next row (RS): Bind off 2 sts, k to end of row—28 (30, 34, 36) sts.
Next row: Purl.
Next row: K1, ssk, k to end—27 (29, 33, 35) sts.
Next row: Purl.
Rep last 2 rows 19 (20, 22, 23) times. When 8 (9, 11, 12) sts rem, ending with a RS row.

Shape neck

At neck edge, bind off 2 sts at beg of next 4 (4, 5, 6) WS rows; dec 1 st at beg on next WS row 0 (1, 1, 0) times. Pull yarn through rem st.

RIGHT FRONT

Work same as Left Front, reversing armhole and neck shaping.

SLEEVE (MAKE 2)

Using smallest needle and A, cast on 39 (41, 43, 45) sts. Change to MC and work 1×1 Rib pat for 2", ending with a RS row.

Next row (WS): Dec 3 sts evenly spaced across row—36 (38, 40, 42) sts. Change to medium-size needle. Work Chart 1 for Color Border for 2 rows.
Next row—Inc row (RS): Inc 1 st at each edge working incs into pattern.
Rep Inc row every 6th row 9 times more, working 18 rows of Color Border, then changing to MC and St st—56 (58, 60, 62) sts.
Work even in St st until Sleeve measures 11 (12, 13, 14)", ending with a WS row.

Shape armhole

Bind off 2 sts at beg of next 2 rows—52 (54, 56, 58) sts.
Next row (RS): K1, ssk, k to last 3 sts, k2tog, k1—50 (52, 54, 56) sts.
Next row: Purl.
Rep last 2 rows 19 (20, 22, 23) times—12 (12, 10, 10) sts. Bind off.

FINISHING

Sew Front and Back to Sleeves along raglan edges. Sew side and sleeve seams.

Neckband

With RS facing and using smallest needle and MC, pick up and knit 77 (81, 85, 89) sts around neck edge. Work 1×1 Rib pat for 3 rows. Change to A; bind off in ribbing.

Left Front button band

With RS facing and using smallest needle and MC, beg at neck edge and pick up and k 77 (79, 81, 83) sts evenly spaced along Left Front edge. Work 1×1 Rib pat for 8 rows. Change to A, rib 1 row, bind off in ribbing. Mark position of 4 (4, 5, 5) buttons evenly spaced along band.

Right Front buttonhole band

With RS facing and using smallest needles and MC, beg at lower edge and pick up and k 77 (79, 81, 83) sts evenly spaced along Right Front edge. Work 1×1 Rib pat for 3 rows. Using button markers as a guide, create buttonholes as foll:
Next row (RS): *Work pat until 1 st before marker, bind off next 3 sts; rep from * 3 (3, 4, 4) times more, rib to end of row.

Next row (WS): Work in rib, casting on 3 sts over bound-off sts.

Rib for 3 rows. Change to A, rib 1 row, bind off in ribbing. Sew buttons to Left Front opposite buttonholes.

CAPELET

Using smallest needle and A, cast on 235 (245, 255, 265) sts. Change to MC and work 1×1 Rib pat for ½", dec 9 sts evenly across last RS row—226 (236, 246, 256) sts. Change to medium or largest needle. Work Chart 2 for Color Border for 9 rows. Change to MC and use largest needle if needed to keep gauge.

Next row (WS): With MC, purl.

Next row: Knit, dec 10 sts evenly spaced across row as follows: k2tog for first 5 decs, ssk for second 5 decs—216 (226, 236, 246) sts.

Next row: Purl. Rep last 2 rows every 2nd (2nd, 4th, 4th) row 6 (2, 9, 4) times, then every 4th (4th, 0, 6th) row 3 (7, 0, 5) times—126 (136, 146, 156) sts rem; p 1 row.

Neck edge

Next row (RS): K2tog, p1, cont in 1×1 Rib pat across row. Work rib even for 2 more rows. Change to A; rib 1 row; bind off in ribbing.

FINISHING
Left edge button band

Work same as Cardigan button band, picking up 43 (49, 55, 61) sts along Right Front edge and marking positions for 3 (3, 4, 4) buttons.

Right edge buttonhole band

Work same as Cardigan buttonhole band, picking up 43 (49, 55, 61) sts along Front edge and creating 3 (3, 4, 4) buttonholes opposite button markers.

Sew buttons to Left Front edge opposite buttonholes.

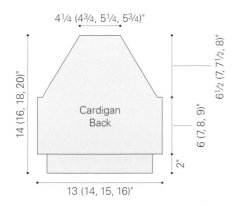

4¼ (4¾, 5¼, 5¾)"

14 (16, 18, 20)"

6½ (7, 7½, 8)"

6 (7, 8, 9)"

Cardigan Back

2"

13 (14, 15, 16)"

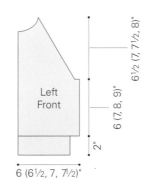

6½ (7, 7½, 8)"

6 (7, 8, 9)"

Left Front

2"

6 (6½, 7, 7½)"

2¼ (2¼, 2, 2)"

6½ (7, 7½, 8)"

11 (11½, 12, 12½)"

Sleeve

9 (10, 11, 12)"

2"

7 (7½, 8, 8½)"

nostalgic
GIRL'S CARDIGAN & BOY'S V-NECK

This pair will look lovely on a brother/sister duo. The lacy cardigan is worked in one piece to the armholes and edged in crochet, while the comfy V-neck has generous swaths of 2-inch ribbing at the lower edge and sleeve ends.

Designed by **Gayle Bunn** (cardigan)
and **Ann E. Smith** (V-neck)
Photographed by **Tony Lattari**

Nostalgic Pink Cardigan

■ ■ ■ □ ■ **Experienced**

Sizes

2 (4, 6, 8, 10) years
Instructions are written for the smallest size with changes for larger sizes given in parentheses. When only one number is given, it applies to all sizes.
Note: For ease in working, circle all numbers pertaining to the size you're knitting.

Finished Measurements

Chest = 22½ (25½, 27½, 29, 30½)"
Length (Back) = 11 (12½, 14, 15½, 17½)"

Materials

Yarns

Worsted weight, 670 (670, 895, 895, 1,120) yds. [605 (605, 810, 810, 1,015) m] in pink

Needles & Extras

- Size 7 (4.5 mm) needles OR SIZE NEEDED TO OBTAIN GAUGE
- Size 4 (3.5 mm) needles
- Size G/5 (3.75 mm) crochet hook
- Cable needle
- Two stitch holders
- Five ⅜"-diameter buttons
- Blunt-end yarn needle

Notes

Gauge

20 sts and 26 rows = 4" (10 cm) over Lace pat with larger needles. TAKE TIME TO CHECK YOUR GAUGE.

Knit

PATTERN STITCHES

Lace Pattern (multiple of 8 sts + 1 st; a 12-row rep)

Row 1 (RS): *K2, k2tog, yo, k1, yo, ssk, k1; rep from *, ending last rep with k1.

Row 2 and all WS rows: Purl.

Row 3: *K1, k2tog, yo, k3, yo, ssk; rep from *, ending last rep with k1.

Row 5: Rep Row 1.

Row 7: *K1, yo, ssk, k3, k2tog, yo; rep from *, ending last rep with k1.

Row 9: *K2, yo, ssk, k1, k2tog, yo, k1; rep from *, ending last rep with k1.

Row 11: Rep Row 7.

Row 12: Purl.

Rep Rows 1–12 for Lace pat.

BODY

Note: Body is worked in one piece to armholes.

Using smaller needles, cast on 108 (124, 132, 140, 148) sts. Work 5 rows in Garter st (knit every row), increasing 5 sts evenly spaced across last row—113 (129, 137, 145, 153) sts. Change to larger needles; k 1 row, p 1 row. Work

Lace pat until piece measures 6 (7, 8, 9, 10)" from beg, ending with a WS row.

Divide for armholes

Next row (RS): Keeping to pat, work across 27 (30, 32, 34, 36) sts for Right Front, place these sts on a holder. Bind off 4 (6, 6, 6, 6) sts, work across 51 (57, 61, 65, 69) sts for Back (include st on needle after binding off), place these sts on a holder, bind off 4 (6, 6, 6, 6) sts, work across 27 (30, 32, 34, 36) sts for Left Front.

LEFT FRONT

Next row (WS): Working on Left Front sts only, purl.

Next row (RS): Cont in pat, dec 1 st at armhole edge. Rep these 2 rows twice more—24 (27, 29, 31, 33) sts.

Work even until Left Front measures 8½ (10, 11½, 13, 14½)", ending with a RS row.

Shape neck

Next row (WS): Bind off 8 (8, 9, 9, 10) sts, p to end of row—16 (19, 20, 22, 23) sts. Dec 1 st at neck edge 7 (8, 8, 9, 9) times—9 (11, 12, 13, 14) sts. Work even in pat until armhole measures 5 (5½, 6, 6½, 7)", ending with a WS row.

Shape shoulder

Next row (RS): Bind off 4 (5, 6, 6, 6) sts—5 (6, 6, 7, 8) sts. P 1 row. Bind off rem sts.

BACK

With WS facing, join yarn and p across 51 (57, 61, 65, 69) Back sts from holder. Keeping to pat, dec 1 st at each edge every RS row 3 times—45 (51, 55, 59, 63) sts. Work even in pat until armholes measure same as on Left Front, ending with a WS row.

Shape shoulders

Next row (RS): Bind off 4 (5, 6, 6, 6) sts at beg of next 2 rows—37 (41, 43, 47, 51) sts. Bind off 5 (6, 6, 7, 8) sts at beg of next 2 rows—27 (29, 31, 33, 35) sts. Dec 3 sts evenly spaced across rem sts—24 (26, 28, 30, 32) sts; slip these sts onto holder for Back neck.

RIGHT FRONT

With WS facing, join yarn and p across 27 (30, 32, 34, 36) sts from holder. Work same as Left Front, reversing shaping.

SLEEVE (MAKE 2)

Using smaller needles, cast on 35 (35, 43, 43, 51) sts. Work 5 rows in Garter st (k every row), increasing 6 sts evenly spaced across last row—41 (41, 49, 49, 57) sts.

Change to larger needles; k 1 row, p 1 row. Work in Lace pat for 8 rows, ending with a WS row.

Inc 1 st each edge of next RS row and every 12th row 2 (4, 2, 4, 2) more times—47 (51, 55, 59, 63) sts.

Work even until Sleeve measures 8 (10, 11, 12, 13)" from beg, ending with a WS row.

Shape cap

Bind off 2 (3, 3, 3, 3) sts at beg of next 2 rows—43 (45, 49, 53, 57) sts. Dec 1 st at each edge every RS row 4 (2, 4, 2, 3) times; then at each edge 13 (16, 15, 19, 19) times— 9 (9, 11, 11, 13) sts. Bind off all sts.

FINISHING

Sew shoulder seams.

Neckband

With RS facing and using smaller needles, pick up and k23 (23, 25, 25, 27) sts along Right Front neck, 24 (26, 28, 30, 32) sts from Back holder, and 23 (23, 25, 25, 27) sts along Left Front neck—70 (72, 78, 80, 86) sts. K 4 rows. Bind off all sts.

Buttonhole band

Row 1: With RS facing and using crochet hook, work 42 (46, 50, 54, 58) sc evenly spaced along Right Front edge to top edge of neckband; turn.
Row 2: Ch 1, sc in each sc across; turn.
Row 3—Buttonholes: Ch 1, sc in each of first 2 sc, *ch 2, sk next 2 sc, sc in each of next 7 (8, 9, 10, 11) sc; rep from * 3 more times, ch 2, sk next 2 sc, sc in each of last 2 sc. Fasten off.

Button band

Row 1: With RS facing, work 42 (46, 50, 54, 58) sc evenly spaced along Left Front edge to bottom edge; turn.
Rows 2 and 3: Ch 1, sc in each st across; fasten off at end of Row 3.

Edging

With RS facing, join yarn with sl st at bottom corner of buttonhole band, ch 1, (sc, ch 2, dc) in same sp, *sk next 2 sts, (sc, ch 2, dc) in next sc; rep from * along buttonhole band, across bound-off edge of neckband and along button band. Fasten off.

Sew Sleeves to armhole openings. Sew sleeve seams. Sew on buttons opposite buttonholes.

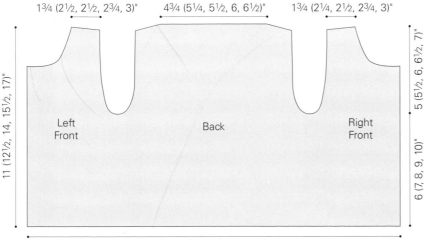

1¾ (2½, 2½, 2¾, 3)" 4¾ (5¼, 5½, 6, 6½)" 1¾ (2¼, 2½, 2¾, 3)"

11 (12½, 14, 15½, 17)"

Left Front   Back   Right Front

5 (5½, 6, 6½, 7)"

6 (7, 8, 9, 10)"

22½ (25½, 27½, 29, 30½)"

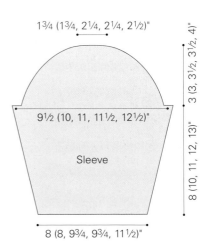

1¾ (1¾, 2¼, 2¼, 2½)"

3 (3, 3½, 3½, 4)"

9½ (10, 11, 11½, 12½)"

Sleeve

8 (10, 11, 12, 13)"

8 (8, 9¾, 9¾, 11½)"

Boy's V-Neck ▪▪▪▪▢ Intermediate

Sizes

2 (4, 6, 8) years

Instructions are written for the smallest size with changes for larger sizes given in parentheses. When only one number is given, it applies to all sizes.

Note: For ease in working, circle all numbers pertaining to the size you're knitting.

Finished Measurements

Chest = 23 (25, 27, 29)"
Length (Back) = 13½ (15, 16½, 18)"

Materials

Yarns

Bulky weight, 826 yds. (752 m)—all sizes— in light sage

5 BULKY

Needles & Extras

- Size 10 (6 mm) needles OR SIZE NEEDED TO OBTAIN GAUGE
- Size 9 (5.5 mm) needles
- Size 7 (4.5 mm) 16" circular needle
- Cable needle (cn)
- Safety pin
- Stitch holder
- Two stitch markers
- Blunt-end yarn needle

Notes

Gauge

13 sts and 24 rows = 4" (10 cm) in Seed st with largest needles. TAKE TIME TO CHECK YOUR GAUGE.

Special Abbreviations

2/2RC = Slip 2 sts to cn and hold in back, k2; k2 from cn.
2/2LC = Slip 2 sts to cable needle (cn) and hold in front, k2; k2 from cn.

Knit

PATTERN STITCHES

1×1 Rib Pattern (multiple of 2 sts + 1; 2-row rep)
Row 1 (WS): P1, (k1, p1) across.
Row 2: K1, (p1, k1) across.
  Rep Rows 1 and 2 for 1×1 Rib pat.

Seed Stitch (multiple of 2 sts + 1; 1-row pat rep)
Pat row: K1, (p1, k1) across.
  Rep Pat row for Seed st over odd number of sts.

BACK

Using size 9 needles, cast on 37 (41, 45, 49) sts. Work 1×1 Rib pat for 2", ending with a RS row. Change to larger needles and work Seed st until piece measures 8 (9, 10, 11)" from beg, ending with a WS row.

Shape armholes

Bind off 4 sts at beg of next 2 rows— 29 (33, 37, 41) sts. Work even until piece measures 13½ (15, 16½, 18)" from beg, ending with a WS row. Bind off all sts in Seed st.

FRONT

Using size 9 needles, cast on 39 (43, 47, 51) sts. Work same as Back to completion of 1×1 Rib, ending with a RS row. Change to largest needles and set up Cable pats as follows:
Row 1 (WS): (K1, p1) twice, k1, place marker (pm), k1, p4, k1, pm; (p1, k1) 8 (10, 12, 14) times; p1, pm, k1, p4, k1, pm, k1, (p1, k1) twice.
Row 2: (K1, p1) 3 times, k4, p2; (k1, p1) 8 (10, 12, 14) times; p1, k4, (p1, k1) 3 times.
Rows 3–7: Rep Rows 1 and 2 twice more, then rep Row 1 again.
Row 8 (RS): (K1, p1) 3 times; 2/2RC, p2; (k1, p1) 8 (10, 12, 14) times; p1, 2/2LC, (p1, k1) 3 times. Rep Rows 1–8 for pat. Work even until piece measures 6½ (8, 9, 10½)" from beg, ending with a WS row.

Shape V-neck and armhole
(LEFT FRONT)

Work pat across first 19 (21, 23, 25) sts; turn. Place center st on safety pin and rem sts on holder. Work 1 row even.

Dec row (RS): Work pat across row, dec 1 st at neck edge 9 (10, 11, 12) times more and AT THE SAME TIME, when piece measures same as Back to underarm, bind off 4 sts for armhole. Work even on 6 (7, 8, 9) sts until piece measures same as Back from beg, ending with a WS row. Bind off all sts in Seed st.

Shape V-neck and armhole
(RIGHT FRONT)

With RS facing, skip center st, join yarn and work pattern across rem sts. Work same as Left Front, reversing neck and armhole shaping.

SLEEVE (MAKE 2)

Using size 9 needles, cast on 23 (25, 27, 27) sts. Work 1×1 Rib pat for 2", ending with a RS row. Change to largest needles and Seed st. Work 3 (9, 9, 9) rows even. Cont in Seed st pat, inc 1 st each edge— 25 (27, 29, 29) sts. Work 5 rows even. Rep last 6 rows 6 (6, 6, 7) more times—37 (39, 41, 43) sts. Work even in Seed st pat until piece measures 10 (12, 12½, 13½)" from beg, ending with a WS row. Bind off all sts in Seed st.

FINISHING

Sew shoulder seams.

Neckband

With RS facing and using circular needle, pick up and k37 (37, 39, 39) sts evenly spaced along left neck edge, pm, k1 from safety pin, pm, pick up and k37 (37, 39, 39) sts along right neck edge, pick up and k17 (19, 19, 23) sts along Back neck—92 (94, 98,102) sts; pm for beg of rnd.

Rnd 1: (K1, p1) to 3 sts before marker, k1, ssk, k1, k2tog, k1, (p1, k1) to marker at beg of rnd, decreasing 0 (0, 0, 2) sts before marker at beg of rnd—90 (92, 96, 98) sts.

Rnd 2: Work rib to 2 sts before marker, ssk, k1, k2tog, rib around—88 (90, 94, 96) sts.

Rnds 3 and 4: Rep Rnds 1 and 2 without decreasing on Back neck on Rnd 3.

Next rnd: Bind off in 1×1 Rib pat to 2 sts before marker, ssk, and bind off; k1 and bind off; k2tog and bind off; bind off all rem sts in pat.

Sew Sleeves to Front and Back armholes. Sew side and sleeve seams.

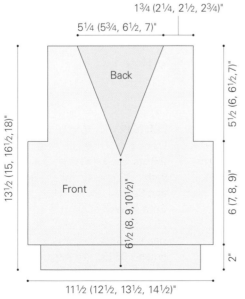

1¾ (2¼, 2½, 2¾)"

5¼ (5¾, 6½, 7)"

Back

5½ (6, 6½, 7)"

13½ (15, 16½, 18)"

Front

6 (7, 8, 9)"

6½ (8, 9, 10½)"

2"

11½ (12½, 13½, 14½)"

11½ (12, 12½, 13)"

10 (12, 12½, 13½)"

Sleeve

8 (10, 10½, 11½)"

2"

7 (7½, 8½, 8½)"

red flecked
GIRL'S COAT

Wide bands of garter stitch and a matching collar adorn this cozy oversized sweater coat stitched in a bright confetti novelty yarn. A two-button closure keeps out the chill.

Designed by **Vladimir Teriokhin**   Photographed by **King Au**

■■□□ **Easy**

Sizes

8 (10, 12) yrs.

Instructions are written for the smallest size with changes for larger sizes given in parentheses. When only one number is given, it applies to all sizes.

Note: For ease in working, circle all numbers pertaining to the size you're knitting.

Finished Measurement

Chest = 30¾ (35, 39½)"
Length (Back) = 21¾ (22¾, 23¾)"

Materials

Yarns

Bulky weight (suedelike), 244 (244, 366) yds. [220 (220, 330) m] in dark red (A)

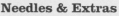

Super bulky weight (novelty), 385 (433, 530) yds. [335 (378, 462) m] in red with multicolor flecks (B)

Worsted weight (wool mix), 400 (600, 600) yds. [360 (540, 540) m] in dark red (C)

Needles & Extras

- Size 9 (5.5 mm) knitting needles OR SIZE NEEDED TO OBTAIN GAUGE
- Two ⅞"-diameter buttons
- Stitch markers
- Blunt-end yarn needle
- Sewing needle and matching thread

Notes

Gauge

12 sts and 24 rows = 4" (10 cm) in Garter st (knit all rows) using A.
12 sts and 18 rows = 4" (10 cm) in St st (knit on RS, purl on WS) using one strand each of B and C held together. TAKE TIME TO CHECK YOUR GAUGE.

Knit

BACK

Using A, cast on 42 (48, 54) sts. Work 30 rows in Garter st (k every row). Leaving a long tail, cut yarn. With one strand each of B and C held tog, work St st (k RS rows, p WS rows) until piece measures approx 20½ (21½, 22½)" from beg, ending with a WS row.

Shape shoulders

Bind off 4 (5, 6) sts at beg of next 4 rows; then bind off 4 sts at beg of next 2 rows. Bind off rem 18 (20, 22) sts for Back neck.

LEFT FRONT

Using A, cast on 25 (29, 33) sts. Mark end of first row for front edge. Work same as for Back and AT THE SAME TIME inc 1 st at front edge every 12th row 7 times—32 (36, 40) sts.

Work even until Front measures approx 19½ (20½, 21½)" from beg.

Shape neck and shoulders

Bind off 6 sts at Front edge 1 (1, 2) times; 4 sts 2 (4, 3) times; then 3 sts 2 (0, 0) times. AT THE SAME TIME, when piece measures approx 20½ (21½, 22½)" from beg, bind off 4 (5, 6) sts at side edge every RS row twice; then bind off 4 sts next RS row.

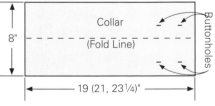

RIGHT FRONT

Work same as for Left Front,
but mark beg of first row for front edge.

SLEEVE (MAKE 2)

Using A, cast on 42 (45, 48) sts. Work
24 rows in Garter st; cut yarn. Using one
strand each of B and C held tog, work St
st until piece measures approx 12 (13, 14)"
from beg; ending with a WS row. Bind off.

FINISHING

Sew shoulder seams. Mark for Sleeve
placement 7 (7¼, 8)" down from
shoulder seams. Sew Sleeves between
markers. Sew side and sleeve seams.

Collar

With RS facing and using A, beg at Right
Front edge, pick up and k57 (63, 70) sts
evenly across neck opening. Knit 9 rows.

Buttonhole

Row 1 (RS): K3 (4, 4), bind off 2 sts
k6 (7, 7), bind off 2 sts, k to end of row.
Row 2 (WS): Knit across, casting on
2 sts over each buttonhole space from
previous row.

K 24 rows; rep buttonhole Rows 1
and 2; k 10 rows. Bind off all sts loosely.

Fold collar to WS, making certain
buttonholes are aligned. Sew bound-off
edge of collar to inside neck edge. Sew
side edges of collar closed. Using sewing
needle and thread, sew inside and
outside buttonhole edges tog. Overlap
collar and sew buttons to correspond
with buttonholes. Weave in ends.

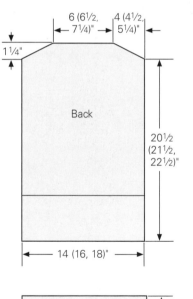

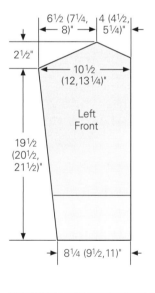

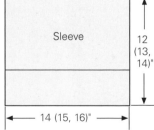

Your favorite young guy will be all the more handsome in this comfy pullover. The overall rib pattern is easy to do—then just add the variegated slip-stitch patch accents to the shoulders and elbows.

Designed by **Svetlana Avrakh**
Photographed by **Greg Scheidemann**

BOY'S RIBBED PULLOVER

Sizes

2 (4, 6, 8) years

Instructions are written for the smallest size with changes for larger sizes given in parentheses. When only one number is given, it applies to all sizes.

Note: For ease in working, circle all numbers pertaining to the size you're knitting.

Finished Measurements

Chest = 23½ (26½, 28, 31)"
Length (Back)= 13½ (15¼, 17, 18½)"

Materials

Yarns

Worsted weight, 600 (600, 600, 720) yds. [545 (545, 545, 654 m] in light blue (MC)

Worsted weight, 95 yds. (86 m)—all sizes—in light blue variegated (CC)

Needles & Extras

- Size 7 (4.5 mm) needles OR SIZE NEEDED TO OBTAIN GAUGE
- Size 6 (4 mm) needles
- Blunt-end yarn needle
- Two stitch holders
- Two stitch markers

Notes

Gauge

21 sts and 26 rows = 4" (10 cm) in Rib pat with larger needles. TAKE TIME TO CHECK YOUR GAUGE.

Knit

PATTERN STITCHES

Rib Pattern (worked over a multiple of 4 + 2 sts; 2-row repeat)

Row 1 (RS): *K2, p1, k1; rep from * to last 2 sts, k2.

Row 2: *P2, k1, p1; rep from * to last 2 sts, p2.

Rep Rows 1–2 for Rib pat.

Slip Stitch (worked over a multiple of 2 sts + 1 st; 4-row repeat)

Row 1 (RS): K1, *with yarn in front (wyif), sl next st pwise; with yarn in back (wyib), k1; rep from * across.

Row 2: K1, p to last st, k1.

Row 3: K1, *k1; wyif, sl 1 st pwise; wyib; rep from * to last 2 sts, k2.

Row 4: Rep Row 2.

Rep Rows 1–4 for Slip st pat.

BACK

Using smaller needles and MC, cast on 62 (70, 74, 82) sts. Work in Rib pat for 6 rows. Change to larger needles and cont in Rib pat until piece measures 7 (8½, 10, 11)" from beg; ending with a WS row.

Shape armholes

Keeping to Rib pat, bind off 6 sts at beg of next 2 rows—50 (58, 62, 70) sts. Work even until armholes measure 6½ (6¾, 7, 7½)", ending with a WS row.

Shape shoulders

Bind off 11 (14, 15, 18) sts at beg of next 2 rows. Sl rem 28 (30, 32, 34) sts onto holder.

FRONT

Work same as Back until armholes measure 4 (4, 4, 4½)"; ending with a WS row.

Shape neck and left shoulder

Next row (RS): Work across 14 (17, 18, 21) sts, k2tog. Sl rem 34 (39, 42, 47) sts onto spare needle.

Keeping to Rib pat, dec 1 st at neck edge on this row and next row, then every other row until 11 (14, 15, 18) sts rem. Work even in pat until armhole measures same as Back to shoulder, ending with a WS row. Bind off all sts.

Shape neck and right shoulder

With RS facing, sl sts from spare needle to larger needle. With RS facing, sl 18 (20, 22, 24) sts from needle onto holder for center neck. Join yarn to rem sts; ssk, work to end of row.

Keeping to pat, dec 1 st at neck edge on this row and next row, then every other row until 11 (14, 15, 18) sts rem. Work even in pat until armhole measures same as Back to shoulder, ending with a WS row. Bind off all sts.

SLEEVE (MAKE 2)

Using smaller needles and MC, cast on 38 (40, 40, 42) sts.

Sizes 2 and 8 only:

Work same as Back for 6 rows.

Sizes 4 and 6 only:

Row 1 (RS): K1, *k2, p1, k1; rep from * to last 3 sts, k3.

Row 2: P1, *p2, k1, p1; rep from * to last 3 sts, p3.

Rep these 2 rows twice more.

All sizes:

Note: On sizes 2 and 4, end last rep at **.
Change to larger needles. Keeping to
pat, *work 2 rows, inc 1 st each edge
on next row; ** work 3 rows, inc 1 st
each edge on next row; rep from * until
there are 64 (66, 68, 74) sts.

Work even in pat until piece measures
9 (10½, 12, 14)" from beg, ending with a
WS row; place a marker at each end of
last row. Work 6 more rows in pat. Bind
off 6 sts at beg of next 8 rows. Bind off
rem 16 (18, 20, 26) sts.

PATCH (MAKE 4)

Using larger needles and CC, cast on
17 (17, 19, 21) sts. Work Slip st pat until
piece measures 6"; end with a WS row.
Bind off all sts.

FINISHING

Neck edging

Sew right shoulder seam.

With RS facing and using smaller
needles and MC, pick up and k18 sts
along left neck edge, 18 (20, 22, 24) sts
from Front neck holder, 18 sts along right
neck edge, and 28 (30, 32, 34) sts from
Back neck holder—82 (86, 90, 94) sts.
Next row (WS): P2, *k2, p2; rep from *
across.
Next row: K2, *p2, k2; rep from *
across.

Rep last 2 rows once. Bind off in
ribbing. Sew left shoulder and neck
seam. Sew in Sleeves, placing rows
above markers along bound-off sts at
armhole. Sew side and sleeve seams.
Sew a Patch in vertical position to center
of each Sleeve 1" up from cast-on edge.
Sew a Patch centered across each
shoulder seam positioning the cast-on
edge at the Back and the bound-off
edge at the Front.

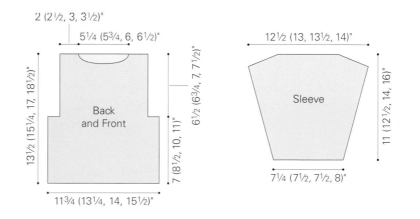

2 (2½, 3, 3½)"

5¼ (5¾, 6, 6½)"

13½ (15¼, 17, 18½)"

6½ (6¾, 7, 7½)"

7 (8½, 10, 11)"

Back
and Front

11¾ (13¼, 14, 15½)"

12½ (13, 13½, 14)"

Sleeve

11 (12½, 14, 16)"

7¼ (7½, 7½, 8)"

furry

Keep her warm with a matching hat and muff set knitted with furlike yarn for a super cuddly combo. A handy I-cord loop makes the muff easy to carry when it's not being worn.

Designed by **Ann E. Smith**   Photographed by **King Au**

■■□□ Easy

Sizes
Finished Measurements
Hat: Circumference = 20"
Muff: 7" tall and 16" in circumference

Materials
Yarns
Super bulky weight (furlike), 160 yds. (140 m) in blue with multicolor flecks (A)

6 SUPER BULKY

Bulky weight (suedelike), 490 yds. (440 m) in blue (B)

5 BULKY

Note: If making both the Hat and the Muff, you will need the full quantity of each yarn. If knitting only one item, you will need only half the amount of each yarn.

Needles & Extras
• Size 13 (9 mm) needles OR SIZE NEEDED TO OBTAIN GAUGE
• Blunt-end yarn needle

Notes
Gauge
8 sts and 12 rows = 4" (10 cm) in Reverse St st (purl all RS rows, knit all WS rows), using two strands of B held together. 8 sts and 14 rows = 4" (10 cm) in St st (knit all RS rows, purl all WS rows), using one strand each of A and B held together. TAKE TIME TO CHECK YOUR GAUGE.

Knit
HAT
Using two strands of B, cast on 40 sts. (P 1 row, k 1 row) 3 times. With one strand each of A and B, (k 1 row, p 1 row) 4 times.

Shape crown
Row 1 (RS): K3; (k2tog, k6) 4 times, k2tog, k3.
Row 2: P35.
Row 3: K3; (k2tog, k5) 4 times, k2tog, k2.
Row 4: P30.
Row 5: K3; (k2tog, k4) 4 times, k2tog, k1.
Row 6: P25.
Row 7: K3; (k2tog, k3) 4 times, k2tog.
Row 8: P20.
Row 9: K3; (k2tog, k2) 3 times, k2tog, k3.
Row 10: P16.
Row 11: K3; (k2tog, k1) 3 times, k2tog, k2.

Row 12: P12.
Row 13: (K2tog) across.
Row 14: P6.
   Leaving long strands for sewing, cut yarn. Thread strands through yarn needle and back through rem sts. Pull up tightly to close opening. Fold cuff up as shown in the photo, *opposite.* Sew seam to top of cuff; then use B only to sew cuff seam.

MUFF
Using one strand each of A and B, cast on 30 sts.
Rows 1–6: (P 1 row, k 1 row) 3 times.
Rows 7–9: With two strands of B, k 1 row, p 1 row, k 1 row.
Row 10: With one strand each of A and B, k 1 row.
   Rep Rows 1–10 for 4 times total, then rep Rows 1–9 once more.

Last row: With one strand each of A and B, bind off loosely.

FINISHING
Make trim
With RS facing and using two strands of B, pick up and k35 sts evenly spaced along one side edge. Bind off.
   Sew short ends of cast-on edge to bound-off edge, also connecting trim edge. Take the untrimmed edge inside the tube for double thickness. Sew in place just beneath the trim.

Handle
Using two strands of B, cast on 30 sts. Bind off. Sew in place near the seam at the trimmed edge.

Garden-variety granny squares spiff up a pair of jeans and a pullover shirt, giving everyday separates a fresh, coordinated look. An embroidered border of blanket stitches in the same thread trims the set neatly.

Designed by *Knit It!* **Staff**
Photographed by **Greg Scheidemann**

garden
OF GRANNIES
EMBELLISHEMENTS

Sizes

Finished Measurements

Large Granny Square: 2" square
Small Granny Square: 1½" square

Materials

Yarns

Sport weight, 150 yds. (137 m) *each* in light pink, yellow, and white

Hooks & Extras

- Size D/3 (3.25 mm) crochet hook OR SIZE NEEDED TO OBTAIN GAUGE
- Blunt-end yarn needle

Notes

Gauge

For jeans: 1 motif = 2" square (5 cm). For shirt: 1 motif = 1½" square (3.8 cm). TAKE TIME TO CHECK YOUR GAUGE.

Crochet

GRANNY SQUARE MOTIFS

Large Granny Square

Foundation Ring: Using any color, ch 5; join to beg ch with sl st to form a ring.

Rnd 1 (RS): Ch 3, 2 dc in ring; (ch 2, 3 dc in ring) 3 times, ch 2; join with sl st in top of beg ch-3. Fasten off.

Rnd 2: With RS facing, join a 2nd color in 2nd ch-2 sp before join of rnd just completed. Ch 3, in same sp work 2 dc, ch 2, 3 dc—first corner made. (Ch 1, in next ch-2 sp work 3 dc, ch 2, and 3 dc—corner made) 3 times; ch 1, join with sl st to top of beg ch-3. Fasten off.

Rnd 3: With RS facing, join 3rd color in 2nd ch-2 sp before join of rnd just completed and work a first corner (refer to instructions for Rnd 2); (ch 1, in next ch-1 sp make 3 dc; ch 1, in next ch-2 sp make a corner (see Rnd 2) 3 times; ch 1, work 3 dc in next ch-1 sp; ch 1, join with sl st to top of beg ch-3. Fasten off.

Small Granny Square

Work as for Large Granny Square, omitting Rnd 3.

Note: You may need to make fewer or more squares, depending on the size and style of your garments.

Work blanket stitches around Shirt neckline and cuffs and around Jeans' cuffs, using light pink yarn.

JEANS

Make 16 Large Granny Squares, using 3 colors for each square and varying the color sequences.

Pin 8 of the squares to each pant leg 1" above the hem; sew in place.

SHIRT

Make 22 Small Granny Squares: 11 with white centers, 11 with light pink centers.

Alternating colors, pin 8 of the squares around each sleeve 1" above the lower edge; sew in place.

Pin 3 squares on each side of the neck edge, alternating colors, and sew in place.

This sweater-and-purse combo is sweet in both look and color. The pink sweater is trimmed in stockinette stripes of purple and green, and the coordinating purse features a twisted strap and funky button closure.

Designed by **Aliza Gebiner**   Photographed by **Jay Wilde**

cotton-candy
CARDIGAN & PURSE

■■□□ Easy

Sizes

4 (6, 8) years

Instructions are written for the smallest size with changes for larger sizes given in parentheses. When only one number is given, it applies to all sizes.

Note: For ease in working, circle all numbers pertaining to the size you're knitting.

Finished Measurements

Cardigan
Chest = 26 (31, 34)"
Length (Back) = 15 (16, 18)"

Purse
Width: 10"; Length: 7"
Strap length: 34", not including side-edge fringes.

Materials

Yarns

Bulky weight (nubby), 370 yds. (335 m)— all sizes—in light pink (MC)

Bulky weight 185 yds. (167 m)—all sizes—*each* in light green (A) and lavender (B)

Needles & Extras

- Size 9 (5.5 mm) needles OR SIZE NEEDED TO OBTAIN GAUGE
- Size 7 (4.5 mm) double-pointed needles (dpns)
- Stitch holders
- Blunt-end yarn needle
- Four buttons about 1" diameter (three for the cardiagn, one for the purse)

Notes

Gauge

14 sts and 22 rows = 4" (10 cm) in St st (knit all RS rows, purl all WS rows). TAKE TIME TO CHECK YOUR GAUGE.

For the Purse, use leftover yarns from the Cardigan and size 9 (5.5 mm) needles.

Special Abbreviations

inc = Knit into the front loop, then into back loop of same stitch.

Knit

CARDIGAN
BACK

Using larger needles and B, cast on 46 (54, 60) sts. Cont with B and beg with WS row, work in St st for 4 rows.
Next row (WS): Knit. This will form purl turning ridge on RS of work. Work next 4 rows in St st (k1 row, p 1 row).

Change to MC and work even in St st until piece measures 15 (16, 18)" from purl row turning ridge. Bind off 12 (16, 19) sts for shoulder, work across next 22 (22, 22) sts (including 1 st already on RH needle from bind-off), then place these sts on holder for back of neck; bind off rem 12 (16, 19) sts for other shoulder.

RIGHT FRONT

Note: The self-facing is knit at the same time as the front. On every RS row, beg with K4, sl 1, then cont in pat. P these same 5 sts at the end of WS rows.

Using larger needles and B, cast on 28 (32, 35) sts. Beg with WS row and keeping the first 5 sts as self-facing, work 4 rows in St st.

Next row (WS): Knit. This will form purl-st turning ridge on RS of work. Work next 4 rows in St st.

Next RS row: Change to MC and work in St st until piece measures 13 (14, 16)" from turning ridge, ending with a WS row.

Shape neck

Row 1 (RS): Starting at beg of row, bind off 5 self-facing sts and 4 front sts, k to end of row.

Rows 2, 4, and 6: Purl.

Row 3: Bind off 3 sts, k to end of row.

Row 5: Bind off 2 sts, k to end of row.

Row 7: Bind off 2 sts, k to end of row.

Row 8: Purl.

Work even in St st on rem sts until piece measures same as Back. Bind off rem 12 (16, 19) sts.

LEFT FRONT

Work same as Right Front, reversing all shaping.

SLEEVE (MAKE 2)

Using larger needles and B, cast on 40 (46, 48) sts. Beg with WS row, work 4 rows in St st.

Next row (WS): Knit. This will form turning ridge on RS of work. Work 2 rows in St st. *Join A, work next 2 rows in St st. Change to B, work 2 rows in St st. Rep from * once more, then work 2 more rows in A. Join MC and work 2 rows.

Next Inc row (RS): Inc in first st, k across row to last st, work inc—42 (48, 50) sts. Work even until Sleeve measures 2½" from Inc row, then rep Inc row— 44 (50, 52) sts. Work even in St st until Sleeve measures 11 (12, 13½)" from turning ridge. Bind off all sts.

POCKET (MAKE 2)

Using larger needles and A, cast on 20 sts. Beg with WS row, work 2 rows St st.

Next row (WS): Knit (turning ridge). *Work 2 rows St st with A, 2 rows with B. Rep from * 3 more times. Bind off all sts with B.

BUTTON LOOP (MAKE 3)

With smaller dpns and B, cast on 6 sts. Beg with RS row, work 4 rows St st.

Next row (RS): K3, place next 3 sts on holder.

Work I-cord on 3 sts as foll: *With RS facing, slide 3 sts to other end of needle (yarn will be at opposite end); pull yarn snugly across back of work to the first st, k3; do not turn. Rep from * 10 more times. Remove rem 3 sts from holder and place on dpn with RS facing. Align both needles with RS tog; using 3rd dpn, join sts with 3-needle bind-off (see *page 268*). Make 2 more Button Loops the same way.

COLLAR

Join shoulders tog using backstitch seam. Fold front facings to WS and sl st facing to Cardigan across top edge. Using larger needles and with RS of Cardigan facing, pick up (do not knit) 15 loops along Cardigan Right Front neck, 20 (22, 22) Back neck sts from holder, 15 loops along Left Front neck—50 (52, 52) sts. With WS of Cardigan (RS of Collar) facing, *join B, k 1 row, p 1 row. Join A, k 1 row, p 1 row*; rep from * to * 3 more times (16 rows), then end with 1 row B. Bind off knitwise on WS.

FINISHING

Sew Sleeves to Cardigan; sew sleeve seams, then fold sleeve hem to WS and whipstitch in place. Sew side seams.

Lower edge facing

Fold hem to WS at turning ridge and whipstitch in place.

Front facings

On WS of Cardigan, whipstitch facing edge to Cardigan.

Attach Pockets

Fold each Pocket top facing to WS at turning ridge and whipstitch to Pocket. Place WS of Pockets, with facing at top, on RS of Cardigan fronts, centered between center front edges and side seams, about 2" up from lower edge, and stitch in place around 3 sides.

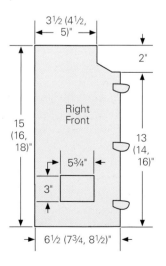

3½ (4½, 5)"
Right Front
2"
15 (16, 18)"
13 (14, 16)"
5¾"
3"
6½ (7¾, 8½)"

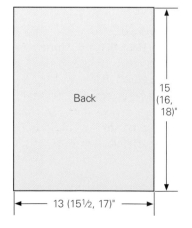

Back
15 (16, 18)"
13 (15½, 17)"

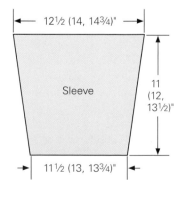

12½ (14, 14¾)"
Sleeve
11 (12, 13½)"
11½ (13, 13¾)"

Button Loops

On the Right Front, place the button Loops along the center front edge, beg about ½" down from neck. Stitch around the 4-row block of St st, leaving the I-cord loop free to close around the button. Sew buttons on Left Front, positioning them to align with Button Loops. Weave in loose ends.

PURSE

Using larger needles and B, cast on 70 sts. Cont with B, and beg with WS row, work 4 rows in St st.

Next row (WS): Knit (creates turning ridge). Work 2 rows in St st.

Next row (RS): *Join A, work 2 rows St st. Join B, work 2 rows St st. Rep from * 8 more times. Bind off knitwise on WS.

 With RS facing, backstitch center back seam. Turn Purse to RS, place seam at center back, and smooth Purse out flat at top and bottom edges.

 Close bottom with backstitch seam along bound-off edge. The seam will be visible on the RS.

Complete top opening

Fold top facing to WS of Purse at turning ridge and whipstitch in place.

Tab: With RS of Purse facing and using B, pick up and k8 sts centered across the turning ridge at the back seam. Beg with WS row, work in St st until tab measures about 3" long.

Buttonhole

On next RS row, k2, bind off 4, k to end.

Next row (WS): P2; using the backward loop method, cast on 4 sts, p2—8 sts. Work 4 rows in St st.

Shape tab end

Next row (RS): *K1, ssk, k to last 3 sts, k2tog, k1.

Next row: Purl**. Rep from * to ** once more—4 sts rem. Bind off. Fold tab over front as if to close Purse, locate position for button to align with button-hole, and attach button to Purse front.

STRAP

Cut 4 strands each of MC, A, and B, each about 50" long. Separate strands into 2 groups of 6 strands (2 strands of each color).

 Working with one group of strands, loosely tie the 6 strands tog at each end using an overhand knot. Loop one end over a doorknob, and insert knitting needle through center at other end. Twist the knitting needle end clockwise until the strands form a tightly twisted cord.

 Secure the twist by knotting both ends tog temporarily. Work the other set of 6 strands the same. Holding onto the twist, untie all the temporary knots at one end of each cord and reknot both cords tog about 3" from one end. Holding the other end of both cords tightly, allow both cords to twist around each other. Help them along if necessary by twisting them by hand.

 Knot both cords tog about 3" from this end. Both cords are now twisted tog to form one cord and are secured at each end with an overhand knot. Sew one knot to the Purse top at one side edge; sew the other end to the other side edge. Smooth out the loose 3"-strand ends and tie an overhand knot in each to prevent raveling.

Just right for a beloved little girl, this three-button cardigan requires a fair amount of expertise. The pattern very cleverly simulates woven ribbons throughout and features ruffled edges.

girl's ruffled cardigan

Designed by **Linda Medina**
Photographed by **Greg Scheidemann**

▬▬ ▬ ▬ ▬ **Experienced**

Sizes

18 (24, 2T, 4T) months
Instructions are written for the smallest size with changes for larger sizes given in parentheses. When only one number is given, it applies to all sizes.
Note: For ease in working, circle all numbers pertaining to the size you're knitting.

Finished Measurements
Chest = 22 (23, 24, 26)"
Length (Back before ruffle) = 11 (12, 13, 14)"

Materials

Yarns
Light worsted weight, 410 (410, 615, 615) yds. [372 (372, 558, 588) m] *each* in blue (A) and bright chartreuse (B)

Light worsted weight, 205 (205, 410,410) yds. [186 (186, 372, 372) m] in magenta (C)

Light worsted weight, 205 yds. (186 m)—all sizes—in white (D)

Needles & Extras
• Size 5 (3.75 mm) 32" circular needle OR SIZE NEEDED TO OBTAIN GAUGE
• Size D (3.25 mm) crochet hook
• Blunt-end yarn needle
• 4 stitch holders
• Three ⅝"-diameter buttons

Notes

Gauge
23 sts and 40 rows = 4" (10 cm) in Woven Ribbons pat. TAKE TIME TO CHECK YOUR GAUGE.

Special Abbreviations
ch-2 picot = Chain 2, slip st into second chain from hook.
skp = Slip 1, k1, pass slipped st over.

Knit

PATTERN STITCHES
Ruffle Pattern (multiple of 12 sts + 3 sts at beg; multiple of 4 sts + 3 at end of 9-row rep)
Row 1 (RS): P3, *k9, p3; rep from * across.
Row 2: K3, *p9, k3; rep from * across.
Row 3: P3, *skp, k5, k2tog, p3; rep from * across—10 sts + 3.
Row 4: K3, *p7, k3; rep from * across.

Row 5: P3, *skp, k3, k2tog, p3; rep from * across—8 sts + 3.
Row 6: K3, *p5, k3; rep from * across.
Row 7: P3, *skp, k1, k2tog, p3; rep from * across—6 sts + 3.
Row 8: K3, *p3, k3; rep from * across.
Row 9: P3, *sl 1, k2tog, psso, p3; rep from * across—4 sts + 3.
 Work Rows 1–9 for Ruffle pat.

Woven Ribbons Pattern
(multiple of 4 sts; 20-row rep)
Note: Slip sts pwise; slip sts wyib on RS rows; slip sts wyif on WS rows; carry A along side edges, attach and cut other colors for each section.
Row 1 (RS): Using A, knit.
Row 2: Using A, purl.
Row 3: Using D, *k3, sl 1; rep from * across.

Row 4: Using D, *sl 1, k3; rep from * across.

Rows 5 and 6: Rep Rows 1 and 2 using A.

Row 7: Using B, k1, *sl 1, k3; rep from * to last 3 sts, sl 1, k2.

Row 8: Using B, k2, *sl 1, k3; rep from * to last 2 sts, sl 1, k 1.

Rows 9 and 10: Rep Rows 7 and 8.

Rows 11–16: Rep Rows 1–6.

Rows 17–20: Using C, rep Row 7–10.

Rep Rows 1–20 for Woven Ribbons pat.

BODY

Note: Cardigan is worked back and forth in rows on circular needle and as one piece from lower edge to armholes.

Ruffle

Using B, cast on 387 (411, 423, 447) sts. Work Rows 1–9 of Ruffle pat—131 (139, 143, 151) sts. Cut yarn. Slide sts to opposite end of needle to prepare for

a RS row again. Attach C.

Row 1 (RS): K2tog, k to last 2 sts, k2tog—129 (137, 141, 149) sts.

Row 2: K2tog, k to end—128 (136, 140, 148) sts.

Cut C; attach A and work Woven Ribbons pat until piece measures 6 (6½, 7, 7½)" from cast-on edge, end with a WS row.

Divide for Fronts and Back

Next row (RS): Keeping to Woven Ribbons pat, work 32 (34, 35, 37) sts for Right Front, sl these sts to holder; work next 64 (68, 70, 74) sts for Back, sl these sts to second holder—32 (34, 35, 37) sts rem for Left Front.

LEFT FRONT
Shape armhole

Row 1 (RS): Keeping to Woven Ribbons pat, work across 32 (34, 35, 37) sts on needle.

Row 2: Work to last 2 sts, p2tog—31 (33, 34, 36) sts.

Rows 3 and 4 : Rep Rows 1 and 2—30 (32, 33, 35) sts.

Work even until piece measures 2½ (2½, 3, 3)" from beg of armhole shaping, ending with a RS row at neck edge.

Shape neck

Row 1 (WS): Bind off 9 (10, 10, 11) sts, work across row—21 (22, 23, 24) sts.

Row 2: Work across row.

Row 3: Work 2 sts tog, work even across row—20 (21, 22, 23) sts.

Rep Rows 2–3 five times—15 (16, 17, 18) sts. Work even until piece measures 11 (12, 13, 14)" from cast-on edge; cut yarn; sl sts onto holder.

BACK

Slip 64 (68, 70, 74) Back sts onto needle. With WS facing, attach yarn for next pat row.

Row 1 (WS): Work 2 sts tog at beg and end of row—62 (66, 68, 72) sts.

Row 2: Work even.

Rep Rows 1 and 2 once—60 (64, 66, 70) sts.

Work even until piece measures 10½ (11½, 12½, 13½)" from cast-on edge, ending with a WS row.

Shape neck

Next row (RS): Work 19 (20, 21, 22) sts, sl these sts to holder for right shoulder; bind off 22 (24, 24, 26) sts for Back neck.

Work across rem 19 (20, 21, 22) sts for left shoulder.

Shape left shoulder

Row 1 (WS): Work to last 2 sts, dec 1 st at neck edge—18 (19, 20, 21) sts.

Row 2: Dec 1 st, work to end of row—17 (18, 19, 20) sts.

Rows 3 and 4: Rep Rows 1 and 2—15 (16, 17, 18) sts.

Row 5: Work even across sts.

Sl sts to holder for left shoulder.

Right shoulder

Sl right shoulder sts to needle ready for a WS row. Work as for left shoulder, reversing shaping—sl rem 15 (16, 17, 18) sts to holder for right shoulder.

RIGHT FRONT

Sl 32 (34, 35, 37) Right Front sts onto needle ready for a WS row; attach yarn at armhole edge.

Shape armhole

Row 1 (WS): Work 2 sts tog, work to end—31 (33, 34, 36) sts.
Row 2: Work even.
Rows 3 and 4: Rep Rows 1 and 2—30 (32, 33, 35) sts.

Work even until piece measures 2½ (2½, 3, 3)" from beg of armhole shaping with a WS row at neck edge.

Shape neck

Row 1 (RS): Bind off 9 (10, 10, 11) sts, work across row—21 (22, 23, 24) sts.
Row 2: Work across row.
Row 3: Work 2 sts tog, work across row—20 (21, 22, 23) sts.

Rep Rows 2–3 five times—15 (16, 17, 18) sts. Work even until piece measures 11 (12, 13, 14)" from cast-on edge; cut yarn; sl sts onto holder.

SLEEVE (MAKE 2)
Ruffle

Using B, cast on 111 (123, 123, 135) sts. Work Rows 1–9 of Ruffle pat—39 (43, 43, 47) sts. Cut yarn. Slide sts to opposite end of needle to work a RS row again. Attach C.
Row 1 (RS): Inc 1 st, k across—40 (44, 44, 48) sts.
Row 2: Knit.

Change to A and begin Woven Ribbons pat.
Row 1: Work even.

Cont in pat, inc 1 st at beg and end of every 5 (6, 6, 8) rows 10 (10, 12, 12) times—60 (64, 68, 72) sts.

Work even until Sleeve measures 7 (7½, 8, 9½)" from cast-on edge, ending with a WS row.

Shape cap

Row 1 (RS): Dec 1 st at beg and end of row—58 (62, 66, 70) sts.
Row 2: Work even.

Rep Rows 1 and 2 twice—54 (58, 62, 66) sts.

Work 4 rows even; bind off all sts.

COLLAR

Using C, cast on 118 (126, 130, 138) sts.
Row 1: Knit.
Row 2: Knit, inc 1 in 29th (31st, 32nd, 35th) st and in 89th (91st, 92nd, 95th) st—120 (128, 132, 140) sts.
Row 3: Knit, inc 1 in 30th (32nd, 33rd, 36th) st and in 90th (92nd, 93rd, 96th) st—122 (130, 134, 142) sts.
Row 4: Knit, inc 1 in 31st (33rd, 34th, 37th) st and in 91st (93rd, 94th, 97th) st—124 (132, 136, 144) sts.
Row 5: Knit, dec 1 st at beg and end of row—122 (130, 134, 142) sts.
Row 6: Knit.
Rows 7–10: Rep Rows 5 and 6 twice—118 (126, 130, 138) sts.
Rows 11 and 12: Rep Row 5 twice—114 (122, 126, 134) sts.

Bind off all sts.

FINISHING

Join shoulder seams using 3-needle bind-off (see *page 268*). Set in Sleeves; sew sleeve seams.

Attach collar

Fold long edge of Collar in half; mark center using pin for center Back. Fold each half-section in half; mark folds with pins for shoulder seams. Fold Back neck edge in half; mark center with pin.

With RS of Collar and Body facing, pin cast-on edge of Collar to Cardigan, matching Collar pins to shoulder seams and center Back edge (stretch or gather to fit if necessary).

With RS facing and using C and crochet hook, sc Collar to Body, working through both thicknesses. Do not fasten off.

Collar edging

Cont along outer edge of Collar, work 2 sl sts in Collar edge, *ch 2-picot, work 3 sl sts along Collar edge, rep from * along outer Collar edge. Fasten off.

Left front edging

Using A and crochet hook, beg at neck edge with RS facing and sc evenly down front edge ending at top of ruffle. Fasten off.

Right front button-loop edging

Row 1 (RS): Beg at top of ruffle, work sc evenly up front edge, ending at neck edge, ch 1, turn.
Row 2: Sc in first sc, *ch 3, sk 2 sc, sc in next 3 (4, 5, 6) sc, rep from * twice; sc in rem sc. Fasten off.

Sew buttons to Left Front opposite button loops.

2½ (2¾, 3, 3¼)"

5¼ (5½, 5½, 6)"

10½ (11, 11¾, 12½)"

1"

11 (12, 13, 14)"

5 (5½, 6, 6½)"

Left Front

Back

Right Front

6 (6½, 7, 7½)"

Sleeve

7 (7½, 8, 9½)"

1½"

22 (23, 24, 26)"

COZY
BOY'S
VEST

Add a cozy element to a little boy's wardrobe by layering this zip-up vest over a shirt. It boasts side pockets for stashing stuff and a stand-up collar for extra warmth.

Designed by **Svetlana Avrakh**
Photographed by **Greg Scheidemann**

Sizes

4 (6, 8, 10) years
Instructions are written for the smallest size with changes for larger sizes given in parentheses. When only one number is given, it applies to all sizes.

Note: For ease in working, circle all numbers pertaining to the size you're crocheting.

Finished Measurements
Chest = 27½ (29½, 31, 33)"
Length (Back) = 13 (15½, 17½, 18½)"

Materials

Yarns
Super bulky weight, 272 (340, 340, 408) yds. [248 (310, 310, 372) m] in denim

6 SUPER BULKY

Hooks & Extras
- Size L/11 (8 mm) crochet hook OR SIZE NEEDED TO OBTAIN GAUGE
- One separating zipper
- Blunt-end yarn needle
- Three ⅝"-diameter buttons

Notes

Gauge
7 sc and 8 rows = 4" (10 cm).
TAKE TIME TO CHECK YOUR GAUGE.

Special Abbreviations
sc2tog = [Insert hook in next st and draw up a loop (lp)] twice, yarn over and draw through all 3 lps on hook.

Crochet

BACK
Ch 25 (27, 28, 30).
Row 1 (RS): Sc in 2nd ch from hook and in each ch to end—24 (26, 27, 29) sts; turn.
Row 2: Ch 1, sc in each sc to end.
Rep Row 2 until Back measures 7½ (9½, 11, 12)" from beg, ending with a WS row.

Shape armholes
Next row: Sl st in first 3 sts; ch 1, sc2tog over same st as last sl st and next sc, sc in each sc to last 4 sc, sc2tog over next 2 sc—18 (20, 21, 23) sts; turn.
Next row: Ch 1, sc2tog over first 2 sc, sc in each sc to last 2 sc, sc2tog over last 2 sc, turn. Rep last row once more—14 (16, 17, 19) sts.
Next row: Ch 1, sc in each sc to end, turn. Rep last row until armhole measures 5½ (6, 6½, 6½)", ending with a WS row; fasten off. Place markers 3 sts in along top edge for shoulders on each side.

LEFT FRONT
Ch 13 (15, 15, 16).
Row 1 (RS): Sc in 2nd ch from hook and in each ch to end—12 (14, 14, 15) sts; turn.
Row 2: Ch 1, sc in each sc to end of row. Rep Row 2 until Left Front measures 7½ (9½, 11, 12)" from beg, ending with a WS row; turn.

Shape armhole
Next row (RS): Sl st in first 3 sts; ch 1, sc2tog over same st as last sl st and next sc, sc in each sc to end; turn—9 (11, 11, 12) sts.
Next row: Ch 1, sc in each sc to last 2 sc, sc2tog over next 2 sc; turn.
Next row: Ch 1, sc2tog over first 2 sc, sc in each sc to end—7 (9, 9, 10) sts; turn.
Next row: Ch 1, sc in each sc to end; turn. Rep last row until armhole measures 6 rows less than Back; end at shoulder edge.

Shape neck
Next row (RS): Ch 1, sc in each sc to last 4 (5, 5, 6) sc, sc2tog over next 2 sts—4 (5, 5, 5) sts; turn.
Next row: Ch 1, sc2tog over first 2 sts, sc in each sc to end—3 (4, 4, 4) sts; turn.

Sizes 6, 8, and 10 only:
Next row: Ch 1, sc in each sc to last 2 sts, sc2tog over last 2 sts—3 (3, 3) sts; turn.

All Sizes:
Work 4 (3, 3, 3) rows even; fasten off.

RIGHT FRONT
Work same as Left Front to armhole.

Shape armhole
Next row (RS): Ch 1, sc in each sc to last 4 sc, sc2tog over next 2 sc—9 (11, 11, 12) sts; turn.
Next row: Ch 1, sc2tog over first 2 sts, sc in each sc to end.

Next row: Ch 1, sc in each sc to last 2 sts, sc2tog over next 2 sts—7 (9, 9, 10) sts; turn.

Next row: Ch 1, sc in each sc to end; turn.

Rep last row until armhole measures 6 rows less than Back; fasten off.

Shape neck

Next row (RS): Sk first 2 (3, 3, 4) sc, join yarn with sl st in next sc; ch 1, sc2tog over first 2 sts, sc in each sc to end—4 (5, 5, 5) sts; turn.

Next row: Ch 1, sc in each sc to last 2 sts, sc2tog over last 2 sts—3 (4, 4, 4); turn.

Sizes 6, 8, and 10 only:

Next row: Ch 1, sc2tog over first 2 sts, sc in each sc to end—3 (3, 3) sts; turn.

All sizes:

Work 4 (3, 3, 3) rows even; fasten off.

POCKET (MAKE 2)

Ch 10.

Row 1: Sc in 2nd ch from hook and in each ch to end—9 sts; turn.

Row 2: Ch 1, sc in each sc to end; turn.

Rep last row 8 more times; fasten off. Place Pockets 2 rows from lower edge and align with Fronts of Vest. Sew along top, 1 st in from zipper edge and bottom edges; sew outer sides of Pockets 2" up from bottom edge.

FINISHING

Collar

Sew shoulder seams. With RS facing, join yarn with sl st at Right Front edge. Ch 1, work 9 sc along Right Front neck edge, sc in 8 (10, 11, 13) sc across Back neck edge, 9 sc along Left Front neck edge—26 (28, 29, 31) sts; turn.

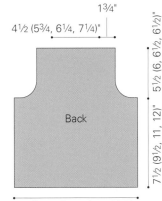

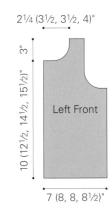

13/4"

41/2 (53/4, 61/4, 71/4)"

51/2 (6, 61/2, 61/2)"

71/2 (91/2, 11, 12)"

Back

13¾ (14¾, 15½, 16½)"

21/4 (31/2, 31/2, 4)"

3"

10 (12½, 14½, 15½)"

Left Front

7 (8, 8, 8½)"

Next row: Ch 1, sc in each sc to end; turn. Rep last row 5 more times; fasten off.

Sew side seams. Sew in zipper from foundation ch to Row 3 of collar. Fold collar in half along Row 3 to WS and sew in place, enclosing zipper.

Armhole edging

Sew side seams. Join yarn with sl st to underarm seam. Ch 1, sc evenly around armhole edge. Join with sl st to first sc; fasten off. Rep for other armhole.

Kids and misplaced mittens go hand in hand—but with this trio of colorfully coordinated striped mittens, you'll always be ready with a spare. All three mittens match a striped rolled-brim cap with a fun tasseled pom-pom atop.

Designed by **Elena Malo**
Photographed by **Akin Girav**

STRIPED
CAP & MITTENS

Sizes
One size fits child 4–6 years old.

Materials
Yarns
Bulky weight (nubby), 185 yds. (167 m) *each* in red (A), green (B), blue (C), and light yellow (D)

5 BULKY

Needles & Extras
• Sizes 7 (4.5 mm) and 9 (5 mm) needles OR SIZE NEEDED TO OBTAIN GAUGE
• Stitch markers
• Stitch holder (short)
• Blunt-end yarn needle

Notes
Gauge
15 sts and 22 rows = 4" (10 cm) over St st (knit all RS rows, purl all WS rows) with larger needles. TAKE TIME TO CHECK YOUR GAUGE.

Special Abbreviations
M1 (make one stitch) = Work an increase by lifting the horizontal thread lying between the needles; insert the tip of the left-hand needle from front to back under the thread, place it onto the left-hand needle; knit the stitch through the back loop.

Knit
PATTERN STITCHES
Stripe Pattern (worked in St st)
4 rows with A
8 rows with B
4 rows with D
4 rows with B
4 rows with C
4 rows with B

CAP
Using larger needles and B, cast on 67 sts.
Row 1 (WS): Purl.
Row 2: Knit.
  Rep Rows 1 and 2 until piece measures 2½", ending with a WS row.
  Beg Stripe pat and work for 18 rows.
  Cont with Stripe pat and shape crown as foll:
Row 1 (RS): K1, *k2tog, k5; rep from * to last 3 sts, k2tog, k1—57 sts.
Row 2 and all WS rows: Purl.
Row 3: K1, *k2tog, k4; rep from * to last 2 sts, k2—48 sts.
Row 5: K1, *k2tog, k3; rep from * to last 2 sts, k2—39 sts.

Row 7: K1, *k2tog, k2; rep from * to last 2 sts, k2—30 sts.
Row 9: K1, *k2tog, k1; rep from * to last 2 sts, k2tog—20 sts.
Row 11: *K2tog; rep from * to end—10 sts.
  P 1 row. Fasten off, leaving a 6" tail. Thread tail through yarn needle, then through rem sts; pull tightly to gather and fasten securely.

FINISHING
Sew seam, reversing seam for lower 2½" for roll-back on lower edge.

Tie
Cut 2-yd. strands of A, B, C, and D. Tightly twist strands of A and D tog, then strands of B and C. Twist these 2 double strands tog until strands begin to curl; then fold all strands in half to form twisted cord. Tie cord into bow and sew knot of bow to top of Cap as shown, *opposite.*

Pom-pom (MAKE 2)
Wind all 4 colors tog around a 2" piece of cardboard approx 20 times. Tie a separate strand tightly around center. Cut ends. Trim with sharp scissors until 1" in diameter. Sew one pom-pom to each end of the twisted cord.

MITTEN (MAKE 3)
Note: Written for Version 1. Directions for Versions 2 and 3 are shown in parentheses. When only one direction is given, it applies to all versions.
  Using smaller needles and B (C, A), cast on 24 sts. Work 15 rows in k1, p1 ribbing, ending with a RS row and inc 1 st in center of last row—25 sts.
  Change to larger needles and purl 1 row.
  Change to C (A, D) and work 4 rows St st.
  Change to B (C, A) and shape thumb gusset as foll:
Row 1 (RS): K12, place marker (pm), make 1 (M1), k1, M1, pm, k12.
Row 2: Purl.
Row 3: K to marker, slip marker (sm), M1, k to next marker, M1, sm, k to end.

Rep last 2 rows until there are 11 sts between markers.

Change to D (B, C).

Next row (RS): K12, remove markers and place next 11 sts on stitch holder, M1, k last 12 sts—25 sts rem.

Work even for 3 more rows.

Change to B (C, A) and work 4 rows, ending with a WS row and placing a marker on each side of center st.

Change to A (D, B) and shape top.

Row 1 (RS): K1, ssk, k to within 2 sts of marker, k2tog, sm, k1, sm, ssk, k to last 3 sts, k2tog, k1.

Row 2: Purl.

Rep last 2 rows once more.

Change to B (C, A) and rep last 2 rows twice more.

Next row: K1, (k2tog) 4 times.

Next row: Purl. Fasten off, leaving a tail. Thread tail through yarn needle, then through rem sts; pull tightly to gather and fasten securely.

Shape thumb

Transfer 11 sts from holder to larger needle. With WS facing, join yarn and p across; cast on 1 st at end of row—12 sts. Work 4 sts even in St st, beg with a k row.

Work even on these 12 sts for 4 rows.

Next row: (K2tog) 6 times.

Next row: Purl. Fasten off, leaving a tail. Thread tail through yarn needle, then through rem sts; pull tightly to gather and fasten securely. Sew thumb seam and close opening beneath thumb. Sew side seam. Weave in loose ends.

VERSION 1

VERSION 2

VERSION 3

She'll be pretty as
a posy when she dons
this hat-and-purse
combo. Stitched
in single crochet and
chain stitches, both
accessories feature
bright, happy flowers.

Designed by **Michele Maks Thompson**
Photographed by **Greg Scheidemann**

flower
power coordinates

■■■▢▢ Easy

Sizes
Youth S (M, L)
Instructions are written for the smallest size with changes for larger sizes given in parentheses. When only one number is given, it applies to all sizes.
Note: For ease in working, circle all numbers pertaining to the size you're crocheting.

Finished Measurements
Hat: Circumference = 17½ (18½, 20)"
Purse: 7½×8½"

Materials
Yarns (for both)
Bulky weight, 185 (185, 370) yds. [167 (167, 334) m] in blue (MC)

Bulky weight, 185 yds. (167 m) *each* in light green (A), pink (B), and yellow (C)

Hooks & Extras
- Size J/10 (6 mm) crochet hook OR SIZE NEEDED TO OBTAIN GAUGE
- Blunt-end yarn needle

Notes
Gauge
12 sc and 14 rows = 4" (10 cm). TAKE TIME TO CHECK YOUR GAUGE.

Crochet
HAT
Using MC, ch 3; join with sl st to form a ring.
Rnd 1: Ch 1, work 8 sc in ring; join with sl st in first sc.
Rnd 2: Ch 1, 2 sc in each sc around—16 sts; join.
Rnd 3: Ch 1, (sc in sc, 2 sc in next sc) around—24 sts; join.
Rnd 4: Ch 1, (sc in next 2 sc, 2 sc in next sc) around—32 sts; join.
Rnd 5: Ch 1, (sc in next 3 sc, 2 sc in next sc) around—40 sts; join.
Rnd 6: Ch 1, (sc in next 4 sc, 2 sc in next sc) around—48 sts; join.
Rnd 7: Ch 1, [sc in next 11 (5, 5) sc, 2 sc in next sc] around—52 (56, 56) sts; join.

Size L only:
Ch 1, (sc in next 13 sc, 2 sc in next sc) around—60 sts; join.

All sizes:
Rnd 1 (RS): With MC, ch 1, sc in 52 (56, 60) sts; join and turn.

Rnd 2 (WS): Ch 1, sc in 52 (56, 60) sts; join and turn. Rep Rows 1 and 2 for 1 (2, 2) more times. Fasten off.

Stripes
With RS facing, join A with sl st in first sc, ch 1, sc in same sc and in each sc across; turn.
Next Rnd: Ch 1, sc in each sc around. Fasten off.
　Rep last 2 rnds once with B, then once with C.

Brim
With RS facing, join MC and work 6 (7, 8) rnds of sc. Fasten off.

Flower I (make 2)
Using B, ch 3; join with sl st to form a ring.
Rnd 1 (RS): Ch 1, 6 sc in ring; join with sl st in first sc. Fasten off.
Rnd 2: With RS facing, join C with sl st in any sc; (ch 5, sl st in next sc) 6 times. Fasten off.

Flower II (make 1)
Using C, ch 3; join with sl st to form a ring.
Rnd 1 (RS): Ch 1, 10 sc in ring; join with sl st in first sc. Fasten off.
Rnd 2: With RS facing, join B with sl st in any sc; * ch 2—counts as hdc; 2 dc in same sc; in next sc work 2 dc and hdc, sl st in next sc; rep from * around—5 petals made. Fasten off.
　Sew flowers to side of Hat as shown in photograph, *opposite*.

PURSE
Base
Using MC, ch 17; sc in 2nd ch from hook and in each ch across—16 sts; turn.
Row 2: Ch 1, sc in each sc across; turn.
Rows 3 and 4: Rep Row 2.

Body
Rnd 1 (RS): Ch 1, sc in 16 sc, 3 sc along side of bottom, sc across 16 ch of foundation ch edge, 3 sc along other side—38 sc; join with sl st in first sc; turn.

Rnd 2 (WS): Ch 1, sc in each sc around; turn.

Rnd 3: Ch 1, sc in each sc around; turn.

Rep Rnds 2 and 3 until there are 18 total rnds, ending with Rnd 2.

Eyelets

Ch 5—counts as dc and ch 2; sk next sc, dc in next sc; (ch 2, sk next 2 sc, dc in next sc) around, ending ch 2, sk last 2 sc, sl st in 3rd ch of beg ch-5. Do not turn. Ch 1, (2 sc in ch-2 sp, sc in next dc) 12 times, 2 sc in last ch-2 sp—38 sc; join and turn. With WS facing, ch 1, sc in each sc around; join and fasten off.

Pocket

Using A, ch 13; sc in 2nd ch from hook and in each ch across—12 sts; turn.

Work evenly in sc over 12 sts until there are a total of 10 rows.

Make 3 sc in first sc for corner, sc across row until last st, make 3 sc in last st; sc evenly along next side, make 3 sc in first ch at beg ch edge, sc across beg ch until last ch, make 3 sc in last ch; sc evenly along rem side; sl st to top of first sc to join. Fasten off.

Sew pocket to side of Purse.

Purse flower

Using C, ch 3; join with sl st to form a ring.

Rnd 1: Ch 1, work 6 sc in ring; join with sl st to to first sc. Fasten off.

Rnd 2: With B, attach yarn in any sc, (ch 7, sl st in next sc) 6 times. Fasten off.

Sew purse flower in center of pocket.

Drawstring

With A, ch 70. Fasten off.

Join B in beg of ch with a sl st; then sl st in each ch across. Fasten off.

Join C in first color-B sl st then sl st in each sl st across. Fasten off.

Weave drawstring through eyelets. Tie overhand knots at each end of drawstring. Weave loose ends securely into knots.

Strap

Using MC, ch 100; sl st into 2nd ch and in each ch across. Fasten off.

Attach strap to Purse on each inside edge just under eyelet row.

As bright as a field of summer daisies, this breezy poncho consists of dozens of lacy chain-stitch petals. The pom-pom trims will bounce joyfully with every step your little girl takes.

Designed by **Joyce Nordstrom**
Photographed by **Greg Scheidemann**

daisy
PONCHO

Sizes

One size fits childen 4 to 6 years old.

Finished Measurement

Approx 10" from neck to edge

Materials

Yarns

Chunky, 270 yds. (246 m) in bright yellow (MC)

Light bulky weight, 135 yds. (123 m) in white (CC)

Hooks & Extras

• Size H/8 (5 mm) crochet hook OR SIZE NEEDED TO OBTAIN GAUGE
• Blunt-end yarn needle

Notes

Gauge

1 flower motif = 3¼" (8.25 cm), measuring from side to side.
TAKE TIME TO CHECK YOUR GAUGE.

Except for Motif #1, the motifs are not worked separately; they are joined to a preceding motif as you work the second round. Follow the Daisy Motif Chart, *opposite,* for their placement as you work. As you work the motifs, connect them in rows and assemble them from right to left. The motifs are made in a counterclockwise direction as you make and connect them to each other.

Crochet

DAISY MOTIF PATTERNS

Motif 1 (make 1)

Note: This motif forms the center front point. It is the only block that's completed without making any connections.

Rnd 1 (RS): Using CC, ch 2; work 8 sc in 2nd ch from hook; join with sl st in first sc. Fasten off.

Rnd 2: [Working in back lps, with RS facing, join MC in any sc, ch 13, sl st in same sc—first corner made; sl st in next sc, ch 9, sl st in same sc—side made, sl st in next sc]; * ch 13, sl st in same sc, sl st in next sc, ch 9, sl st in same sc, sl st in next sc; rep from * twice more. Sl st in same sc as beg corner. Fasten off.

Motif 2 (make 9)

Note: Motif 2 is joined on one side to each preceding motif. Make 6 motifs for Row 1.

Rnd 1: Same as Motif 1.

Rnd 2: Rep from [to] in Rnd 2 of Motif 1. Ch 6, sl st in ch-13 lp of Motif 1, ch 6, sl st in same st of Motif 2; sl st in next sc of Motif 2, ch 4, sl st in ch-9 lp of Motif 1, ch 4, sl st in same st of Motif 2, sl st in

next sc of Motif 2, ch 6, sl st in ch-13 lp of Motif 1, ch 6, sl st in same st and next sc of Motif 2. Complete motif as for Motif 1.

Motif 3 (make 10)

Note: In Row 2, Motif 3 connects to 2 motifs. Make 6 motifs for Row 2.

Rnd 1: Same as Motif 1.

Rnd 2: Rep from [to] in Rnd 2 of Motif 1. Ch 6, sl st in ch-13 of Motif 2, ch 6, sl st in same st of Motif 3, sl st in next sc of Motif 3, ch 4, sl st in ch-9 lp of Motif 2; ch 4, sl st in same st of Motif 3, sl st in next sc of Motif 3, ch 6, sl st in the sl st connection bet first and 2nd motifs, ch 6, sl st in same st of Motif 3, sl st in next sc of Motif 3—2 motif connections made; connect to side and corner of next motif, then complete motif as est with no more connections.

Half Motif 4 (make 2)

Note: Motif 4 makes the right shoulder of the poncho on Row 3 and the left shoulder on Row 4. It is one-half of a square and connects to top of Motif 3 on 2nd row and side of Motif 5 on Row 3.

Rnd 1 of Motif 4 on Row 3 (right shoulder): With CC, ch 2, 5 sc in first ch. Fasten off.

Join MC in first sc, ch 9, sl st in same sc, * sl st in next sc; ch 6, sl st in connecting st of ch-13 lp of Motif 3, ch 6, sl st in same sc of Motif 4, sl st in next sc, ch 4, sl st in ch-9 lp of next motif, ch 4, sl st in same sc of Motif 4; rep from * once more; sl st in next sc of Motif 4. Fasten off.

Rnd 1 of Motif 4 on Row 4 (left shoulder): With CC, ch 2, 5 sc in 2nd ch from hook. Fasten off.

Join MC in first sc, ch 4, and connect to ch-9 lp of Motif 5 as est, then connect to the sl st connection bet Motif 5 and Motif 3 in Rows 3 and 4. Cont to connect side and corner lps as est; work last ch-9 lp with no connections. Fasten off.

Three-quarter Motif 5 (make 2)

Note: This motif establishes the center V at the front and back. They are connected to Motifs 3 and 4 on Row 3. Follow the Daisy Motif Chart, *opposite,* as you connect them.

**Rnd 1 of first Motif 5 on
Row 3:** With CC, ch 2, work
7 sc in 2nd ch from hook. Fasten off.

Join MC in first sc and work the first
ch-9 lp (not connected); then connect the
next 5 lps as est, work the last ch-9 lp
(not connected). Fasten off.

Rnd 1 of second Motif 5 on Row 3:
With CC, ch 2, work 7 sc in 2nd ch from
hook. Fasten off.

Join MC in first sc and work first 3 lps
free, then work next 4 lps connected to
Motifs 3 and 4.

PONCHO

Row 1: Make Motif 1, then add 6 of
Motif 2.

Row 2: Join Motif 2 to Motif 1 along
one side, then join 6 of Motif 3, joining
2 sides of each to preceding motifs on
Rows 1 and 2.

Row 3: Join Motif 2 to Motif 2 along
one side, then join Motifs 3, 5, 4, and 5,
joining 2 sides of each to preceding
motifs on Rows 2 and 3.

Row 4: Join Motif 2 to Motif 2 along
one side, then add Motifs 3 and 4. When
you make Motif 4, note that the C side is
joined to the C side of Motif 5 in Row 3.

Row 5: Motif 6 is worked liked Motif 3,
except these 2 motifs are joined to each
other and at the same time connected
to the 2 motifs at end of Row 2 and to
Motif 5 at end of Row 3. Work the 2nd
Motif 6 (the one above Motif 3) before

working the first one. Note that it also
connects to side D of Motif 5 on Row 3
and side E of Motif 3 on Row 2.

The first Motif 6 connects to the sides
of Motifs 6 and 2 and along the D side
of Motif 3 of Row 2.

FINISHING
Border

Rnd 1: With RS facing, join MC with sl
st in any ch-9 lp along lower edge, (ch 5,
sc in sl st connection bet corner [ch-13]
lps, ch 5, sc in ch-9 lp) around, ending
ch 5, sc in sl st connection bet corner lps.
Rnd 2: Sc in first sc; * work 2 sc in next
ch-5 lp; in same lp work sl st, ch 3, and
sl st—picot made; work 2 sc in same lp;
**, sc in next sc; rep from * around,
ending last rep at **; join with sl st in
first sc. Fasten off.

Neck edging

With RS facing, join MC with sl st in the
sl st of any corner connection, (ch 1, sc,
ch 4, sl st in same sp); * 2 sc in side of
lp, sc in edge of center, (sc, ch 4, sl st)
in center of flower; sc in edge of center;
rep from * around, ending 2 sc in side of
lp; join with sl st in first sc. Fasten off.

Tie

Using double strand of MC, ch 85.
Fasten off. Weave through each ch-4 sp
along neck edge, beg and ending at center
front.

For the child's safety, try the Poncho on
the child, adjusting and tying the tie so
the garment easily pulls on and off.
Securely stitch the tie to the Poncho at
any point where the tie threads through
the edging to anchor the tie so it cannot
be pulled tighter.

Pom-pom (make 2)

Wind CC around the palm of your hand
50 times. With a separate CC strand,
tightly tie around center.

Cut and trim ends to form the pom-pom.
Sew to ends of ties.

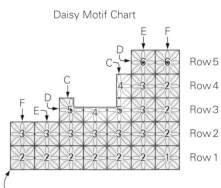

Daisy Motif Chart

Center back point

rainbow
CARDIGAN & BLUEBERRY PULLOVER

Boys and girls alike will love the comfortable styling of these versatile sweaters, which will hold up to even the most demanding playtimes. Using super bulky weight yarns, you can stitch both up in a flash.

Designed by **Traci Bunkers** (cardigan) and **Shanta Moitran** (pullover)
Photographed by **Jay Wilde**

Rainbow Cardigan ■■■□□ Easy

Sizes

18 months (2, 3, 4 years)
Instructions are written for the smallest size with changes for larger sizes given in parentheses. When only one number is given, it applies to all sizes.
Note: For ease in working, circle all numbers pertaining to the size you're knitting.

Finished Measurements
Chest (buttoned) = 24 (26, 28, 30)"
Length (Back before neckband) = 13 (14, 15, 16)"

Materials

Yarns
Super bulky weight, 252 (336, 336, 420) yds. [228 (304, 304, 380) m] in variegated multicolor

6 SUPER BULKY

Needles & Extras
- Size 15 (10 mm) knitting needles OR SIZE NEEDED TO OBTAIN GAUGE
- Size 15 (10 mm) 24" circular needle
- Five ¾"-diameter buttons
- Stitch markers
- Blunt-end yarn needle

Notes

Gauge
8 sts and 16 rows = 4" (10 cm) over Garter st (knit all rows).
TAKE TIME TO CHECK YOUR GAUGE.

Knit

Note: Body is worked in one piece to armholes, then divided for fronts and back.

BODY

Using circular needle, cast on 46 (50, 54, 58) sts.

Work 3 rows in k1, p1 ribbing.

Work back and forth on needle in Garter st (k every row) until piece measures 7 (8, 8½, 9)" from beg, ending with a WS row.

Divide for underarms

K8 (9, 9, 10) sts and place on holder for right front, bind off 6 (6, 8, 8) sts for underarm, k18 (20, 20, 22) sts for back and place on holder, bind off 6 (6, 8, 8) sts for underarm, k8 (9, 9, 10) for left front.

Shape left front

Cont in Garter st on 8 (9, 9, 10) sts for left front until armhole measures 4 (3½, 3½, 4)", ending at front edge.

Shape neck

Bind off 2 (2, 3, 3) sts at front edge of next row, then dec 1 st at neck edge on next 2 rows—4 (5, 4, 5) sts rem. Work even until armhole measures 6 (6, 6½, 7)". Bind off 4 (5, 4, 5) shoulder sts.

Shape back

With WS facing, join yarn to 18 (20, 20, 22) back sts and work even in Garter st until armhole measures 6 (6, 6½, 7)". Bind off.

Shape right front

With WS facing, join yarn to 8 (9, 9, 10) right front sts and work as for left front, reversing the shaping.

SLEEVE (MAKE 2)

Using straight needles, cast on 13 (13, 14, 15) sts. Beg with a k row, work 3 rows St st (k 1 row, p 1 row) for cuff. **Next row (WS):** Knit, inc 1 (1, 0, 1) st in center of row—14 (14, 14, 16) sts.

Cont in Garter st, inc 1 st each end of next and every 4th row 1 (1, 2, 2) time(s), then every 6th row 3 times—24 (24, 26, 28) sts. Work even until piece measures 9 (9¾, 10½, 11)" with cuff rolled. Bind off all sts.

FINISHING
Sew shoulder seams.

Buttonhole band
With RS facing, pick up and k21 (22, 23, 26) sts along right front edge for girls or left front edge for boys.
Buttonhole row (WS): K1 (2, 2, 1), (k2tog, yo, k2 (2, 2, 3) 5 times, k0 (0, 1, 0). Knit 1 row. Bind off kwise.

Buttonband
With RS facing, pick up and k21 (22, 23, 26) sts along right front edge for girls or left front edge for boys. Knit 2 rows. Bind off knitwise.

Neckband
With RS facing, pick up and k5 (6, 6, 6) sts along right front band and up front neck edge, 10 (10, 12, 12) sts across back neck edge and 5 (6, 6, 6) sts down left front neck edge and buttonhole band— 20 (22, 24, 24) sts. Beg with a purl row, work 3 rows in St st. Bind off knitwise.

Place markers 1½ (1½, 2, 2)" down from top of Sleeve on each side. Sew sleeve seams to markers, leaving rolled edge of cuffs unsewn. Sew in Sleeves, placing rows above markers along bound-off sts of front and back to form square armholes. Sew on buttons.

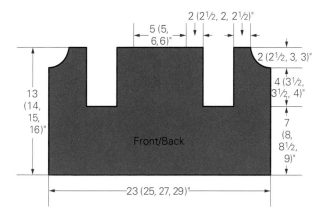

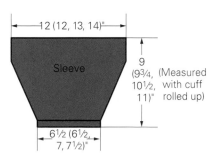

Blueberry Pullover ■■□□ Easy

Sizes

4 (6, 8) years

Instructions are written for smallest size with changes for larger sizes given in parentheses. When only one number is given, it applies to all sizes. **Note:** For ease in working, circle all numbers pertaining to the size you're knitting.

Finished Measurements

Chest = 28 (32, 36)"
Length (Back)= 15 (16½, 18)"

Materials

Yarns

Bulky weight, 285 (285, 342) yds. [260 (260, 312) m] in dark blue (MC)

Super bulky weight, 114 yds. (104 m)—all sizes—in variegated green (CC)

Needles & Extras

- Sizes 10 (6 mm) and 10½ (6.5 mm) needles OR SIZE NEEDED TO OBTAIN GAUGE
- Size 10 (6 mm) 16" circular needle
- Stitch markers
- Blunt-end yarn needle

Notes

Gauge

12 sts and 18 rows = 4" (10 cm) over St st (knit all RS rows, purl all WS rows) with larger needles. TAKE TIME TO CHECK YOUR GAUGE.

Knit

PATTERN STITCHES

1×1 Rib Pattern (multiple of 2 sts + 1; 2-row rep)
Row 1 (RS): (K1, p1) across; end k1.
Row 2: (P1, k1) across; end p1.
  Rep Rows 1 and 2 for 1×1 Rib pat.

Stripe Pattern

Beg with a knit row and CC, work 4 rows St st.
  Beg with a knit row and MC, work 4 rows St st.
  Rep last 8 rows for Stripe pat.

BACK

Using smaller needles and MC, cast on 41 (47, 53) sts. Work 1½" in 1×1 Rib pat, ending with WS row and inc 1 st in center of last row—42 (48, 54) sts.
  Change to larger needles and beg with a knit row, work 2 rows in St st. Work 20 rows in Stripe pat. Cont with MC only until piece measures 8½ (9, 10)" from beg, ending with a purl row.

Shape armholes

Bind off 4 (4, 5) sts at beg of next 2 rows—34 (40, 44) sts. Work even until armholes measure 5½ (6, 7)", ending with a purl row.

Shape neck

Next row (RS): K12 (14,15), join 2nd ball of yarn and bind off center 10 (12,14) sts; k to end. Working both sides at the same time with separate balls, dec 1 st at each neck edge on next 4 rows—8 (10, 11) sts rem for each shoulder. Work even until armhole measures 6½ (7, 8)", ending with a purl row. Bind off.

FRONT

Work as for Back until armhole measures 4½ (5, 6)", ending with a purl row.

Shape neck

Next row (RS): K13 (16, 17), join 2nd ball of yarn and bind off center 8 (8,10) sts; k to end. Working both sides at the same time with separate balls, dec 1 st at each neck edge on next 5 (6, 6) rows—8 (10, 11) sts. Cont even until armhole measures 6½ (7, 8)" ending with a purl row. Bind off.

SLEEVE (MAKE 2)

Using smaller needles and MC, cast on 19 (21, 24) sts. Work 1½" in 1×1 Rib pat, ending with WS row.

Change to larger needles and work in Stripe pat for 20 rows and AT THE SAME TIME inc 1 st on each edge on 5th and every 4th row 3 (4, 5) times, every 6th row 6 (6, 0) times, then every 8th row 0 (0, 6) times—39 (43, 48) sts. Cont with MC only until Sleeve measures 13 (14, 15)" from beg, ending with a purl row. Bind off. Place markers (pm) on side edges of each sleeve 1¼ (1¼, 1½)" down from bound-off edge.

FINISHING

Block to measurements. Join shoulder seams.

Shape neckband

With RS facing and using circular needle and CC, beg at left shoulder seam, pick up and k58 (60, 64) sts around neck opening. Pm, join, and work 1" in 1×1 Rib pat. Bind off loosely in pat.

Sew in Sleeves, placing the rows above the markers along bound-off sts of Front and Back to form square armholes. Sew side and sleeve seams.

Weave in loose ends.

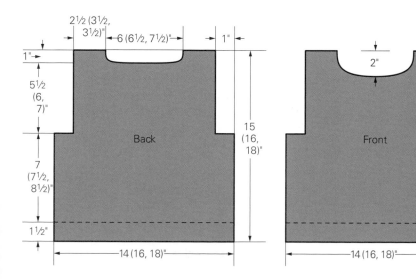

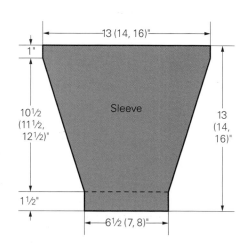

Take a jumbo hook, soft chunky yarn, and a pattern in easy single crochet, and what can you make? This pint-size cardi that's as soft and comfortable as it looks.

Designed by **Svetlana Avrakh**
Photographed by **Greg Scheidemann**

girl's
JACKET

Sizes

4 (6, 8, 10) years

Instructions are written for the smallest size with changes for larger sizes given in parentheses. When only one number is given, it applies to all sizes.

Note: For ease in working, circle all numbers pertaining to the size you're crocheting.

Finished Measurements

Chest = 27½ (29½, 31, 33)"
Length (Back before Collar) = 13½ (15½, 18, 19½)"

Materials

Yarns

Super bulky weight, 340 (408, 476, 476) yds. [310 (372, 434, 434) m] in coral

Hooks & Extras

- Size L/11 (8 mm) crochet hook OR SIZE NEEDED TO OBTAIN GAUGE
- Five 1⅛"-diameter buttons
- Sewing needle and matching thread
- Blunt-end yarn needle

Notes

Gauge

7 sc and 8 rows = 4" (10 cm). TAKE TIME TO CHECK YOUR GAUGE.

Special Abbreviations

sc2tog = [Insert hook in next st and draw up a loop (lp)] twice, yarn over and draw through all 3 lps on hook.

Crochet

BACK

Ch 25 (27, 28, 30).

Row 1 (RS): Sc in 2nd ch from hook and in each ch to end—24 (26, 27, 29) sts; turn.

Row 2: Ch 1, sc in each sc to end.

Rep Row 2 until Back measures 7½ (9½, 11, 12)" from beg, ending with a WS row.

Shape armholes

Next row: Sl st in first 4 sts; ch 1, sc in same st as last sl st and in each sc to last 3 sc—18 (20, 21, 23) sts; turn.

Next row: Ch 1, 1 sc in each sc to end of row; turn.

Rep last row until armholes measure 6 (6½, 7, 7½)", end with a WS row; fasten off. Place markers (pm) 4 (5, 5, 5) sts in along top edge for shoulders on each side.

LEFT FRONT

Ch 17 (18, 18, 19).

Row 1 (RS): Sc in 2nd ch from hook and in each ch to end—16 (17, 17, 18) sts; turn.

Row 2: Ch 1, sc in each sc to end.

Rep Row 2 until Left Front measures 7½ (9½, 11, 12)" from beg, ending with WS row.

Shape armhole

Next row (RS): Sl st in first 4 sts; ch 1, sc in same st as last sl st and in each sc to end—13 (14, 14, 15) sts; turn.

Next row: Ch 1, sc in each sc to end; turn. Rep last row until armhole measures 6 rows less than Back, ending at armhole edge.

Shape neck

Next row (RS): Ch 1, sc in each sc to last 8 (8, 8, 9) sc, sc2tog over next 2 sts—6 (7, 7, 7) sts; turn.

Next row: Ch 1, sc2tog over first 2 sts, sc in each sc to end—5 (6, 6, 6) sts; turn.

Next row: Ch 1, sc in each sc to last 2 sts, sc2tog over last 2 sts—4 (5, 5, 5) sts; turn.

Work 3 rows even; fasten off.

Pm for 5 buttons, with first button 2 rows up from bottom edge, last button 2 rows down from neck edge, and rem 3 buttons evenly spaced bet.

RIGHT FRONT

Work same as Left Front to armhole, working buttonholes to correspond with markers as foll:

Next row (RS): Ch 1, sc in first 2 sc, ch 1, sk next sc, sc in each sc to end; turn.

Next row: Ch 1, sc in each ch and sc across; turn.

Shape armhole

Next row (RS): Ch 1, sc in each sc to last 3 sts—13 (14, 14, 15) sts; turn.

Next row: Ch 1, sc in each sc to end of row; turn.

Rep last row until armhole measures 6 rows less than Back; fasten off.

Shape neck

Next row (RS): Sk first 6 (6, 6, 7) sc, join yarn with sl st in next sc; ch 1, sc2tog over first 2 sts, sc in each sc to end—6 (7, 7, 7) sts; turn.

Next row: Ch 1, sc in each sc to last 2 sts, sc2tog over last 2 sts; turn.

Next row: Ch 1, sc2tog over first 2 sts, sc in each sc to end—4 (5, 5, 5) sts; turn. Work 3 rows even; fasten off.

SLEEVE (MAKE 2)

Ch 11 (12, 12, 13).

Row 1 (RS): Sc in 2nd ch from hook and in each ch to end—10 (11, 11, 12) sts; turn.

Row 2: Ch 1, sc in each sc to end; turn. Inc row: Ch 1, 2 sc in first sc, sc to last sc, 2 sc in last sc. Cont to rep Row 2, working inc row every other row to 20 (19, 21, 18) sts, then every 4th row to 22 (23, 25, 26) sts. Work even until Sleeve measures 9½ (11, 12½, 15½)" from beg; fasten off. Pm at each side edge, 1¾" down from last row.

FINISHING

Collar

Sew shoulder seams.

With RS facing and starting at right front edge, sk 3 sc, join yarn with sl st in next sc; ch 1, starting in same sp, work 9 sc along Right Front neck edge, 10 (10, 11, 13) sc across Back neck edge, 9 sc along Left Front neck edge—28 (28, 29, 31) sts; turn.

Inc row (RS of Collar): Ch 1, 2 sc in first sc, sc in each sc to last sc, 2 sc in last sc; turn.

Rep last row twice more. Work 1 row even. Work inc row on next, then every other row twice.

Next row: Ch 1, sc2tog over first 2 sts, sc in each sc to last 2 sts, sc2tog over last 2 sts; turn. Rep last row once; fasten off.

POCKET (MAKE 2)

Ch 8 (8, 9, 9).

Row 1: Sc in 2nd ch from hook and in each ch to end—7 (7, 8, 8) sts; turn.

Row 2: Ch 1, sc in each sc to end; turn. Rep last row 5 (5, 7, 7) more times; fasten off.

Set in Sleeves, placing rows above markers along skipped sts. Sew side and Sleeve seams. Sew buttons to correspond to buttonholes. Sew Pockets in place.

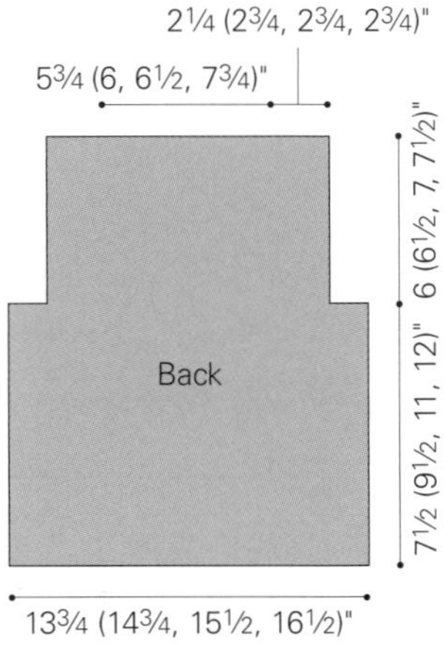

2¼ (2¾, 2¾, 2¾)"

5¾ (6, 6½, 7¾)"

6 (6½, 7, 7½)"

7½ (9½, 11, 12)"

Back

13¾ (14¾, 15½, 16½)"

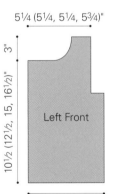

5¼ (5¼, 5¼, 5¾)"

3"

10½ (12½, 15, 16½)"

Left Front

9¼ (9¾, 9¾, 10¼)"

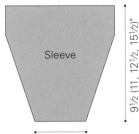

12½ (13, 14¼, 14¾)"

Sleeve

9½ (11, 12½, 15½)"

5¾ (6¼, 6¼, 6¾)"

Perfect for girls on the go, this sweater packs plenty of punch in its colorful stripes. Knit-3, purl-3 ribbing adds growing room and comfort along with style.

CHILD'S STRIPED
hoodie

Designed by **Ann E. Smith**   Photographed by **King Au**

Sizes

6 (8, 10) years

Instructions are written for the smallest size with changes for larger sizes given in parentheses. When only one number is given, it applies to all sizes.

Note: For ease in working, circle all numbers pertaining to the size you're knitting.

Finished Measurements

Chest (buttoned) = 30 (34, 37¾)"
Length (Back without Hood) = 18 (19, 20)"

Materials

Yarns

Worsted weight, 600 yds. (540 m)—all sizes— in medium blue (MC)

Worsted weight, 364 yds. (333 m)—all sizes—in dark blue (A)

Worsted weight, 200 yds. (180 m)—all sizes—*each* in pale blue (B) and aqua (C)

Worsted weight, 302 yds. (276 m)—all sizes—in lime green (D)

4 MEDIUM

Needles & Extras

- Size 8 (5 mm) knitting needles OR SIZE NEEDED TO OBTAIN GAUGE
- Size 6 (4.25 mm) knitting needles
- Five ⅝"-diameter buttons
- Blunt-end yarn needles

Notes

Gauge

17 sts and 24 rows = 4" (10 cm) in body pat with larger needles.
TAKE TIME TO CHECK YOUR GAUGE.

Knit

BACK

Beg at the lower edge and using larger needles and A, cast on 93 (105, 117) sts.

Shape lower body

Row 1 (WS): Using A, p3; (k3, p3) across.
Row 2: Using A, k3; (p3, k3) across.
Row 3: Rep Row 1.
Rows 4 and 5: Using D, rep Rows 2 and 3.
Rows 6 and 7: Using A, rep Rows 2 and 3.
Rows 8 and 9: Using C, rep Rows 2 and 3.
Rows 10 and 11: Using A, rep Rows 2 and 3.
Rows 12 and 13: Using B, rep Rows 2 and 3.
Rows 14 and 15: Using A, rep Rows 2 and 3.
Rows 16–21: Using MC, rep Rows 2 and 3.
 Rep Rows 2–20 once more.
Dec row: Using MC, p3; * sl 1, k2tog, psso, p3; rep from * across—63 (71, 79) sts. Piece should measure approx 7" from beg.

Shape upper body

Row 1 (RS): Using A, k3; (p1, k3) across.
Row 2: Using A, p3; (k1, p3) across.

Rows 3 and 4: Using D, rep Rows 1 and 2.
Rows 5 and 6: Using A, rep Rows 1 and 2.
Rows 7 and 8: Using C, rep Rows 1 and 2.
Rows 9 and 10: Using A, rep Rows 1 and 2.
Rows 11 and 12: Using C, rep Rows 1 and 2.
Rows 13 and 14: Using C, rep Rows 1 and 2.
Rows 15–20: Using MC, rep Rows 1 and 2. Rep Rows 1–20 until piece measures approx 11½ (12, 12½)" from beg, ending with a WS row.

Shape armholes

Bind off 5 sts at beg of next 2 rows, then dec 1 st each edge every other row 1 (2, 3) time(s)—51 (57, 63) sts. Keeping 1 st each edge in St st, cont pat to approx 18 (19, 20)" from beg, ending with a WS row. Bind off straight across and kwise using color from previous row.

RIGHT FRONT

Beg at lower edge and using larger needles and A, cast on 45 (51, 57) sts. Work lower body as for Back. After Dec row, 31 (35, 39) sts rem. Work upper body as for Back until piece measures approx 11½ (12, 12½)" from beg, ending with a RS row.

Shape armhole

At armhole edge, bind off 5 sts once, then dec 1 st at armhole edge every other row 1 (2, 3) time(s)—25 (28, 31) sts. Keeping 1 st at armhole edge in St st, cont pat to approx 16 (17, 18)" from beg, ending with a WS row.

Shape neck

At neck edge, bind off 6 (7, 7) sts once, 3 sts once, 2 sts once, and 1 st once. Work even on rem 13 (15, 18) sts to same length as Back, ending with WS row. Bind off kwise using color from previous row.

LEFT FRONT

Work as for Right Front, reversing armhole and neck shaping.

SLEEVE (MAKE 2)

Using larger needles and A, cast on 31 (35, 39) sts. P3; (k1, p3) across for first WS row. Rep Rows 1–20 of upper body pat as for Back for entire Sleeve. When piece measures approx 2" from beg, end Using a WS row. Including new sts into pat as they accumulate, inc 1 st each edge every 4th row 10 (8, 5) times and every 6th row 2 (4, 7) times. Work even on 55 (59, 63) sts to approx 11 (12, 13)" from beg, ending with a WS row.

Shape armhole as for Back. On next RS row, bind off rem 43 (45, 47) sts kwise using color from previous row.

HOOD

Using larger needles and A, cast on 87 (91, 95) sts. P3; (k1, p3) across for first WS row. Rep Rows 1–20 of upper body pat as for Back until piece measures approx 10½ (11¼, 12)" from beg, ending with WS row. Bind off kwise using color from previous row.

FINISHING

Join shoulder seams. Set in Sleeves. Join underarm and side seams. Fold Hood in half lengthwise, and join ends to form top seam. Holding RS tog, sew Hood to neck edge. With the RS facing and using smaller needles and A, pick up and k88 (92, 96) sts evenly spaced around Hood. K 5 rows. Bind off loosely kwise.

Make Left Front band

Row 1: With the RS facing, using smaller needles and A, pick up and k69 (73, 77) sts evenly spaced along edge. K 5 more rows. Bind off kwise. Sew top of band to Hood band.

Make Right Front band

Row 1: Work as for Left Front band through completion of first k row.
Row 2: K31 (35, 39); * (yo, k2tog, k6) 4 times, yo, k2tog, k4. K 3 more rows. Bind off kwise. Sew top of band to Hood band.

Sew buttons to Left Front opposite buttonholes.

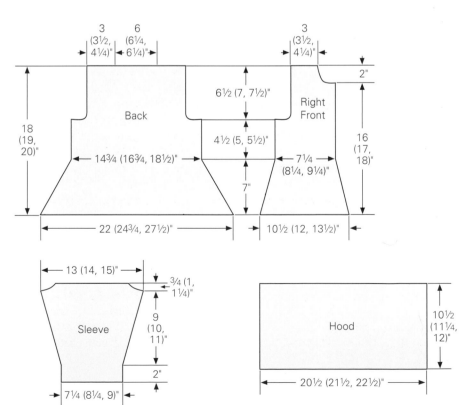

home decor

Add texture and warmth to your living spaces
with cozy afghans and pillows.

Knit your own room accessories to breathe new life into your decor.

Designed by **Heather Lodinsky** (button pillows and throw)
and **Joyce Nordstrom** (stripe pillow)
Photographed by **Greg Scheidemann**

RIGHT AT home

Textured-Blocks Throw and Button-Flange Pillows

■■■□□ Easy

Sizes

Finished Measurements

Throw: Approximately 36×44"
Pillows: Approximately 12×20"

Materials

Yarns

Throw:

Bulky weight (we used nubby yarn), 740 yds. (668 m) in tan (MC)

Bulky wieght, 185 yds. (167 m) *each* in blue (A), forest green (B), and ivory (C)

Pillow:

Worsted weight, 600 yds. (540 m) in forest green

Worsted weight, 400 yds. (360 m) *each* in brown, blue, and tan

Needles & Extras

Throw:

• Size 10½ (6.5 mm) 24" circular needle OR SIZE NEEDED TO OBTAIN GAUGE

Pillow:

• Size 8 (5 mm) needles OR SIZE NEEDED TO OBTAIN GAUGE
• Stitch markers
• Blunt-end yarn needle
• Ten ¾"-diameter buttons for each pillow
• Four 12×16" pillow forms

Notes

Gauge

Throw: 12 sts and 21 rows = 4" (10 cm) in St st (knit 1 row, purl 1 row).
Pillow: 18 sts and 24 rows = 4" (10 cm) in St st. TAKE TIME TO CHECK YOUR GAUGE.

CHECKER PATTERN

SEED STITCH PATTERN

ALTERNATE GARTER PATTERN

BROKEN RIB PATTERN

Knit

PATTERN STITCHES

Alternate Garter Pattern
(multiple of 8 + 4 sts)
Row 1 (RS): Knit.
Row 2: P4, *k4 , p4; rep from *.
  Rep Rows 1 and 2 for pat.

Broken Rib Pattern
(multiple of 2 sts)
Rows 1–3 (RS): *K1, p1; rep from *.
Row 4: Purl.
Rows 5–7: *P1, k1; rep from *.
Row 8: Purl.
  Rep Rows 1–8 for pat.

Seed Stitch Pattern
(multiple of 2 sts)
Row 1 (RS): *K1, p1; rep from *.
Row 2: *P1, k1; rep from *.
  Rep Rows 1 and 2 for pat.

Checker Pattern (multiple of 4 sts)
Row 1 (RS): *K2, p2; rep from *.
Row 2: Same as Row 1.
Rows 3 and 4: *P2, k2; rep from *.
  Rep Rows 1–4 for pat.

THROW

Note: Always KNIT first row of color block when there is a color change.

Using MC, cast on 108 sts. Work in Garter st (k every row) for 2", ending with a WS row.

Next row (RS): K6, place marker (pm), k to last 6 sts, pm, k6.

Next row: K6, slip marker (sm), p to last marker, sm, k6.

Cont to slip markers for each row, rep last 2 rows until piece measures 4" from beg, ending with a WS row.

Next row: K6, work Row 1 of Chart, *page 236*, in stitches and colors indicated over next 96 sts, k last 6 sts. (Also see Note above.)

Maintaining 6-st Garter st edges, cont to work Chart between markers. When first joined blocks of Chart are complete, cont to work center sts in MC and St st for 2", ending on a WS row.

Next row: Starting at Row 58 of Chart, work Chart in stitches and colors as indicated for 2nd set of joined blocks (see Note in first column) between markers. Then work in St st and MC for 2", ending with a WS row.

Starting with Row 117 of Chart, work Chart in stitches and colors indicated for 3rd set of joined blocks (see Note in first column). Then work MC in St st for 2", then cont in MC and Garter st for 2". Bind off.

PILLOWS

With color of choice, cast on 90 sts.
Next row (RS): K7, pm, work Row 1 of pat of choice to last 7 sts, pm, k7.
Next row: K7, work Row 2 of pat of choice to last 7 sts, k7. Maintaining 7-st Garter st edges, cont to work pat st between markers until piece measures 1", ending with a WS row.

Next row (Buttonhole row): K2, k2tog, yo, k3, work in pat to last 7 sts, k2, k2tog, yo, k3. Cont in pat, working buttonhole row every 2½" four more times (piece should measure 11"). Work even in pat as est until piece measures 24" from beg. Bind off.

FINISHING

Block pieces to size. Fold pillows lengthwise with wrong sides together and with buttonhole band side on top. Mark placement for buttons on inside of bottom side of pillow. Sew buttons on inside to correspond to buttonholes. Sew lengthwise seam and weave in ends. Button one side of pillow and insert form. Button opposite side of pillow.

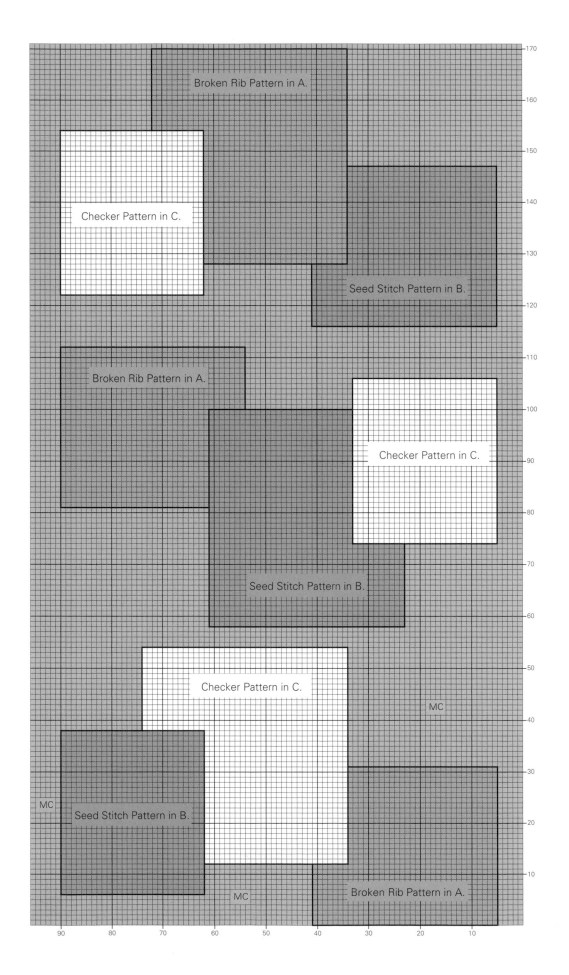

Striped Chenille Pillow ■■□□ Easy

Sizes

Finished Measurements

12×22"

Materials

Yarns

Bulky weight chenille, 100 yds. (90 m) *each* in tan (MC), blue (A), ivory (B), and forest green (C)

Needles & Extras

- Size 11 (8 mm) needles OR SIZE NEEDED TO OBTAIN GAUGE
- Rectangular pillow form 12×22"
- Blunt-end yarn needle

Notes

Gauge

8 sts and 16 rows = 4" (10 cm) over St st (k RS rows, p WS rows). TAKE TIME TO CHECK YOUR GAUGE.

Knit

FRONT

Using MC, cast on 24 sts.

Beg with a k row (RS), work 4 rows St st.

Using A, k 1 row.

Cont with A and beg with a k row (WS), work 5 rows Reverse St st. (knit WS row, purl RS row).

Using B and beg with a k row, work 4 rows St st.

Using C, k 1 row.

Cont with C and beg with a k row, work 3 rows Reverse St st.

Using A, beg with a k row, work 6 rows St st.

Using MC, k 1 row.

Cont with MC and beg with a k row, work 5 rows Reverse St st.

Using B, beg with a k row, work 2 rows St st.

Using C, work 4 rows St st.

Using B, k 1 row.

Cont with B and beg with a k row, work 3 rows Reverse St st.

Using A, beg with a k row, work 6 rows St st.

Using C, k 2 rows.

Using B and beg with a k row, work 2 rows St st.

Using C, k 1 row. Cont with C and beg with a k row, work 5 rows Reverse St st.

Using MC, beg with a k row, work 4 rows St st.

Using A, k 1 row. Cont with A and beg with a k row, work 3 rows Reverse St st.

Using B and beg with a k row, work 4 rows St st.

Using MC, k 1 row. Cont with MC and beg with a k row, work 3 rows Reverse St st.

Using C and beg with a k row, work 4 rows St st.

Using B, k 1 row. Cont with B and beg with a k row, work 3 rows Reverse St st.

Bind off.

BACK

Using MC, cast on 24 sts.

Work as for Front with MC only, omitting all color changes.

FINISHING

Sew Front and Back tog, leaving one end open. Insert pillow form. Sew opening closed.

Weave in loose ends.

mixed-stripes
PILLOW & AFGHAN

Three different yarns gently stripe this sumptuous set.
Beginners will love the designs because both pieces are
crafted in single crochet. Slight pattern and stitch
variations add impact to the look.

Designed by **Stitchworx**   Photographed by **Greg Scheidemann**

■■■□□ **Easy**

Sizes
Finished Measurements
Pillow: 14×14"
Afghan: 36×48", excluding fringe

Materials
Yarns
Bulky weight, 555 yds.
(500 m) in beige (A)

Bulky weight, 365 yds. (330 m)
in ivory (B)

Bulky weight, 400 yds. (375 m)
in tan (C)

Hooks & Extras
• Size K/10 (6 mm) crochet hook OR
  SIZE NEEDED TO OBTAIN GAUGE
• 14×14" pillow form
• Blunt-end yarn needle

Notes
Gauge
10 sts and 10½ rows = 4" (10 cm)
in Stripe pat. TAKE TIME TO CHECK
YOUR GAUGE.

A new color may begin on a RS or WS
row; cut and join yarns as needed. Work
over ends as you work to weave them
in. Afghan is fringed along the short
sides rather than at the long top and
bottom edges.

Crochet

PATTERN STITCHES

Stripe Pattern

Row 1 (RS): Ch 1, turn, sc under both lps of each sc across.

Row 2: Ch 1, turn, sc in front lp of each sc across.

Row 3: Ch 1, turn, sc in back lp of each sc across.

Rows 4 and 5: Rep Rows 2 and 3 as directed.

Note: After Stripe pat is complete, continue working single crochet under both loops.

PILLOW
FRONT

Using A, ch 35.

Row 1: Sc into 2nd ch from hook and in each ch across—34 sc.

Row 2: Ch 1, turn, sc in each sc across.

Row 3: With A, rep Row 2.

Row 4: With B, rep Row 2.

Rows 5–7: With C, work Stripe pat, Rows 1–3.

Row 8: With B, rep Row 2.

Row 9: With A, rep Row 2.

Row 10: With B, rep Row 2.

Rows 11–15: With C, work Stripe pat, Rows 1–5.

Row 16: With B, rep Row 2.

Rows 17–19: With A, rep Row 2.

Row 20: With B, rep Row 2.

Rows 21–25: With C, work Stripe pat, Rows 1–5.

Row 26: With B, rep Row 2.

Row 27: With A, rep Row 2.

Row 28: With B, rep Row 2.

Rows 29–31: With C, work Stripe pat, Rows 1–3.

Row 32: With B, rep Row 2.

Rows 33–35: With A, rep Row 2.
  Fasten off.

BACK

Using A, ch 35.

Row 1: Sc into 2nd ch from hook and in each ch across—34 sc.

Row 2: Ch 1, turn, sc in each sc across. Cont in sc with A for 33 more rows.
  Fasten off.

FINISHING

With RS tog, sew Front to Back on 3 sides. Turn pillow right side out and insert pillow form. Sew rem side tog.

AFGHAN

Using A, ch 121.

Row 1: Sc in 2nd ch from hook and in each ch across—120 sc.

Row 2: Ch 1, turn, sc in each sc across.

Rows 3–6: Rep Row 2.

Rows 7 and 8: With B, rep Row 2.

Rows 9–11: With C, work Stripe pat, Rows 1–3.

Row 12 (WS): With B, rep Row 2.

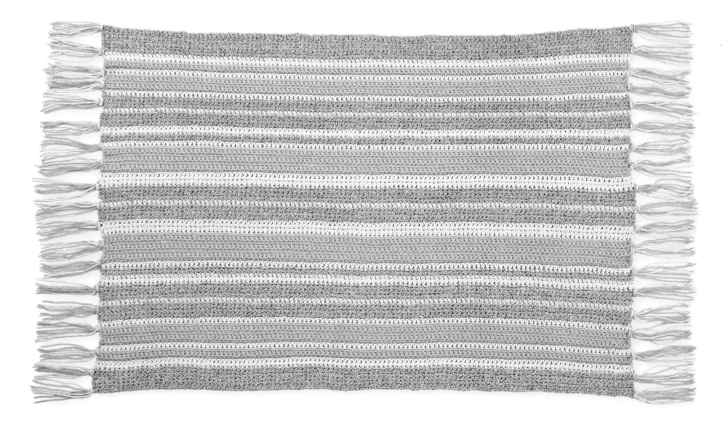

Rows 13–17: With C, work Stripe pat, Rows 1–5.

Row 18: With B, rep Row 2.

Rows 19–22: With A, rep Row 2.

Row 23: With B, rep Row 2.

Rows 24–27: With A, rep Row 2.

Rows 28 and 29: With B, rep Row 2.

Rows 30 and 31: With A, rep Row 2.

Row 32: With B, rep Row 2.

Rows 33–39: With C, work Stripe pat, Rows 1–5, and then Rows 2 and 3.

Rows 40–42: With B, rep Row 2.

Rows 43–46: With A, rep Row 2.

Row 47: With B, rep Row 2.

Rows 48–51: With A, rep Row 2.

Rows 52–54: With B, rep Row 2.

Rows 55–61: With C, work Stripe pat, Rows 1–5, and then Rows 2 and 3.

Row 62: With B, rep Row 2.

Rows 63 and 64: With A, rep Row 2.

Rows 65 and 66: With B, rep Row 2.

Rows 67–70: With A, rep Row 2.

Row 71: With B, rep Row 2.

Rows 72–75: With A, rep Row 2.

Row 76: With B, rep Row 2.

Rows 77–81: With C, work Stripe pat, Rows 1–5.

Row 82: With B, rep Row 2.

Rows 83–85: With C, work Stripe pat, Rows 1–3.

Rows 86 and 87: With B, rep Row 2.

Rows 88–93: With A, rep Row 2.
Fasten off.

TASSEL FRINGE

Fringe consists of 19 Tassels evenly spaced across each short side of the afghan.

Cut a piece of cardboard measuring 7" wide. Holding B and C tog, wrap yarn around cardboard 2 times. Cut yarn at 1 end (4 strands, each 14" long).

Insert hook from back to front through 1 stitch at edge of Afghan; fold yarn lengths in half over the hook, pull the folded yarn halfway through the stitch, pull the yarn ends through the loop, and tighten. Trim as needed.

comforts
of home

Use your crochet skills to liven up a couch or a chair
with these cozy mitered pillows and bobble-blocks throw.

Designed by **Stitchworx**, adapted from a block-motif design by **Jan Eaton** (pillows) and **Cindy Grosch**
adapted from a block-motif design by **Jan Eaton** (throw)   Photographed by **Greg Scheidemann**

Four-Patch Mitered Pillows

■■■■□ Intermediate

Sizes

Finished Measurements

16×16"

Materials

Yarns

Worsted weight, 600 yds. (540 m) Main Color (MC)

5 BULKY

Worsted weight, 600 yds. (180 m) *each* in Contrasting Colors (A) and (B)

Hooks & Extras

- Size H/8 (5 mm) crochet hook OR SIZE NEEDED TO OBTAIN GAUGE
- Three 16×16" pillow forms
- Blunt-end yarn needle

Notes

Gauge

13 sc and 14 rows = 4" (10 cm). TAKE TIME TO CHECK YOUR GAUGE.

Special Abbreviations

sc3tog: Dec 2 sts by working the next 3 sc tog as follows: Draw up a lp in each of the next 3 sc, yo, draw through 4 lps on hook.

Crochet

FRONT (MAKE 4 IDENTICAL SECTIONS TO COMPLETE FRONT)

Using MC, ch 58.

Foundation Row (WS): Sc in 2nd ch from hook and in each ch across; turn— 57 sc; turn.

Row 1: Ch 1, sc in each of next 27 sc, sc3tog, sc in each of rem 27 sc— 55 sc; turn.

Row 2: Ch 1, sc in each of next 26 sc, sc3tog, sc in each of rem 26 sc— 53 sc; turn.

Row 3: Ch 1, sc in each of next 25 sc, sc3tog, sc in each of rem 25 sc— 51 sc; turn.

Row 4: Ch 1, sc in each of next 24 sc, sc3tog, sc in each of rem 24 sc— 49 sc; turn. Drop MC.

Cont in this manner, following the color scheme below, working 1 st fewer each side of sc3tog. When Row 26 is complete, 5 sts rem.

COLOR SCHEME FOR REM FRONT

Rows 5 and 6: Use A.
Rows 7–10: Use MC.
Rows 11 and 12: Use B.
Rows 13–26: Use MC.
Row 27: Using MC, ch 1, sc into first sc, sc3tog, sc in last sc; turn.
Row 28: Ch 1, sc3tog. Fasten off.

BACK

Using MC, ch 51.

Row 1 (Foundation Row): Sc in 2nd ch from hook and in each ch across— 50 sc; turn.

Row 2: Ch 1, sc in each sc across; turn.
  Rep Row 2 for 56 more rows. Fasten off.

FINISHING

Sew 2 corner squares tog, matching stripes. Rep with rem 2 corner squares. Sew the 2 sets of squares to each other, matching stripes to form the Pillow Front. With RS facing, sew Front to Back on 3 sides. Weave in loose ends. Insert pillow form; sew rem side closed.

Bobble-Blocks Throw

■■■□□ Easy

Sizes

Finished Measurements

Each Block: Approximately 8½×8½".

Bedspread: 60×76" (fits a twin-size bed)

Materials

Yarns

Worsted weight, 4,000 yds. (3,600 m) in blue (MC)

Worsted weight, 600 yds. (540 m) *each* in tan (A) and ivory (B)

Hooks & Extras

- Size I/9 (5.5mm) crochet hook OR SIZE NEEDED TO OBTAIN GAUGE
- Blunt-end yarn needle

Notes

Gauge

13 sc and 14 rows = 4" (10 cm). TAKE TIME TO CHECK YOUR GAUGE.

Pattern Stitches

MB (make bobble): Working in same st, yo, draw up lp, yo, draw through 2 lps on hook 4 times; yo, draw yarn through all 5 lps on hook. Ch 1 to close.

To change colors in single crochet, work up to one stitch before next color, draw up a loop in next stitch with color in use; with new color, complete the single crochet. Before beginning the bobble, lay color A across the single crochet in which the bobble will be made and work the bobble over the yarn as you work the stitch. Between bobbles, the contrast color is carried across the wrong side to the next bobble stitch.

Crochet

BLOCK (MAKE 63)

Using MC, ch 28.

Foundation Row (WS): Sc in 2nd ch from hook and in each ch across, turn—27 sc.

Rows 1–3: Ch 1, sc in each sc, turn.

Row 4 (WS): Ch 1, sc in each of the next 3 sc, MB using A; * using MC, sc into each of the next 4 sc (carrying A across back of work on WS), MB using A*; rep from * to * across, ending row with 3 sc using MC.

Rows 5–11: Rep Row 1.

Row 12: Rep Row 4, using B for the bobbles.

Rows 13–19: Rep Row 1.

Rows 20–28: Rep Rows 4–12.

Rows 29–32: Rep Row 1.

Fasten off yarn.

ASSEMBLY

Using yarn needle and MC, whipstitch squares together into 9 rows of 7 Blocks each.

Note: To join Blocks, always sew them together working in the same direction, starting at the bottom of the Blocks and working to the top. Join the rows, sewing them together in the same direction, too.

FINISHING

Weave in all loose ends.

Sc 2 rnds around the entire bedspread to finish the edges, working 3 sc in each corner st.

urban
COMFORTS

Opulent tones of fuchsia, eggplant, olive, and cream create a palette of warm colors for your home, infusing style through a cozy afghan and coordinating pillows. A subtle miter pattern, worked completely in garter stitch, dominates the set.

Designed by **Barbara Nudelman** and **Susan Prince** of **Stitchworx**
Photographed by **King Au**

Sizes
Finished Measurements
Afghan: 40×56"
Square Pillows: 14×14"
Rectangular Pillow: 12×16"

Materials
Yarns
Bulky weight, 555 yds. (500 m) in variegated multicolor (A)

Bulky weight, 370 yds. (335 m) *each* in purple (B), tan (C), fuschia (D), and dark green (E)

Needles & Extras
• Size 10.5 (6.5 mm) knitting needles OR SIZE NEEDED TO OBTAIN GAUGE
• Two 14" square pillow forms
• One 12×16" pillow form
• Blunt-end yarn needle

Notes
Gauge
20 sts and 24 rows = 4" (10 cm) in Garter st (knit every row) in mitered pattern.
12 sts = 4" (2.54 cm) in plain Garter st. TAKE TIME TO CHECK YOUR GAUGE.

Knit
AFGHAN

Note: Each blanket rectangle measures 20×28".

RECTANGLE I (MAKE 2, LOWER RIGHT AND UPPER LEFT)
Using B, cast on 142 sts.
Row 1 and all RS rows: Knit.
Row 2: K58, k3tog, k81—140 sts.
Row 4: K57, k3tog, k80—138 sts.
 Cut B and join A to beg Row 5.
Row 6: K56, k3tog, k79—136 sts.
 Cont in this manner, knitting every row and working 2 sts less on every even-numbered row. **Note:** Do not work k3tog on odd-numbered rows.
 AT THE SAME TIME, change colors as follows: beg with Row 5, 10 rows A; 10 rows B; 10 rows C; 10 rows D; 16 rows E; 20 rows A; rem 38 rows B. At end of Row 116, 26 sts rem.
Row 117: Knit.
Row 118 (last row): K3tog and bind off all sts.

PILLOW I

PILLOW II

PILLOW III

RECTANGLE II (MAKE 2, LOWER LEFT AND UPPER RIGHT)

Using B, cast on 142 sts.

Row 1 and all RS rows: Knit

Row 2: K81, k3tog, k58.

Row 4: K80, k3tog, k57, break B and join D to beg Row 5.

Row 6: K79, k3tog, k56.

Cont in this manner, knitting every row and working 2 sts less on each side on every even-numbered row.

AT THE SAME TIME, change colors as follows: beg with Row 5, 10 rows D; 10 rows C; 10 rows A; 10 rows E; 16 rows C; 20 rows D; rem 38 rows A. At end of Row 116, 26 sts rem.

Row 117: Knit.

Row 118 (last row): Bind off to within last 3 sts, k3tog and bind off.

FINISHING

With RS facing, position 4 sections so matching rectangles do not meet. Backstitch seams, matching stripes.

PILLOW I FRONT

Using B, cast on 77 sts.

Row 1 and all RS rows: Knit.

Row 2: K37, k3tog, k37—75 sts.

Row 4: K36, k3tog, k36—73 sts.

Cut B and join A to beg Row 5.

Cont in this manner, knitting every row and working 1 st less on each side of k3tog.

AT THE SAME TIME, change colors as follows: 10 rows A; 10 rows B; 10 rows C; 10 rows D; 10 rows E; rem 22 rows A. Bind off.

BACK

Using A, cast on 38 sts. Work Garter st until piece measures 13" from beg. Bind off.

FINISHING

With RS tog, sew along 3 edges. Turn RS out. Insert pillow form. Sew rem side.

PILLOW II FRONT

Work as for Pillow I through Row 4, then cont in the following color sequence: 10 rows D; 10 rows C; 10 rows A; 10 rows E; 10 rows C; rem 22 rows D. Bind off.

BACK

Using E, cast on 38 sts. Work Garter st until piece measures 13" from beg. Bind off.

FINISHING

Rep instructions for Pillow I.

PILLOW III

Using C, cast on 84 sts. K 4 rows. Cont Garter st in the following color sequence: 4 rows B, 2 rows C, 10 rows D, 2 rows C, 4 rows B, 8 rows C, 2 rows E, (8 rows A, 2 rows E) twice, 8 rows C, 4 rows B, 2 rows C, 10 rows D, 2 rows C, 4 rows B, 4 rows C. Bind off.

FINISHING

With WS facing, fold pillow fabric in half. Sew 2 sides tog. Turn RS out, insert pillow form, and sew rem side closed.

sports fan
BEDSPREAD & PILLOW

Designed by **Michelle Maks Thompson**   Photographed by **Greg Scheidemann**

■■■□□ **Easy**

Sizes
One Size

Finished Measurements
Bedspread = 50×60"
(excluding borders)
Pillow = 14" square
(excluding borders)

Materials
Yarns
Bedspread
Chunky weight, 985 yds.
(900 m) in denim (A);
approx 490 yds. (450 m) in
dark red (B); approx 340 yds. (300 m)
in light brown (C); approx 1,475 yds.
(1,359 m) in cream (D)

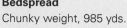

Pillow
Chunky weight, 165 yds. (150 m)
each in denim (A), dark red (B),
light brown (C), and cream (D)

Hooks & Extras
- Size J/10 (6 mm) crochet hook OR SIZE NEEDED TO OBTAIN GAUGE
- 14" pillow form
- Assorted appliqués or cutouts from sports pennants
- Sewing needle and thread OR fabric glue
- Blunt-end yarn needle

Notes
Gauge
27 sc and 34 rows = 10". TAKE TIME TO CHECK YOUR GAUGE.

Crochet
BEDSPREAD

Note: Bedspread is worked in 5 strips; strips are then sewn or slip-stitched tog.

STRIP I (MAKE 3)
Color Sequence I: *(4 rows A, 2 rows B, 4 rows A, 2 rows C) twice, 4 rows A, 2 rows B, 4 rows A; 34 rows D; rep from * twice more.

Using A, ch 29, sc in 2nd ch from hook and in each ch across—28 sts; turn.

Row 1: Ch 1. Sc in each sc across. Cont to rep Row 1 until Color Sequence I is complete—204 rows; fasten off.

STRIP II (MAKE 2)
Color Sequence II: *34 rows D, (4 rows A, 2 rows B, 4 rows A, 2 rows C) twice, 4 rows A, 2 rows B, 4 rows A; rep from * twice more.

Using D, ch 29. Work same as Strip I, foll Color Sequence II.

FINISHING
Work 6 rows of cross-stitches to complete the plaid pattern on striped blocks as foll: Beg stitching in 2nd row and in 2nd st from left side of block with C. Work toward top of block and make a cross-stitch in every other row—17 cross-stitches.

Sk 4 sts to right of first row of C cross-stitches and work B cross-stitch in next st. Complete row of B cross-stitches—17 cross-stitches.

Be a sport and make this bedspread and pillow set for a special little guy. Make the afghan with fast-finish squares worked in chunky weight yarn; the logos are cut from pennants and sewn or glued on.

Cont to make 4 more rows of cross-stitches to complete plaid pat, alternating colors B and C. Work cross-stitches in the same manner in all colored blocks. Alternate strips, beg and ending with Strip I; join strips.

Side edges

With RS facing and working at side edge, (join A and sc evenly along side of plaid section, join D and sc evenly along side of solid section) 3 times; fasten off. Rep on opposite side edge.

Border

Join B in any sc.
Rnd 1 (RS): Ch 1, sc evenly around entire Bedspread, working 3 sc in each corner; end join with sl st to first sc; turn.
Rnds 2–3 (WS): Ch 1, sc in each sc around, working 3 sc in each corner; join with sl st to top of first sc; do not turn; fasten off at end of Rnd 3. Weave in loose ends.

Cut appliqués into desired shapes. Sew or glue shapes onto solid D sections of Bedspread.

PILLOW FRONT

Using D, ch 38. Sc in 2nd ch from hook and in each ch across—37 sts.
Row 1: Ch 1, sc in each sc across.
Rep Row 1 for a total of 46 rows; fasten off.

Side edges and border

With RS facing and using D, sc evenly along each side edge of Pillow. Join B in any sc and work 3 rnds sc same as for Bedspread.

BACK

Color sequence: (4 rows A, 2 rows B, 4 rows A, 2 rows C) 3 times, 4 rows A, 2 rows B, 4 rows A.
Using A, ch 38. Sc in 2nd ch from hook and in each ch across—37 sts.
Cont rep Row 1 until color sequence is complete—46 rows; fasten off.

Side edges and border

With RS facing and using A, sc evenly along each side edge of Pillow. Join B in any sc and work 3 rnds sc same as for Bedspread.

FINISHING

Work 8 rows of cross-stitch embroidery in the same manner as for Bedspread. Sew desired appliqué(s) onto front of Pillow.
Sew 3 sides of Pillow tog, insert pillow form, sew rem side closed.

girl's
floral
BED COORDINATES

Any little girl will love this posy-covered bedspread and
matching pillow. Green stripes crocheted into the afghan serve
as stems for the three-dimensional flowers and leaves that
are later attached to the surface.

Designed by **Michelle Maks Thompson** (afghan) and **Svetlana Avrakh** (pillow)
Photographed by **Greg Scheidemann**

Hooks & Extras
- Size K/10.5 (6.5 mm) crochet hook OR SIZE NEEDED TO OBTAIN GAUGE
- Blunt-end yarn needle
- Polyester fiberfill for Pillow

Sizes
Finished Measurements
Bedspread = 48×64" (not including edging)
Pillow = 14" diameter

Materials
Yarns
Chunky weight:
Bedspread
1,210 yds. (1,105 m) in yellow (MC); 370 yds. (255 m) in light green (CC); 185 yds. (170 m) *each* in light pink (A) and light blue (B)
Pillow
185 yds. (170 m) *each* in light blue (MC) and light pint (CC)

Notes
Gauge
Bedspread
14 dc and 8 rows = 6" (15 cm)
Pillow
14 sts = 6" (15 cm) and 11 rnds = 5" (12.5 cm) in sc.
TAKE TIME TO CHECK YOUR GAUGE.

Special Abbreviations
sc2tog = Draw up a lp in next 2 sts, yo, and draw through all 3 lps on hook.

Crochet

BEDSPREAD

Note: Bedspread is worked side to side. Flowers and Leaves are sewn on afterward.

Using MC, ch 152.
Row 1 (RS): Dc in 4th ch from hook and in each ch across—150 sts; turn.
Rows 2–6: Ch 3—counts as dc; dc in each st across; turn; do not fasten off.
Row 7: With RS facing, join CC; ch 1, sc in each st across—150 sts; fasten off; do not turn; join MC.
Rows 8–19: Ch 3, dc in each sc across—150 sts.

Rep Rows 7–19 for 3 more times, then work Rows 7–13; do not fasten off.

Edging
Rnd 1 (RS): Using MC, 2 sc in first dc, sc to last dc, 3 sc in last dc; rotate to work next side, sc evenly across top edge, 3 sc in corner, sc along beg ch edge, 3 sc in corner, sc evenly across bottom edge, join with sl st to first sc; fasten off.
Rnd 2 (RS): Join CC in any sc, ch 1, sc in each sc around, working 3 sc in each corner sc, join with sl st to top of first sc; turn.
Rnd 3 (WS): Ch 3, dc in each sc around, working 3 dc in each corner sc, join with sl st to top of beg ch-3; fasten off.

FLOWER (MAKE 18)
Using B, ch 3, join with sl st to form ring.
Rnd 1: Ch 3, 14 dc in ring; join with sl st in top of beg ch-3—15 dc: fasten off.
Rnd 2: Join A in any dc, ch 1, [(sl st, sc, dc) in dc, 2 tr in next dc, (dc, sc, sl st) in next dc] 5 times, join with sl st to first sl st; fasten off, leaving a long tail for sewing.

LEAF (MAKE 34)
Using CC, ch 10. Sl st in 2nd ch from hook, sc in next ch, dc in next ch, tr in next 3 ch, dc in next ch, sc in next ch, sl st into last ch; fasten off, leaving a long tail for sewing.

FINISHING
Sew Flowers and Leaves to Bedspread along CC sc rows as foll: On first, 3rd, and 5th CC rows, sew a Flower at 12th, 54th, 96th, and 138th sts; then sew 2 Leaves at 33rd, 75th, and 117th sts. On 2nd and 4th CC rows, sew 2 Leaves at 12th, 54th, 96th, and 138th sts; then sew a Flower at 33rd, 75th, and 138th sts.

Sew Flowers with RS facing, Leaves with WS facing. Weave in ends.

PILLOW CENTER (MAKE 2)

Using MC, ch 3; join with sl st to form ring.

Rnd 1: Ch 1, 8 sc in ring; join with sl st to first sc.

Rnd 2: Ch 1, 2 sc in each sc around—16 sts.

Rnd 3: Ch 1, sc in first sc, 2 sc in next sc, (sc in next sc, 2 sc in next sc) around; join—24 sts.

Rnd 4: Ch 1, sc in first 2 sc, 2 sc in next sc, (sc in next 2 sc, 2 sc in next sc) around; join—32 sts.

Rnd 5: Ch 1, sc in first 3 sc, 2 sc in next sc, (sc in next 3 sc, 2 sc in next sc) around; join—40 sts.

Rnds 6–14: Cont inc 8 sts every rnd as est, working 1 more sc before each inc; join—112 at end of Rnd 14.

Rnd 15: Ch 1, sc in first 13 sc, 2 sc in next sc, (sc in next 13 sc, 2 sc in next sc) around; join—120 sts; fasten off on first side; do not cut yarn on 2nd Center piece.

FINISHING

Holding both Center pieces with WS tog, sc three-quarters of the way around, working through both layers and matching sc. Stuff Pillow with fiberfill. Cont to sc around, closing opening and adjusting fiberfill as necessary. Join with sl st to first sc; fasten off.

Petal front (MAKE 5)

Join CC in any sc on Pillow edge.

Row 1: Ch 1, sc in this and next 21 sc; turn.

Rows 2–3: Rep Row 1.

Rows 4–9: Ch 1, sc2tog, sc to last 2 sts, sc2tog; turn; fasten off at end of Row 9. Sk next 2 sts of Pillow, Join CC and rep Rows 1–9 for 4 more times—5 petals.

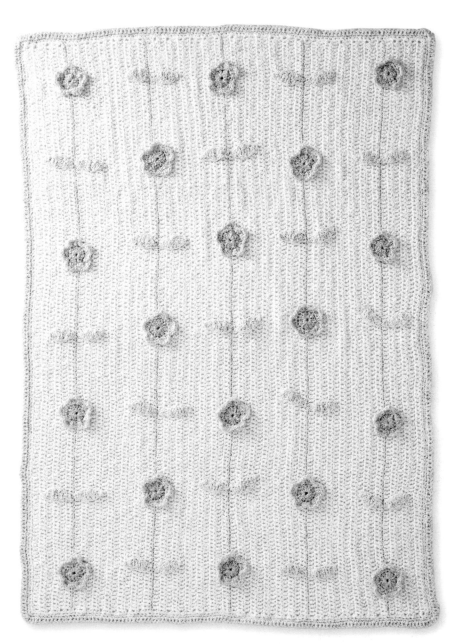

Petal front edging

Join CC in sc bet petals; ch 1, (work sc in skipped sts and sc evenly around edge of petal, working 2 sc in each top corner) 5 times; join with sl st in first sc; fasten off.

Petal back (MAKE 5)

Using CC, ch 23.

Row 1: Sc in 2nd ch from hook and in each ch across—22 sts; turn.

Rows 2–4: Ch 1, sc in each sc across; turn.

Rows 5–10: Ch 1, sc2tog, sc to last 2 sts, sc2tog; turn; fasten off.

Petal back edging

With RS facing, join CC at bottom right; ch 1, sc evenly around curved edge of petal, working 2 sc in each top corner; fasten off, leaving a long tail for sewing.

Flower

Using MC, ch 3, join with sl st to form ring.

Rnd 1: Ch 3, 14 dc in ring, join with sl st in top of beg ch-3; fasten off.

Rnd 2: Join CC in any dc, ch 1, [(sc, dc) in dc, 2 tr in next dc, (dc,sc) in next dc] 5 times, join with sl st to first sc; fasten off, leaving a long tail for sewing. Sew petal backs to petal fronts along curved edges. Stuff lightly. Cont sewing along beg ch edge to close opening, adjusting fiberfill as necessary. Sew Flower to center of Pillow. Weave in ends.

Filled with sunny blooms, this afghan is made using just two easy motifs in seven cheery colors.

pretty, sweet throw

Designed by **Marilyn Losee**
Photographed by **Greg Scheidemann**

■■■□□ Easy

Sizes
Finished Measurements
33×44", not including fringe

Note: To join a new color, complete the stitch in progress until 2 loops remain on the hook, then drop the color in use; with new color, yarn over and draw the new color through the 2 loops on the hook.

Materials
Yarns
Worsted weight, 330 yds. (304 m) *each* in bright pink (A), orange (B), yellow (C), bright green (D), turquoise (E), light purple (F), and dark purple (G)

4 MEDIUM

Note: If adding fringe you will need 330 yards (304 m) more of D, E, and F (*each*).

Hooks & Extra
- Size I/9 (5.5 mm) crochet hook OR SIZE NEEDED TO OBTAIN GAUGE
- Blunt-end yarn needle

Notes
Gauge
Large Flower Motif: 5½" in diameter
Small Circle Motif: 2½" (6.5 cm) in diameter

Gauge is not critical for this project.

Crochet

LARGE FLOWER

**(MAKE 48: 16 IN EACH OF
3 COLORWAYS)**

Work Rnds 1–4 in the foll colorways:

Colorway 1: Beg ch and Rnd 1 (C),
Rnd 2 (B), Rnd 3 (A), Rnd 4 (D).

Colorway 2: Beg ch and Rnd 1 (B),
Rnd 2 (G), Rnd 3 (D), Rnd 4 (E).

Colorway 3: Beg ch and Rnd 1 (A),
Rnd 2 (C), Rnd 3 (G), Rnd 4 (F).

With first color, ch 6, join with a slip st
to form ring.

Rnd 1 (RS): Ch 2—counts as dc; 23 dc
in ring, join 2nd color, and join it with sl st
to top of beg ch-2—24 dc. Fasten off first
color.

Rnd 2: Using 2nd color, ch 4—counts as
dc, ch 2; dc in same st, ch 1, *sk next
2 dc, (dc, ch 2, dc) in next dc, ch 1; rep
from * 6 more times, sk next 2 dc, join
3rd color, and join it with sl st to 2nd ch
of beg ch-4; fasten off 2nd color.

Rnd 3: Using 3rd color, ch 2—counts as
dc; dc in next ch-2 sp, ch 2, 2 dc in same
sp, *sc in ch-1 sp, (2 dc, ch 2, 2 dc) in
next ch-2 sp; rep from * 6 more times,
end sc in ch-1 sp, join 4th color, and join
it with sl st to top of beg ch-2; fasten off
3rd color.

Rnd 4: Using 4th color, sl st in first ch-2
sp, ch 2—counts as dc; (2 dc, ch 1, 3 dc)
in same sp, *sc in sp on each side of
next sc; (3 dc, ch 1, 3 dc) in next ch-2 sp;
rep from * 6 more times, sc in sp on
each side of next sc, and join with sl st
to top of beg ch-2; fasten off. Weave
in ends.

SMALL CIRCLES

**(MAKE 35: 11 IN COLORWAY 1;
12 EACH IN COLORWAYS 2 AND 3)**

**Work Rnds 1 and 2 in the foll
colorways:**

Colorway 1: Beg ch and Rnd 1 (C),
Rnd 2 (E).

Colorway 2: Beg ch and Rnd 1 (B),
Rnd 2 (F).

Colorway 3: Beg ch and Rnd 1 (G),
Rnd 2 (A).

With first color, ch 6, join with sl st to
form ring.

Rnd 1 (RS): Ch 2—counts as dc; 23 dc
in ring, join 2nd color, and join it with sl st
to top of beg ch-2—24 dc; fasten off first
color.

Rnd 2: Using 2nd color, *sc in next
2 sts, 2 sc in next st; rep from * around;
join with sl st to first sc; fasten off.
Weave in ends.

FINISHING

Assemble Large Flower rows

Foll Assembly Diagram, *right,* lay out 1
row of 6 Large Flowers; pin each Flower
to the one beside it at the two points
where they touch (see photo, *page 256*).
Using yarn needle and yarn color to
match one of the Flowers, sew the
points together.

Cont laying out and sewing each row of
Large Flowers, foll Assembly Diagram—
8 rows of 6 Flowers each. Join first and
2nd rows and cont joining rows until all
8 rows are sewn together.

Attach Small Circles

Lay completed piece on a flat surface;
foll Assembly Diagram, position the
Small Circles for first row between Large
Flowers; pin in place.

Using yarn needle and matching yarn
color, attach Small Circles between
the points of the Large Flower. Cont until
all Small Circles have been attached.

Fringe

Cut 13" strands of D, E, and F. Working
around entire Throw, make 7 fringes
evenly around each unattached petal and
3 fringes along side of each attached
petal as foll: Matching colors of Rnd 4,
hold 2 strands tog and fold in half. *Insert
hook from WS to RS into st or ch-1 sp,
pull lps through, insert ends into lp and
pull tight against edge; rep from *.
Trim if necessary.

Assembly Diagram

creating
FOR CHARITY

Want to make a difference while doing something you truly enjoy? Knit or crochet items for those who truly need them and welcome them with open arms.

Organizations in Need

One quick Web search and you'll soon discover that there is no shortage of organizations looking for both knit and crochet donations. From newborn caps to helmet liners for soldiers, you're sure to find a cause you can adopt for your next project. Here are just a few of our favorites:

- **Warm Up America** *craftyarncouncil.com*
  Stitch 7x9" rectangles to make afghans for a variety of charitable agencies, including homeless and battered women's shelters.

- **Project Linus** *projectlinus.org*
  Make a washable blanket for seriously ill and traumatized children. They accept knit or crochet blankets, along with handmade quilts.

- **Shawl Ministry** *shawlministry.com*
  Knit or crochet a prayer shawl to support those dealing with loss or illness or to celebrate life events.

- **Afghans for Afghans** *afghansforafghans.org*
  Bring comfort and warmth to Afghan men, women, and children by donating a knit or crocheted blanket or garment (including sweaters, socks, mittens, and hats).

- **Chemo Caps** *chemocaps.com*
  Knit a cap for a cancer patient who is undergoing treatment.

- **Check with your local hospitals**
  Many are looking for preemie and newborn hats and toys for children.

What You Need to Know

Before you start any charity project, make sure you know the requirements of the organization you plan to send your donation to. Some may require the project yarn to be washable or may require a certain yarn content in order to be accepted. While many organizations provide patterns for projects, others may not—which may allow more flexibility in design. Also be sure that if there are size limitations that you adhere to the required standards.

If you're looking for free charity patterns, try online resources such as *ravelry.com*, *knittingforcharity.org*, *dailyknitter.com*, *dailycrocheter.com*, and *lionbrandyarn.com*. Or try the knit and crochet patterns for baby hats, prayer shawls, and baby blankets on *pages 260–263*.

Knit Prayer Shawl

Adapted by **Nancy Wyatt**; original design by **Victoria Galo** and **Janet Bristow** for the Shawl Ministry Photographed by **Jay Wilde**

■■■□□ Easy

Sizes

Finished Measurements

22×60" (not including fringe)

Materials

Yarns

Bulky weight, 370 yds. (340 m) *each* in light blue (A) and in light green (B)

Needles & Extras

- Size 11 (8 mm) 24" circular needle OR SIZE NEEDED TO OBTAIN GAUGE
- Size J/10 (5.5 mm) crochet hook
- Blunt-end yarn needle

Notes

Gauge

10 sts and 18 rows = 4" (10 cm). TAKE TIME TO CHECK YOUR GAUGE.

Note: The shawl shown, *at right*, is an adaptation of an original design from the Shawl Ministry; *www.shawlministry.com*.

Knit

With A, cast on 57 sts. Do not turn. Slide sts to other end of needle. Join B at the point where you began the cast-on row and work (k3, p3) across, ending k3; turn.
Row 2: With A, (p3, k3) across, ending p3; do not turn.
Row 3: Slide sts to other end of needle. With B, (k3, p3) across, ending k3; turn.
Rep Rows 2 and 3 until Shawl measures 60" from beg, ending with a WS row. Bind off.

FRINGE

Cut one 13" strand of each yarn. Holding the strands tog, fold in half to form a loop.

With the crochet hook, take the loop through the first cast-on st. Take ends through loop and pull up to form a knot. Tie an overhand knot at the end of each single strand. Attach 30 fringes evenly spaced along each short end of Shawl.

Crocheted Prayer Shawl

Designed by **Robyn Chachula**   Photographed by **Brian Richmond**   ■■ ■■ ■■ ▢ **Intermediate**

Sizes

Finished Measurements

22×60" (not including fringe)

Materials

Yarns

Worsted weight, 1,250 yds. (1,135 m) in moss green

Hooks & Extras

- Size K/10.5 (6.5 mm) crochet hook OR SIZE NEEDED TO OBTAIN GAUGE
- Blunt-end yarn needle

Notes

Gauge

15 dc by 8 rows = 4×4". TAKE TIME TO CHECK YOUR GAUGE.

Special Abbreviations

blp (back loop) = Insert hook into back loop only of st indicated

middle bar = Insert hook into the center loop of the wrong side of the dc stitch that is formed by the yarn over in the dc stitch. (The middle bar is directly below the top two loops.)

Crochet

Ch 85.

Row 1 (RS): Dc in 4th ch from hook (sk ch count as dc), dc in each ch across, turn--83 dc.

Row 2: Ch 3 (counts as dc),*dc in the middle bar of next 3 dc, dc blp in next 3 dc, rep from * across to last 4 dc, dc in the middle bar of next 3 dc, dc in top of t-ch, turn.

Rep Row 2 for 118 rows total. Fasten off, and weave in ends.

FINISHING

Block by pinning shawl to size and spraying lightly with water; let dry.

Fringe

Cut 224 15-inch long strands of yarn. Holding 4 strands together, join to edge of Shawl by folding strands in half, pulling center of strands through edge, pulling ends through center, and tightening. Join fringe in every 3rd stitch along the short edges.

Knit Baby Hat with Tie

Designed by **Mary Heaton**
Photographed by **Brian Richmond**
pictured above, right

Sizes

Finished Measurements
Circumference = 15½"

Materials

Yarns
Worsted weight, 100 yds.
(91 m) in multicolor pastel

Needles & Extras
• Size 8 (5 mm) double-pointed
  needles (dpns) OR SIZE
  NEEDED TO OBTAIN GAUGE
• Blunt-end yarn needle

Notes

Gauge
15 sts = 4" (10 cm). TAKE TIME
TO CHECK YOUR GAUGE.

Knit

Cast on 63 sts. Divide onto 3 dpns
(21 sts per needle). Purl 6 rnds. Then knit
every rnd until Hat measures 5 inches
from bottom edge.
Next rnd: Inc 1 st at end of round–64
sts.
Next rnd—Eyelet rnd: *K2, k2tog,
yo, rep from * to end of rnd.
Next rnd: Knit.
Next rnd—Ribbing: *K1, p1, rep from
* to end of rnd.
   Repeat ribbing rnd until Hat measures
7 inches from bottom edge. Bind off in
pattern.

Tie

Make a tie about 10 inches long using
I-cord method or single crochet.
I-cord: Cast 2 sts onto one dpn. Slide
sts to other end of needle. DO NOT
TURN. Knit those 2 sts. Then slide those
sts to other end of needle and knit them.
Repeat until tie is the length you want.
Bind off.

Alternate method for tie: Cast on 75
sts, and on the next row bind them off.

Thread tie through eyelet-row holes; pull
tightly, gathering the body of the Hat into
folds; and tie in a bow.

Knit Baby Hat with I-Cord Loop

Designed by **Mary Heaton**
Photographed by **Brian Richmond**
pictured left, front

Sizes

Finished Measurements
Circumference = 15½"

Materials

Yarns
Worsted weight, 100 yds.
(91 m) in multicolor pastel

Needles & Extras
• Size 8 (5 mm) double-pointed
  needles (dpns) OR SIZE
  NEEDED TO OBTAIN GAUGE
• Blunt-end yarn needle

Notes

Gauge
15 sts = 4" (10 cm). TAKE TIME TO
CHECK YOUR GAUGE.

Knit

Cast on 60 sts. Divide onto 3 dpns. Knit
for 6 rnds.
Next rnd: Increase 4 sts evenly spaced
in rnd–64 sts
   Knit every rnd until Hat measures 6
inches from cast-on row (unrolled).
Dec rnd: *K6, k2tog, rep from * to end
of rnd.
Next rnd: Knit.
Dec rnd: *K5, k2tog, rep from * to end
of rnd.
Next rnd: Knit.
   Rep these last two rnds, decreasing
the number of sts before each k2tog by
1 st until 8 sts remain.
   Bind off the first 5 sts of the 8
remaining sts. With the last 3 sts, make
an I-cord (see *middle column*, this page)
about 4 inches long. Bind off. Stitch the
end of the I-cord to the top of the Hat.
(The other end of the I-cord will be still
attached to the Hat.)

Crocheted Baby Blanket

Designed by **Michelle Maks Thompson**
Photographed by **Greg Scheidemann**

▰▰▱▱▱ Easy

Sizes

Finished Measurements
41½×42"

Materials

Yarns

Medium sport weight, 918 yds. (835 m) *each* in light blue (A) and lavender (B)

2
FINE

Super bulky weight, 108 yds. (100 m) in blue (C)

6
SUPER BULKY

Hooks & Extras

- Size K/10½ (6.5 mm) crochet hook OR SIZE NEEDED TO OBTAIN GAUGE
- Blunt-end yarn needle

Notes

Gauge

With 1 strand each of A and B held tog, 10 dc and 6 rows = 4" (10 cm). TAKE TIME TO CHECK YOUR GAUGE.

Crochet
BLANKET

With 1 strand each of A and B held tog, ch 101.

Row 1 (RS): Dc in 4th ch from hook and in each ch across—99 sts; turn.

Row 2: Ch 3—counts as dc; dc in each dc across; turn.

Rep Row 2 until Blanket measures 40" from beg. Fasten off A and B.

EDGING

Rnd 1: With RS facing, join C with a sl st in top right corner st, ch 1; * in corner st work sc, ch 1, and sc; (ch 1, sk dc, sc in next st) across, end with ch 1, sk dc, in last dc work sc, ch 1, and sc for corner. Ch 1, working across side edge, work sc in each row across and make ch 1 bet each sc; ch 1 before working next corner; rep from * around; join with a sl st in first sc.

Rnd 2: Ch 1, sc in first sc, 2 sc in corner ch-1 sp. Sc in each sc and ch-1 sp around, working 2 sc in each corner ch-1 sp; join with a sl st in first sc. Fasten off.

KNITTING & CROCHET
basics

Here you'll find abbreviations, stitch details, and other helpful information to get you started knitting or crocheting.

Knitting Basics

Abbreviations

The abbreviations used throughout this book—plus other common ones—are listed below.

approx	approximately
beg	begin(ning)(s)
cn	cable needle
dec	decrease(s)(ing)
dpn	double-pointed needle(s)
est	established
foll	follow(s)(ing)
inc	increase(s)(ing)
k or K	knit
kwise	as if to knit
k2tog	knit two stitches together (right-slanting decrease)
M1	make one stitch
p or P	purl
pat	pattern
pm	place marker
psso	pass slipped stitch over

p2sso	pass two slipped stitches over
p2tog	purl two stitches together (right-slanting decrease)
pwise	as if to purl
rem	remain(s)(ing)
rep	repeat(s)(ing)
rev	reverse
rnd(s)	round(s)
RS	right side(s) of work
sl	slip
sm	slip marker
ssk	(slip, slip, knit) slip two stitches, one at a time knitwise, insert left needle and knit two together (left-slanting decrease)
ssp	(slip, slip, purl) slip two stitches, one at a time knitwise, pass back to left needle, purl together through back loops (left-slanting decrease)

st(s)	stitch(es)
St st	stockinette stitch
tbl	through the back loop(s)
tog	together
WS	wrong side of work
wyib	with yarn in back
wyif	with yarn in front
yo	yarn over
yon	yarn over needle
yrn	yarn around needle
( )	work instructions within parentheses in the place directed and the number of times indicated
[ ]	work step in brackets the number of times indicated
*	repeat the instructions following the single asterisk as directed

Standard Yarn Weight System

Categories of yarn, gauge ranges, and recommended needle and hook sizes							
Yarn Weight Symbol & Category Names	0 LACE	1 SUPER FINE	2 FINE	3 LIGHT	4 MEDIUM	5 BULKY	6 SUPER BULKY
Type of Yarns in Category	Fingering, 10-count crochet thread	Sock, Fingering, Baby	Sport, Baby	DK, Light Worsted	Worsted, Afghan, Aran	Bulky, Chunky, Craft, Rug	Super, Bulky, Roving
Knitting Guage Range* in Stockinette Stitch for 4 inches	33–40** sts	27–32 sts	23–26 sts	21–24 sts	16–20 sts	12–15 sts	6–11 sts
Recommended Needle in Metric Size Range	1.5 mm to 2.25 mm	2.25 mm to 3.25 mm	3.25 mm to 3.75 mm	3.75 mm to 4.5 mm	4.5 mm to 5.5 mm	5.5 mm to 8 mm	8 mm and larger
Recommended Needle in U.S. Size Range	000 to 1	1 to 3	3 to 5	5 to 7	7 to 9	9 to 11	11 and larger
Crochet Gauge Range* in Single Crochet to 4 inches	32–42 double crochets**	21–32 sts	16–20 sts	12–17 sts	11–14 sts	8–11 sts	5–9 sts
Recommended Hook in Metric Size Range	Steel*** 1.6 mm to 1.4 mm	2.25 mm to 3.5 mm	3.5 mm to 4.5 mm	4.5 mm to 5.5 mm	5.5 mm to 6.5 mm	6.5 mm to 9 mm	9 mm and larger
Recommended Hook in U.S. Size Range	Steel*** 6, 7, 8 Regular hook B/1	B/1 to E/4	E/4 to 7	7 to I/9	I/9 to K/10½	K/10½ to M/13	M/13 and larger

* GUIDELINES ONLY: The above reflect the most commonly used gauges and needle or hook sizes for specific yarn categories.

** Lace weight yarns are usually knitted or crocheted on larger needles and hooks to create lacy, openwork patterns. Accordingly, a gauge range is difficult to determine. Always follow the gauge stated in your pattern.

*** Steel crochet hooks are sized differently from regular hooks—the higher the number, the smaller the hook, which is the reverse of regular hook sizing.

Skill Levels Defined

■■□□□ BEGINNER

Projects for first-time knitters are labeled "Beginner." These patterns use basic stitches, minimal shaping, and very simple finishing.

■■■□□ EASY

Projects labeled "Easy" use basic stitches, repetitive stitch patterns, simple color changes, and simple shaping and finishing.

■■■■□ INTERMEDIATE

Projects labeled "Intermediate" use a variety of techniques, such as cables and lace or color patterns, with midlevel shaping and finishing.

■■■■■ EXPERIENCED

Projects labeled "Experienced" use advanced techniques and stitches, with detailed shaping and refined finishing.

Making a Gauge Swatch

Using the recommended needles and yarn, cast on a few more stitches than the number indicated by the gauge printed in the pattern for 4" (10 cm). Work the pattern for several rows beyond 4". Loosely bind off or remove the swatch from the needles. Place a ruler over the swatch; count the number of stitches across 4" and the number of rows down 4", including fractions of stitches or rows. If you have too many stitches and rows, switch to larger needles; if you have too few stitches, use smaller needles.

Long Tail Cast-On

Estimate a yarn tail length that is three times the length of what the cast-on edge will be.

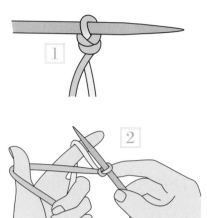

STEP 1
Make a slip knot this distance from the yarn end and place it on the right-hand needle.

STEP 2
*Position thumb and index finger between the two strands of yarn. Close the other fingers into the palm of your hand and securely hold the yarn.

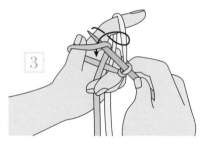

STEP 3
Moving in an upward direction, insert the needle under the yarn on the thumb and into the loop that's formed around the thumb. Take the needle over the top of the yarn in front of the index finger and guide it down into the thumb loop—the strand of yarn from the index finger easily moves along with the needle. Pull the strand through the thumb loop, making a new loop on the right-hand needle.

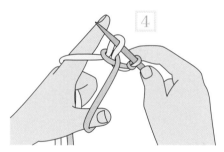

Step 4
Drop the yarn around the thumb, and spread your index finger and thumb to tighten the loop on the needle—one cast-on stitch is made. Repeat from * to make a second cast-on stitch, and so on.

Cable Cast-On

STEP 1
Make a slip knot on the left needle.

STEP 2
Working into the loop of the knot, knit a stitch; transfer it to the left needle.

STEP 3
Insert the right needle between those 2 stitches. Knit a stitch and transfer it to left needle. Repeat this step for each additional stitch.

Basic Stitches

GARTER STITCH

Knit every row using a circular needle, k one round, then p one round; repeat.

STOCKINETTE STITCH

Knit all RS rows and purl all WS rows. Using a circular needle, k every rnd.

REVERSE STOCKINETTE STITCH

Knit all WS rows and purl all RS rows. Using a circular needle, p every rnd.

Knit Stitch

STEP 1

With yarn in back, insert the right-hand needle from front to back into the first stitch on the left-hand needle. Notice that the right-hand needle is behind the left-hand needle.

STEP 2

Form a loop by wrapping the yarn under and around the right-hand needle.

STEP 3

Pull the loop through the stitch so the loop is in front of the work.

STEP 4

Slip the first or "old" knit stitch over and off the tip of the left-hand needle, leaving it on the right-hand needle.

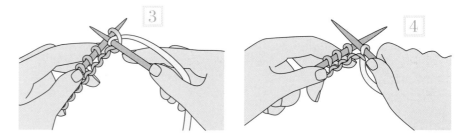

Purl Stitch

STEP 1

With yarn in front of the work, put the right-hand needle from back to front into the first stitch on the left-hand needle.

STEP 2

Form a loop by wrapping the yarn on top of and around the right-hand needle.

STEP 3

Pull the loop through the stitch to make a new purl stitch.

STEP 4

Slip the first or "old" purl stitch over and off the tip of the left-hand needle, leaving it on the right-hand needle.

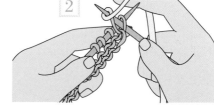
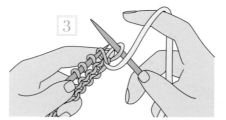
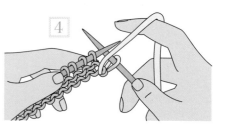

3-Needle Bind-Off

With RS together, hold in one hand two needles with an equal number of stitches on each and with points in the same direction.

STEP 1

Using a third needle of the same size, knit together one stitch from each needle.

STEPS 2 and 3

*Knit together the next stitch from each needle, pass the first stitch worked over the second stitch to bind off; repeat from * across to bind off all stitches.

Duplicate Stitch

This embroidery stitch imitates the knit stitch, covering the original stitch with a different color of yarn to create the pattern.

Thread a blunt-end yarn needle with a short length of the yarn and follow the path of the original stitch. Trim the yarn and weave in the ends so they can't be seen on the right side.

Making a Pom-Pom

Wind yarn around a piece of cardboard or the palm of your hand loosely 100 times. Tie a 10-inch strand tightly around all the loops. Cut the yarn bundle opposite the tied end. Leaving the tails free, trim the pom-pom so that it is rounded and measures 1–2" in diameter. Tie onto piece with tails; trim tails.

Specialty Stitches

INCREASING STITCHES

MAKE ONE (M1)

Version A, increased stitch slants to the right

Insert the tip of the left needle from back to front under the strand that lies between the next stitch on the left needle and the last stitch worked on the right needle. See the illustration, *right*.

Insert the right needle from left to right into the front loop of the lifted strand, and knit it from this position.

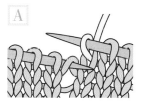

MAKE ONE (M1)

Version B, increased stitch slants to the left

Insert the tip of the left needle from front to back under the strand that lies between the first stitch on the left needle and the last stitch worked on the right needle. See the illustration, *right*.

Knit the strand on the left needle, inserting the needle from right to left into the back loop.

DECREASING STITCHES

KNIT TWO TOGETHER (K2TOG)

Decreased stitch slants to the right

Working from left to right at the point of the decrease, insert the tip of the right needle into the second and then the first stitch on the left needle; knit the two stitches together. See the illustration, *right*.

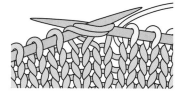

PURL TWO TOGETHER (P2TOG)

Decreased stitch slants to the right

Working from right to left at the point of the decrease, insert the tip of the right needle into the first two stitches on the left needle and purl the two stitches together. See the illustration, *right*.

SLIP, SLIP, KNIT (SSK)

Decreased stitch slants to the left

As if to knit, slip the first two stitches from the left needle one at a time to the right needle. See the illustration, *right*.

Insert the left needle into these two stitches from back to front, and knit them together from this position.

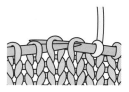

For More Help

Visit *www.YarnStandards .com* for downloadable knitting information compiled by the Craft Yarn Council of America. You'll find standard sizing information, abbreviations, yarn weights and sizes, and more—all valuable data for knitters and crocheters.

Grafting Stockinette Stitches (Kitchener Stitch)

Hold wrong sides together with the needles pointed to the right. Thread the yarn tail into a yarn needle. *Insert the yarn needle knitwise through the first stitch on the front needle and let the stitch drop from the needle.

Insert the yarn needle into the second stitch on the front needle purlwise and pull the yarn through, leaving the stitch on the needle.

Insert the yarn needle into the first stitch on the back needle purlwise and let it drop from the needle. Insert the yarn needle knitwise through the second stitch on the back needle and pull the yarn through, leaving the stitch on the needle. Repeat from * across until all stitches have been joined. Adjust the tension as necessary. Weave in loose ends.

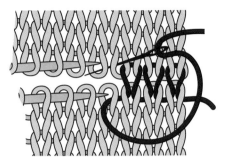

Felting

After you've knitted the fabric for your felted project, place it in a mesh lingerie bag and put it in the washing machine with Ivory Flakes or shampoo (avoid detergents), along with other lint-free items such as old T-shirts or jeans—they provide the necessary friction as the machine agitates to promote the felting. Do not hand-wash the item—without the agitation of the machine and the friction of the other items, the fabric will not felt. Wash the item in hot water and rinse in cold water.

Successful felting occurs when the stitches visually disappear. But there are times when it's a good idea not to let the felting go too far, especially when you're felting with novelty yarns or when fit is important, as in mittens or hats. Remove the felted item from the washer when you think it has reached the size you want. You can always put it back in for another washing if you want it smaller. If you remove it in the middle of a wash cycle, hand-rinse it in cold water, and then roll it in a towel to remove excess water.

Don't put a washed felted item in the dryer at any time. Machine-drying does not promote felting; it only promotes shrinkage. Let the felting process do the shrinking. You'll find that felting will shrink your item from 15 to 20 percent across its width and from 25 to 40 percent in length.

SHAPING IT UP

Shape your project as soon as you remove it from the washing machine. Stretch it, pull it, and, if appropriate, stuff it until it becomes the shape you want. Use items around the house to hold the article's shape as it dries. For example, tuck a book wrapped in plastic snugly inside a straight-sided item. Stuff plastic bags around curved shapes, much as you would stuff fiberfill into a soft toy. Keep the "stuffing" in the project until the shape is established and the article is almost dry. Then remove the stuffing and let the item dry completely, allowing up to two days.

If you don't like the way an item is shaping up, wet it and reshape. For a soft and fuzzy finish, brush the item with a wire brush after it is completely dry.

Crochet Basics

Abbreviations

approx	approximately	**inc**	increase	
beg	begin(ning)(s)	**lp(s)**	loop(s)	
bet	between	**MC**	main color	
BPdc	back post double crochet	**pat**	pattern	
CC	contrasting color	**pc**	popcorn	
ch	chain	**rep**	repeat	
ch-	refers to chain or space previously made	**rem**	remain(ing)(s)	
ch-sp	chain space	**rnd(s)**	round(s)	
cont	continue	**RS**	right side	
dc	double crochet	**sc**	single crochet	
dc cl	double crochet cluster	**sc2tog**	single crochet 2 stitches together	
dc2tog	double crochet 2 stitches together	**sc3tog**	single crochet 3 stitches together	
dec	decrease	**sk**	skip	
est	established	**sl st**	slip stitch	
foll	follow(ing)(s)	**sp(s)**	space(s)	
FPdc	front post double crochet	**st(s)**	stitch(es)	
FPsc	front post single crochet	**tog**	together	
FPtr	front post treble crochet	**tr**	treble crochet	
grp	group	**tr cl**	treble crochet cluster	
hdc	half double crochet	**WS**	wrong side	
hdc2tog	half double crochet 2 stitches together	**yo**	yarn over	

[ ] work instructions within brackets as many times as directed

( ) work instructions within parentheses as many times as directed

* repeat the instructions following the single asterisk as directed

* * repeat instructions between asterisks as many times as directed or repeat from a set of instructions (sometimes you will see as many as three or four sets of asterisks; the same directions apply)

" inches

Slip Knot

STEP 1
Make a loop; then hook another loop through it.

STEP 2
Tighten gently and slide the knot up to the hook.

Chain Stitch (ch)

STEP 1
Yarn over (yo) hook and draw the yarn through to form a new loop without tightening up the previous one.

STEP 2
Repeat to form as many chains as required. Do not count the slip knot as a chain stitch.

1

2

Single Crochet (sc)

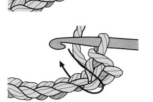

STEP 1

Insert the hook into the work (second chain from hook on the starting chain), *yarn over the hook, and draw yarn through the work only.

STEP 2

Yarn over the hook again and draw the yarn through both loops on the hook—one single crochet made.

STEP 3

Insert the hook into the next stitch; repeat from * in step 1.

Double Crochet (dc)

STEP 1

Yarn over the hook and insert the hook into the work (fourth chain from the hook on the starting chain). *Yarn over the hook and draw through the work only—three loops are on the hook.

STEP 2

Yarn over the hook and draw through the first two loops only.

STEP 3

Yarn over the hook and draw through the last two loops on the hook—one double crochet made.

STEP 4

Yarn over the hook, insert the hook into the next stitch; repeat from * in step 2.

Half Double Crochet (hdc)

STEP 1

Yarn over the hook and insert the hook into the work (third chain from the hook on the starting chain).

STEPS 2 AND 3

*Yarn over the hook and draw up a loop—three loops on the hook. Yarn over the hook again and draw through all three loops on the hook—one half double crochet made.

STEP 4

Yarn over the hook, insert the hook into the next stitch; repeat from * in step 2.

Triple Crochet (tr)

STEP 1

Yarn over the hook two times and insert the hook into the work (fifth chain from the hook on the starting chain).

STEP 2

Yarn over the hook and draw through the work only—four loops are on the hook.

STEP 3

Yarn over the hook and draw through the first two loops on the hook—three loops are on the hook.

STEP 4

Yarn over the hook and draw through the next two loops on the hook—two loops remain on the hook.

STEP 5

Yarn over the hook again and draw through remaining two loops on hook—one triple crochet made. Repeat steps 1–5, working a triple crochet in each chain across.

Slip Stitch (sl st)

This is the shortest crochet stitch and, unlike other stitches, is not used on its own to produce a fabric. It is used for joining, shaping, and where necessary carrying the yarn to another part of the fabric for the next stage.

STEP 1

Insert the hook into the work (second chain from hook), yarn over, and draw the yarn through both the work and the loop on the hook in one movement.

STEP 2

To join chains into a ring with a slip stitch, insert the hook into the first chain, yarn over, and draw through both the work and the yarn on the hook in one movement.